Call to Worship

LITURGY, MUSIC, PREACHING & THE ARTS

Continuing the tradition of
Reformed Liturgy & Music

Published by the Office of Theology and Worship,
Presbyterian Church (U.S.A.), in Association with Geneva Press.
The official journal of the Presbyterian Association of Musicians.

Call to Worship

VOLUME 37.1
2003–2004

LITURGY, MUSIC, PREACHING & THE ARTS

5   Introduction—*Paul Galbreath*

PART ONE: EXPERIENCE

8   Forming Faith: Exploring the Experience of Worship-Centered
     Congregations—*Jane Rogers Vann*

34   In Spirit and in Truth: Experience and Worship in the
     Reformed Tradition—*Joseph D. Small*

50   The Promise for Renewal—*Harold Daniels*

PART TWO: RESOURCES

68   Introducing *Holy Is the Lord*—*Melva Costen*

71   The Presbyterian *Psalter* Revisited—*Hal Hopson*

80   Music Review of Bradley Ellingboe's *Requiem*—*Janet Loman*

82   Book Review of *Interchurch Families*—*Charles Wiley*

PART THREE: AIDS FOR THE *REVISED COMMON LECTIONARY*
     YEAR C—ADVENT 2003 THROUGH REIGN OF CHRIST 2004

87   Introduction to Lectionary Aids

92   Lectionary Aids for 2003–2004: Year C

220 Inclusive Language Text of the Confession of 1967

235 The Confession of 1967

Call to Worship

LITURGY, MUSIC, PREACHING & THE ARTS

Continuing the tradition of *Reformed Liturgy & Music* (1971–2000) and *Reformed Liturgics* (1963–69), *Call to Worship* seeks to further the church's commitment to theological integrity, corporate worship, and excellence in music, preaching, and other liturgical art forms.

Editor: Paul Galbreath
Interior design by Rohani Design
Cover design by Night & Day Design

Congregational Ministries Division,
Presbyterian Church (U.S.A.)
Helen Morrison, Chair
Donald G. Campbell, Director

Office of Theology and Worship
Joseph D. Small III, Coordinator

Presbyterian Association of Musicians
PAM National Office
100 Witherspoon Street
Louisville, KY 40202-1396
Phone: 502-569-5288
Fax: 502-569-8465
Web: http://www.pam.pcusa.org
Alan Barthel, Executive Director,
abarthel@ctr.pcusa.org
Creston Parker, Sr. Administrative Assistant,
pam@ctr.pcusa.org

PAM Board, 2003
Craig Dobbins, CCM, President
David Eicher, Past President
Vicki Fey, President-elect
Mary Beth Jones, Secretary
Wes Ward, Treasurer
Sally Gant
Fannie C. Scott
Scott Miller
Richard Clement
Janet Loman

© 2003 Office of Theology and Worship,
Presbyterian Church (U.S.A.) and Geneva Press
ISSN 1534-8318
ISBN 0-664-50257-1

Indexed with abstract in Religion Index One: Periodicals, American Theological Library Association; available online through BRS (Bibliographic Retrieval Services) and DIALOG; by Music Article Guide and by Religious and Theological Abstracts. This publication is available in microfilm from ProQuest.

Address editorial correspondence, materials for review, and unsolicited manuscripts to
Editor, *Call to Worship*
100 Witherspoon Street
Louisville, KY 40202-1396
Phone: 502-569-5331
Fax: 502-569-8060

Address advertising correspondence to
Bill Falvey
100 Witherspoon Street
Louisville, KY 40202-1396
Phone: 502-569-5085
E-mail: Bfalvey@presbypub.com

Send change of address and subscription requests to
Presbyterian Publishing Corp.
Attn: *Call to Worship* Customer Service
100 Witherspoon Street
Louisville, KY 40202-1396
Phone: 1-800-227-2872

Introduction

I f one is to speak of God, then one must speak of one's self." Years ago my wife created a calligraphy version of these words by Rudolf Bultmann, and it sits atop my desk. These words are one way that I remain focused on the deep conviction that incarnational experience lies at the heart of Christian faith.

Experience: it seems strangely appropriate and highly ironic (or providential as we Calvinists prefer to claim) that I should begin my service as editor of *Call to Worship* with an issue that is linked by the theme of experience. My own experience with the rich heritage of *Reformed Liturgy & Music* brought me to this task. As a pastor for the last ten years, I kept copies of the journal near my desk. Frequently, I found myself referring back to issues on topics as they came up in the life of the parish. Whether it was discussions with the worship committee about reclaiming a balance between Word and Sacrament, planning for the Easter Vigil, or selecting hymns with our church musician, *Reformed Liturgy & Music* provided a resource that grounded, challenged, and at times corrected our practice. *Call to Worship* seeks to extend and renew the tradition of *Reformed Liturgy & Music* by providing timely and pertinent resources that point to current issues that grow out of the worshiping life of the church.

This first big issue includes an array of lectionary aids for help with planning worship during the coming year. It includes many of the past categories as well as offering suggestions for incorporating multicultural and contemporary hymns and songs in conjunction with the liturgical year and lectionary readings. This issue also comes with a series of acknowledgments. I am grateful to my new colleagues in the Office of Theology and Worship for their participation, encouragement, and support in putting this issue together. Special thanks to Alan Barthel, executive director of the Presbyterian Association of Musicians, whose library I frequently plundered to check references, as well as to the Presbyterian Association of Musicians board for their support and encouragement. Finally, a word of thanks goes out to Debbie Chesser, who as temporary support staff in the office, worked diligently to help me get all of the pieces into place.

May your experience in reading and using this issue of *Call to Worship* be one that strengthens, encourages, and confirms the gifts of service which you offer with the people of God in thanksgiving for God's goodness in our lives.

PAUL GALBREATH

Part One

Experience

Forming Faith

Exploring the Experience
of Worship-Centered Congregations

BY JANE ROGERS VANN

Liturgy both shapes and expresses a worshiping community's deepest beliefs and affections toward God, toward one another, and toward the world.

Shortly before his retirement from Eleanore Presbyterian Church in Eleanore, West Virginia, Pastor Frank McCraven, his face glowing with gratitude, told me this story. When he first came to Eleanore some eight years before, he introduced participatory prayers into the service—prayers said by everyone or prayers said by a leader with responses for the whole congregation. Before the introduction of this new pattern, the pastor's voice had been the only voice of prayer for the congregation. Frank encouraged the congregation to try the pattern of shared prayer for three months, after which time the session would evaluate its use in worship. At the end of the three months, Frank waited anxiously to see what the church's "patriarch" would have to say, knowing that the congregation would follow his lead. "Now I can pray, too," said this patient saint. "Now I can participate." Like faithful pastors everywhere, Frank took the experience of worship for his congregation seriously. He knew that experience in worship that is formative begins with "full, active participation."[1]

Humans are pattern-seeking, storytelling, meaning-making beings who hunger for communities and practices that support this natural impulse to reflect on and make sense of life's many and varied circumstances. Anthropologists tell us that among all the levels of meaning—which they name as information, metaphor, and participation—the highest level of meaning is participation.[2]

It should not surprise us that from the smallest churches to the largest and most sophisticated congregations, participation in worship is a natural practice. Liturgy naturally carries out two functions simultaneously. It both shapes and expresses a worshiping community's deepest beliefs and affections toward

God, toward one another, and toward the world. This essay explores the many dimensions of the practice of worship as it gives expression to the faith of congregations and, at the same time, forms them, more faithfully, into the body of Christ.

Liturgical theologians refer to this participatory, embodied communal activity of the believing assembly as *primary liturgical theology*. According to Gordon Lathrop, "The meaning of the liturgy resides first of all in the liturgy itself. If the gathering has a meaning for us, if it says an authentic thing about God and our world—indeed, if it brings us face to face with God—then that becomes known while we are participating in the gathering. The liturgical vision engages us while the order of actions flows over us and while we ourselves perform the patterns and crises of this public work. The liturgy itself is primary theology. . . . Primary liturgical theology is the communal meaning of the liturgy exercised by the gathering itself."[3]

Take, for example, a congregation in Latrobe, Pennsylvania, as it celebrates Pentecost. It is obvious that today is a special day. There is an air of excitement and celebration throughout the church, and everyone—children, youth, adults—everyone is wearing red. A procession of banners, red balloons, choir, ministers, and the whole congregation forms in the sanctuary's gathering space. Music—sometimes celebratory, sometimes mysterious—leads the people into worship and supports their worship of the God who dwells with us through the Holy Spirit given on this day. After worship the celebration continues with birthday cake, conversation, and lots of laughter in the fellowship hall.

As these Christians enact the stories of their faith, in this case the story of the coming of the Holy Spirit at Pentecost, they express their awareness of the Holy Spirit's presence in their own lives and their gratitude to God. At the same time their discernment of and orientation toward God's presence is deepened and their capacity for gratitude is expanded. Thus the communally enacted celebration of Pentecost both shapes and expresses their faith. It is *primary liturgical theology*, to use Lathrop's term, because it flows over participants in enacted patterns as worship's vision is proclaimed.

Worshipers often ask *what* liturgy means, a necessary and important question that we will take up later. Fred Holper reorients the question when he suggests that an equally important approach is to ask *how* liturgy means. Worship, he says, "is an invitation for the whole person and the whole community to participate in a symbolic journey of discovery. Thus, the rites for Baptism and Renewal of the Baptismal Covenant bid us to 'grow into our baptism,' to explore how baptism means to a child, how baptism means to a couple who will follow Christ in the particular relationship of marriage, how baptism means to those whose life has been changed by disease, divorce or disability, how baptism means for those facing death."[4]

As thickly symbolic communal enactments—complex juxtapositions of words and gestures to the assembly's own presence and participation—the worship of the church has meaning that can never be exhausted. How does worship mean? Worship means in a multilayered, complex, communally enacted, and symbolic way that can be known first of all through participation, and then supported by reflection on that participation.

THE EXPERIENCE OF WORSHIP

Worship-centered congregations take experience, especially the experience of worship, seriously. These congregations know that when they are formed in the likeness of Christ, the people of God are responding to "a totally embodied religious experience and religious vision."[5]

Their attentiveness to all the aspects of worship is intended to invite the gathered community into such an experience. The invitation is not manipulative but arises out of their own deep and heartfelt response to the presence of God among them. Worship engages people as whole beings—body, mind, and affections. Worship engages their natural, social, and relational nature. Worship invites people into the ancient and ongoing story of the people of God. But most of all, worship enlivens the imagination in ways that make the presence of God vividly discernable in each of these experiential domains: *physical/ sensory, affective, narrative, cognitive, social, relational,* and *imaginative.*

Not only is worship given depth and detail by its many inherent juxtapositions, worship is also experienced simultaneously on many levels of human receptivity and understanding. Through a sustained pattern of experience and reflection, a single experience is considered and reconsidered from many different perspectives. The dimensions of experience listed above represent some of the opportunities for reflective detours as the people of God continue to learn the Christian life from the experience of congregational life, beginning with the experience of worship.

THE PHYSICAL/SENSORY DIMENSION

There is a famous Norman Rockwell painting that features a family walking to church, dressed in prim finery, through a rough-and-tumble neighborhood where the remnants of Saturday night stand in sharp contrast to Sunday morning. This painting always reminds me of the sheer physical nature of "going to church." This family has engaged in a lot of physical activity in order to prepare themselves for worship. They are scrubbed and starched and polished. Their act of walking together toward the church is full of physical energy. The embodi-

Worship enlivens the imagination in ways that make the presence of God vividly discernible.

ment of worship begins with our preparations for gathering as the worshiping assembly, but it surely does not end there. My colleague Ron Byars says that, "The exercise of our 'royal priesthood' (I Peter 2:9) does not take place only within the mind, but also requires engagement of the whole self, body as well as soul."[6]

Every congregation has a particular way of enacting its worship of God. According to Don Saliers, "[E]ach element of a service of worship is 'performed' in a specific manner. . . . Congregations have tacit understandings of what constitutes integrity and authenticity in the 'realization' of the texts."[7] At Latrobe Presbyterian, the physical dimension of liturgy is a natural part of the larger whole of what it means to participate in worship. When children lead the Pentecost procession with banners and balloons, the natural exuberance of children is displayed physically. Thus they lead the community both physically and expressively in the celebration of God's presence at Pentecost.

Our physical and sensory participation is complex. There is, of course, the visible bodily activity involved in participation, some of which is conscious and volitional while other elements are unconscious or spontaneous. In addition, and maybe more important, there is the simultaneous inner sensation of physical activity, inseparable from bodily activity but at the same time distinct from it. Harold Daniels describes these aspects of human personhood well:

The human person is a soul, a spirit, a body, a mind, a wonderful complex of physical and spiritual realities. There is an inseparable relationship between gesture and our inner feelings and attitudes. In gesture, posture, and action we express our deepest feelings. We clasp another's hand in expressing warmth in greeting. We embrace another in showing affection. Furthermore, we know that the body often communicates more truthfully than one's lips. Since gesture, posture, and action involve our whole being, they reinforce and intensify our attitudes and can even evoke feelings within us.[8]

The consequences for liturgy are significant, given that worship is an enacted, communal affair where all aspects of human participation presume physical presence and participation. "We pray with the body as well as with our lips and minds."[9] The combination of external and internal, conscious and unconscious components of physical activity require sustained reflection in order to discern the deeper meanings they may contain. In addition, they combine with other elements of participation and add to the complexity of human experience, which makes reflection on experience all the more important.

Every congregation has a particular way of enacting its worship of God.

The sacraments of baptism and Eucharist are occasions for a congregation's thorough physical and sensory participation whereby they can be continually formed in the likeness of Christ. Ellen Charry writes of meeting a woman who said she became a Christian because she "needed a God she could eat, take into herself and be continuously transformed by. . . . Sacraments are concrete actions by which Christians may be marked, fed and touched by the Holy Spirit so that the reality of God and the work of Christ become embedded in the body and psyche."[10] Thus the embodied practices of the congregation have formative as well as expressive significance for worshipers. During the Reformation, when much of the ceremonial gesture of worshipers and leaders was abandoned, the criteria for whether or not such practices ought to be included in worship was, according to Calvin, whether or not they led people to Christ. "[C]eremonies, to be exercises of piety, ought to lead us straight to Christ."[11] The congregations in this study are careful in their use of bodily gesture and other physical elements of participation. Many say that the inclusion of new practices has stretched them to understand their faith in new ways. During midweek Lenten Communion services at Immanuel Church in Tacoma, participants form a circle around the Lord's Table and offer the elements to one another with the words, "The bread of life; the cup of salvation." This act of taking and offering, eating and drinking together has marked this community with the reality of God's presence among them. Eucharistic generosity shapes their life together and their care for the community in which they live. They and those to whom they minister are "led to Christ" by their sacramentally formed lives. During the worship committee report at a recent session meeting, personal responses to these weekly Communion services make their way into the conversation. "It wasn't too long ago we only had Communion once every three months," comments one elder. "This is quite a welcome change." "I like saying the words, 'The bread of life; the cup of salvation,'" says another. "When we use the bread that is broken [rather than pre-cut] you can't miss the meaning," observes someone else. "There is a deeper level of participation when we come forward, when we exchange the words and the bread and the cup. That is a really important part of sharing Communion." These elders, the most vocal of whom are middle-aged and older men, are aware of how all of their senses and their physical presence are involved in the way they receive Communion. They receive it physically, but also spiritually in ways that are new and exciting to them.

THE AFFECTIVE DIMENSION

Though it is not always apparent in the practice of some mainline Protestant churches, human experience always brings with it an affective dimension. Brain researchers tell us that all our thoughts and physical sensations are routed first through a part of the brain that governs the emotions. According to Fred Edie, for example, "[E]motion is increasingly understood as both integral and essential to human knowing and acting, and by extension, to human social interaction and moral life. Further, the role of emotion in memory is increasingly well-understood; especially the ways in which the affective tonality of recalled experience shapes the ways persons lean into the future. Finally, emotion is also increasingly framed within the context of relationality; that is, not as a discrete self-contained experience of the individual but as a response which resonates with (and elicits responses from) others in the environment."[12]

Liturgy "moves" people. "Liturgy elicits from God's people a broad sweep of emotion, from ecstasies of praise to the sorrows of lamentation. Its power is a visceral 'felt' power in the hearts and bodies of those who practice it."[13] But attention to liturgy's natural affective component is not manipulative. Rather, it is, as Don Saliers points out, a natural schooling of the affections toward love of God and neighbor. "There is no religious life without our being profoundly affected: doctrine without experience is empty; religious experience without doctrine is blind."[14]

Worship-centered congregations recognize the importance of the affective dimension of worship and give particular attention to it in their enactment of worship. This being the case, and because worship both shapes and expresses religious commitments, congregations are wise to attend carefully to the affective tone of their gatherings for worship. At Covenant Presbyterian in Palo Alto, California, pastor Isaiah Jones is leading the congregation into patterns of worship that include a broader range of emotional expression, and he is doing it in a way that helps worshipers to find their own levels of comfort. "I look for things that are familiar and take them to a new level," he says. Recently when he asked the children to sing "Jesus Loves Me," he asked them to change the words. "Sing 'Jesus Loves You' and look someone in the eye when you sing it." Pretty soon the whole congregation had joined in and the level of involvement was multiplied. "I want them to experience the aliveness of God. I don't want them to just come here and perfunctorily go through the motions of liturgy. So I take something familiar and then have them try something new with it. That makes it more alive, and then when I ask them to relate to each other, then they become a corporate body worshiping together. Worship becomes exciting to them, alive to them. When they leave here they say they feel the spiritual presence of God."

When we speak of religious affections and their necessary inclusion in the practice of worship, we are not speaking of shallow sentiments nor

Liturgy moves people.

expressions of emotionalism. Rather, we have in mind the deeper dispositions and contours of character that are made apparent through a person's actions, perceptions, and feelings over time. "The principal point is that in the moral and religious life, we are more accountable for what we *are* than for what we immediately feel. . . . What we *are* in our intentions and actions, is more adequately revealed by referring to the dispositions which constitute a 'sense' of the heart than by referring to what we feel or what ideas we have at the time."[15]

Thus it is that participation in worship "schools the affections," the deepest commitments of heart and life through encounter with God in the midst of the community. Sometimes gradually, sometimes suddenly, our character is shaped through repeated encounters with God in worship. In order for this to be the case, our coming before God must include a kind of spiritual honesty that surpasses the polite decorum of many kinds of public gatherings. Joining in worship is a gathering of an altogether different sort, where nothing but the truth of our lives will do. Walter Brueggemann observes that "Very many people have the impression that it is 'meet and right and our bounded duty' to pretend that life does not hurt. That is correlated to a false notion of god who does not traffic in grief, rage, and pain. . . . In a society of cover-up and denial, the liturgic practice of honesty can permit new vitality in the community and in communion with God."[16]

Denise Thorpe at West Raleigh Church says that in worship there is an emerging honesty, discernable in the prayers of the people. Whereas in the past various groups in the church came together to form a loosely knit "confederacy" of particular interests, the congregation is beginning to see itself as one congregation. "There were these groups within the church that got along well but had very different interests and commitments. The reason everybody got along is they didn't get close enough to disagree. Everybody knew that if you got too close you would disagree. That was a fear." As the church has become more spiritually centered and has sought to integrate all parts of its life around the centrality of worship, there has emerged a greater willingness to discuss areas of disagreement and, at times, agree to disagree. "I find myself continuing to say it is okay to talk about these things and to disagree about them because of what holds us together. It isn't our politeness. What binds us together is the love of God made known to us in Jesus Christ, and that's really what the church is all about. That is our foundation and we can trust that. We can trust it so much that we can be honest." The centrality of worship and the communal life of prayer shapes all that the congregation is and does. "Our orientation in everything that we do comes from the life of the Spirit, from our understanding of who we are, a people claimed by God. It begins with our worship together.

Our ministry and mission are shaped first of all there. Then our ministry actions and other decisions come back in and shape our life of worship and prayer. A lot of this has been forged in our struggle, in the places where conflict and struggle emerged, and were then surrounded by worship and prayer."

Another way the West Raleigh church practices honesty is in its services for wholeness and healing. Using a liturgy provided by the denomination and adapted for their congregation, those gathered pray, hear the Word, and celebrate Communion. As people come forward to receive Communion, the pastors and elders are available to pray individually with those who request it. The centrality of the Eucharist has emerged as an important element of this congregation's life. As Denise put it, "because of the centrality of the Eucharist, worship is a healing experience. This has really broadened my understanding of all the work of the church as a healing ministry. When we celebrate Communion by intinction, we have people available to pray for celebration, thanksgiving, comfort, and healing, before they receive Communion."

The Narrative Dimension

Many have noted that in the Jewish tradition, when children ask questions, their questions are often answered with a story. During the Passover Seder meal when a child asks, "Why is this night different from all other nights?" the answer comes in the form of the narrative recounting of slavery in Egypt, God's triumphant leading out, and the forming of the people of Israel in the deserts of Sinai. Likewise, Christians are a story-formed people,[17] formed after the likeness of Jesus Christ through the continual remembrance of his life, death, and resurrection. Week by week the story of God's way with humankind in Scripture and history is woven together with the congregational, family, and personal stories of a community of faith. In this way the lives of worshipers become part of a larger narrative, especially the narrative of Scripture. Community and identity are established by means of shared stories, common memories of who we are and to whom we belong. Thus we are called into the "communal memory of those gathered about the font, the book, and the table."[18]

As any good storyteller knows, stories have a way of imaginatively involving hearers in the plot and action of the story. Listeners enter into the world of the story in ways that allow them to share the experience of the characters themselves. Especially with the stories of God's people, told and retold in the church, their stories become "our story" as we become God's people, too. "We experience salvation for our time by remembering and re-encountering the Story of God's saving deeds. When we remind

Community and identity are established by means of shared stories.

God and ourselves of the Story, it is as if even God cannot but be moved by the memory, and for us it becomes a saving 'event' once more."[19] The biblical story becomes our story, as we experience the saving acts of God and take our place alongside others who have gone before us.

Storytelling of any kind has a remarkable way of weaving together the past, the present, and the future. Through the stories of faith Christians can remember a shared and treasured past, orient themselves toward God's saving action in the present, and envision a future which is in the care of this self-same God. While participation in worship always takes place in the present tense, the story of the past and a vision for God's future are pervasively present. Past, present, and future become united as they mutually inform and influence one another. As Christians we live in both the "already" and the "not yet" of the reign of God. Especially in worship we are invited into this eternal vision as the past, present, and future of God's reign are enacted in story, sacrament, prayer, and song. The narrative qualities of worship ensure that we who gather in God's presence will become part of the story of God's redemption. Pam Wilson, who sings in the choir at West Raleigh Presbyterian, says that it is more than just listening to Scripture. "You really must *participate* in worship and in Scripture. First of all you have *read* the Word. Now that sounds pretty simple, but in point of fact, to go about that in a disciplined and sus-tained way is not that easy, at least for me. I have to keep doing it over and over, reminding myself how to read Scripture. Second, you have to open yourself to being shaped by what God reveals to us (and to me personally) in the Word. Scripture is not just a collection of stories or histories. While it is all of these things, it is so much more than that, as the inspired Word of God. It's really one way that God speaks to me and to us simultaneously. So it means to study, whether alone or with other people, and then to be open to what the Word says we should do."

THE COGNITIVE DIMENSION

If, as Saliers says, religious experience without doctrine is blind, then we can be especially thankful for the many theologians across the centuries who have given to the church the gift of sound doctrine. Worship's cognitive dimension is related, at least in part, to the ways liturgy enacts the principal doctrines of Christian faith. At Madison Avenue Presbyterian Church in New York, changes in architecture, furnishings, and their arrangement signal new insight into primary Christian beliefs. "A historic church, the church of Henry Sloane Coffin, George Buttrick, and David Read, Madison Avenue Presbyterian now focuses on a pulpit, a large communion table, and, in the central aisle, a font large enough to immerse an infant. At Madison Avenue, prayer is offered from the communion table; the Scriptures are read where they are preached. The ambiguity of having both a pulpit and a lectern—which all too often reflected an era of topical preaching when Scripture and sermon were isolated entities in the order of worship—is avoided."[20]

A list of cognitive functions typically includes knowledge, comprehension, application, analysis, synthesis, and evaluation.[21] Various levels of cognitive functioning are called upon in the course of participation in worship as worshipers relate previous knowledge to present experience, encounter new knowledge, and seek to comprehend the relationships between previous knowledge and that which is new. Worship also invites participants to compare and contrast aspects of worship with one another and with previous worship occasions. And worship calls participants to evaluate the importance of worship's claims about God and the world, thus leading us to a critical engagement with the world and a deeper commitment to God. An important element in this process is a biblical, theological, and spiritual vocabulary that both shapes and illuminates the experience of encounter with God.

Insights about the cognitive domain of human experience from the field of education can help us here. Teaching can be arranged in two broad categories: teaching *that* and teaching *how*.[22] Teaching *that* includes all of the ways we convey information about a particular subject matter. Teaching *how*, on the other hand, is what we might call "coaching." It includes all the ways we demonstrate an activity, encourage practice, give constructive and

corrective feedback, and initiate novices into details of a skill. The cognitive domain in worship consists much more in "showing how" than in "telling that." There is always information to be given and insights to be shared, but when learning the Christian life, especially in worship, "learning that" is always in service of "showing how." Learning how the community worships God comes primarily through participation in the enactment of worship. Whatever information is necessary to enable, broaden, and deepen that participation is in service of "learning how."

At Covenant, Pastor Isaiah Jones is leading the way, showing how worship can be energetic and lively, even while it upholds the long-standing traditions of the congregation. Diane Jones, a member of Covenant, says that an eagerness to learn has always been a prominent characteristic of the congregation. Pastors over the years, including the current pastor, have included the work of prominent biblical scholars and theologians in their preaching and teaching. "That kind of intellectual curiosity has encouraged me to look at other aspects of the Christian life. I have gotten interested in the practice of Christian spirituality. We have an adult class now where we read Scripture, study together, and practice *lectio divina*." Deeper knowledge of the Christian tradition has inspired people like Diane to take up practices of Christian spirituality that they might never have discovered. Knowing about the Christian spiritual tradition led them into learning how to practice it with heartfelt dedication.

Part of the meaning-making inclination of the human mind is to bring some sort of systematic order to the buzz of activity that pervades our senses. The cognitive domain is fruitfully engaged in worship when worship itself demonstrates *how* the assembly's praise enacts consistent patterns of faithfulness to its own theocentric intentions. The words, symbols, gestures, and actions of the community, repeated during successive occasions, cohere in a way that corresponds with what the community is and does. There is logical consistency in the claims made by worship on the lives of members of the assembly so that the intellect is stretched even as its need for systematic order is satisfied. As Gordon Lathrop reminds us, "A community doing its liturgy will be remembering the series of rituals that the participants have known and will be reorganizing, reinterpreting, and reforming—criticizing—those memories by means of the on-going ritual enactment. The current ritual performs and reforms what is remembered and known 'by heart.' A book and a discussion may help us to sort out the local memories, in relationship to the patterned communal memories from the history of the church, giving us specific tools for doing the next liturgy. So the perceived juxtapositions of the *ordo* or the discussion of strong signs and strong critique of the signs have yielded concrete proposals for the continual reshaping of our local assemblies. But the actual critical force of the ordo, like the primary meaning of liturgical theology, will be found in the next liturgy we do."[23]

Throughout his work Gordon Lathrop uses the structure of the ordo (the fourfold pattern of gathering, service of the Word, Eucharist, and sending) and its inherent "juxtapositions" to note the dependable patterns of Christian worship (the shape of the ordo) and the expansive and surprising possibilities within that ordo. In the practice of the liturgy, texts, actions, objects, songs, gestures, and the assembly itself are "juxtaposed" to one another in ways that proclaim God's surprising grace. Seasons, stories, sound, and silence all interact in unpredictable ways, giving our cognitive faculties both familiarity and novelty through which to discern the patterns of God's presence. Our cognitive faculties naturally search for patterns in the juxtapositions that both break and confirm other elements of the liturgy.

Most Protestants have grown accustomed to the ways the sermon dominates the assembly's worship and generally appeals to a strongly cognitive dimension of human nature. Congregations are finding that when they take into consideration additional important aspects of human experience in worship, their knowledge of God and of their world is strengthened. Thus there is a kind of reciprocal complementary relationship between the cognitive dimension of worship and all its other dimensions.

SOCIAL AND RELATIONAL DIMENSIONS OF WORSHIP

The social structures and relational dynamics of a congregation are manifested in many areas of the community's life. In worship-centered congregations significant attention is given to how these social and relational aspects of congregational life are enacted in worship. In the social domain, various roles, responsibilities, and levels of communal authority are enacted. Acolytes, ushers, eucharistic ministers, pastors, readers, and members of the assembly all have specific roles to play in the enactment of the community's praise. Thus it is important to ask, What patterns of social order are projected by the enactment of our liturgies? What are the implicit manifestations of assumptions about such things as diversity in gender, race, ability, and age? What does our worship say about the social standing and power of lay and clergy members of the assembly? What kinds of imagery predominate, and to whose experience does it refer? What patterns of authority are demonstrated by passivity and/or active participation? How does leadership reflect service to the assembly alone? Or does leadership reflect authority accrued in some other social order? It is critical for congregations to keep these and similar questions in mind as they participate in worship and anticipate future participation.

At St. Paul's Episcopal Church in Bloomsburg, Pennsylvania, planning for the Easter Vigil begins early in Lent and includes a wide variety of members of the church. Leadership for this most important service demonstrates that service to the assembly is primarily focused on the ability of the leader to support and enliven the people's prayer. Matters of social status within and outside the congregation are of little concern here. Rather, worship leaders are chosen for their gifts for leadership and for their maturity in faith. And so when the vigil is celebrated leaders include people of many ages, backgrounds, and abilities. All are well prepared for their roles in the service and demonstrate a kind of spiritual leadership that invites the full participation of the community.

What patterns of social order are projected by the enactment of our liturgies?

One quality that distinguishes worship-centered, spiritually lively congregations is the nature of their relationships. In these congregations there are frequent demonstrations of genuine affection and intimacy among members and leaders. The importance of the Christian spiritual life is apparent in the ways individuals relate to one another. The kind of caring intimacy the community expects is enacted Sunday by Sunday at St. Paul's between Rector Marjorie Menaul and the acolytes who serve with her. Acolytes carry the cross, candles, and Gospel book in the entrance and final procession, and again when the Gospel is read in the midst of the assembly. They also assist her in preparation and serving of the Eucharist. In this congregation of about three hundred members, there are more than twenty-five teenagers who are eager to serve as acolytes. This enthusiastic participation by young people has both advantages and disadvantages. According to Marjorie, the school and activity schedules of the young people, coupled with the liturgical schedule of the church, mean that acolytes serve only once every *six, seven,* or *eight* weeks. Marjorie makes sure the young people have thorough training in their roles as acolytes, both in the local parish and at regional and national acolyte camps. Nevertheless, without frequent enactment of their roles, these young people are apt to need some coaching as they serve the worshiping assembly alongside the priest. Watching the relational enactment of liturgical service between Marjorie and the acolytes is heartwarming in a way that draws worshipers into a kind of communal intimacy, while at the same time contributing to the joyful reverence that is natural to worship. As Marjorie, in quiet words and gestures, reminds and coaches the acolytes through their responsibilities, it is as though they are truly preparing a meal together, not going through the ritual motions of preparing bread and wine. Anxiety about "getting it right" seems completely absent here, as Marjorie presides in ways that support and direct the central actions but do not dominate or control. There is a sense of relaxed and joyful liturgical hospitality demonstrated in the relation-

ship between priest and acolytes that is then extended to eucharistic ministers and to the entire assembly during the celebration of the Eucharist. The participatory practice these Christians share is the centerpoint of their embodied faith and forms a history of shared experience on which they can reflect as they seek to broaden and deepen their communal life of faith. Based on the relationships established in the celebration of the worship of God, these people are able to ask one another, "How goes it with you and God? Where is God in this?" Congregations like these also demonstrate a kind of honesty before God and one another that makes it possible for them to weather the ups and downs of any community. Their relationships are lived out before God, and so their ability to face the truth about themselves is grounded in their knowledge of the steadfast faithfulness of God.

THE IMAGINATIVE DIMENSION

At worship recently one of the texts was Hebrews, chapters 11 and 12, where the writer names and describes the faithful lives of the people of God through the centuries and then calls the attention of readers to the "great cloud of witnesses" that surrounds the community of faith. As the preacher creatively called the attention of the congregation to the many witnesses of the faith that had gone before us in First Presbyterian Church of Bloomsburg, my eyes were drawn to the brilliantly colored windows that surrounded us. The Gothic shapes of the windows reminded me of head-and-shoulder silhouettes of our forebears, surrounding us as we joined them in the worship of God. I imagined the many men and women of faith, some of whom I knew and some whom I had heard about in Scripture, song, and congregational story. I felt their presence nearby and gave thanks for their witness. The designers of those windows did not intend that they be seen as silhouettes of the cloud of witnesses. I imagined their presence. Or, to put it more accurately, I discerned their presence through the experience of the biblical witness "juxtaposed" to artistic expression.

Acts of faithful imagination are to be found everywhere in worship. In the communal enactments of the praise of God, congregations call upon story and song, metaphor and symbol, image and gesture, in order to give expression to the unfathomable mystery of God. The human imagination, enlivened and faithfully shaped through disciplined worshiping communities, learns to discern the presence of God through the many aspects of the liturgy. Thus the meaning of Word and Sacrament "is discovered again and again in new depth and breadth as sacramental celebration draws us into the mystery of God's covenant relationship with us in Jesus Christ, a relationship whose depth and breadth is never fully exhausted or comprehended. God presents Godself to us in new ways each time we encounter God in the sacraments no matter how often we celebrate them."[24]

It has been common to be wary of human imagination, fearing that its fruits are "imaginary." Recent research in fields as diverse as philosophy, neurology, and learning theory repeatedly points out, however, that when imagination is understood simply as the act of making present in the mind that which is absent to the senses, the use of the imagination is understood more thoroughly. The natural strategy of the mind is to reach for understanding of the here-and-now by searching for similarities with previous experience and by noticing new patterns of meaning that have not been encountered before. Both the calling on memory and the noticing of patterns are acts of the imagination. In remembering, we recall into the present that which is past. In discovering patterns within present experience, we naturally pose imaginative "What if?" questions and explore their implications. When we are called to envision the future, our imaginative capacities are oriented to that which is "not yet." In our efforts at meaning-making we naturally link past and present in ways that are ever new. This requires the use of imagination, our active engagement with the world around us. Understood in this way the term "imagination" does not refer to some outlandish, fly-away mental abandon that will inevitably lead us astray. Rather, the imagination is our active participation in meaning-making that allows metaphors to sing and images to resonate with the very presence of God. Imagination works indirectly, bringing various aspects of experience, memory, and expectation together in order to construct meaning. Imagination serves to interpret metaphorical language and image, as well as to deepen the symbolic interpretation of concrete experience.

Worship proposes a world that is different from (though not separate from) the world of our ordinary experience. By immersing us in the very presence of God, worship enables us to notice and attend to the presence of God at other times and places. "'Worldmaking' is a prime activity of the artistic imagination," says Leland Ryken,[25] and, I would contend, a prime activity of the faithful liturgical imagination. "There is emancipation in the imagination: It frees us in an instant from our time and place and transports us to another world."[26]

Theologians in all branches of Christendom agree that proposing and inviting people into an alternative world—a world where all praise and honor, glory, and power are ascribed to the triune God—is a primary intention of worship. In order to accomplish this—to hold present in the mind those things that are absent to the senses—our capacities for discerning God's pervasive presence throughout creation must be enlivened and disciplined. The God we know is the God of Scripture, especially known in the life, death, and resurrection of Jesus Christ. As we are shaped by scriptural story, image, and

metaphor, so our capacities for imaginative discernment of God's presence become more acute. Many worshipers sitting near me a few Sundays ago might have noticed the beautifully colored windows. They might have admired them, or worried about needed repairs to them, or they might have been irritated by the windows' particular design and colors. It required active, discerning imagination to see the congregation surrounded by the great cloud of witnesses. It is these sorts of sustained, disciplined acts of imagination that worship continually calls forth.

Faithful worship, says Stan Hall, "is in service of and in the reign of God as the reign of God is proclaimed by the Word of God, embodied in Jesus Christ, rendered through the Spirit. . . . [T]he church participates in the 'already' and the 'not yet' of the reign of God. . . . Worship according to the Word of God is at once already our engagement in the reign of God, and it is also the sign of that reign for which we pray, which in God's freedom is yet to come."[27] Of course most people do not live, day in and day out, with a consciousness of God's reign. It is in worship that this consciousness is lifted up, shared, embodied, and embraced. In order to perceive the reign of God in worship (and to extend one's perceptions into all of life), sustained, disciplined, faithful use of the imagination is required. Worshipers learn to "see through" the stories, songs, symbols, gestures, and ritual enactments into the reign

Worship proposes a world that is different from (though not separate from) the world of our ordinary experience.

of God in ways that enable them to discern that reign wherever it appears and pray for its emergence where it does not. Calvin urged Christians to view the world as the "theater of God's glory," and it is through faithful imagination that the contours of God's glory can be discerned. Walter Brueggemann has said, "The church does its subversive work not by ethical admonition and heavy-handed coercion but by making available an alternative construction of reality which legitimates and makes possible a life more faithful, more obedient, and more joyous." The church's worship, he suggests, does not need to be relevant "as much as it needs to be honest, intentional, and nervy about the practice of reality that is done in this liturgy."[28]

When worship's natural imaginative dimensions are allowed to flourish through Scripture and storytelling, through poetic and metaphorical language, through gesture and enacted praise, through robust use of the church's own symbols, human imagination can be faithfully shaped in ways that give expression to deepening relationships with God.

MAKING WORSHIP "EXPERIENTIAL"

Let us now shift our attention from aspects of human experience relevant to the practice of worship to a discussion of worship's intrinsic aesthetic qualities and the theological, pastoral, and symbolic questions that they raise. The worship wars have so polarized the church's conversations about liturgy that one hesitates to speak about the aesthetics or "style" inherent in worship. But if, as we have claimed, worship both shapes and expresses our beliefs about God and ourselves, we cannot escape such discussions. Added complexity comes from the fact that the environment for worship is made up of so many varied aspects. In addition to the structure and sequence of the liturgy itself, along with its seasonal variations in mood, the liturgical environment is made up of architectural space and how it is used, the decorations and appointments of the space, the rhythm and pacing of liturgical time, liturgical speech and song, and the actions, movements, and gestures of the assembly and its leaders. Each of these aspects contains its own symbolic "language." Gilbert Ostdiek reminds us that "The liturgy is meant to speak to us as one total language, richly and harmoniously varied. It seeks to evoke in us an experience of ourselves as God's people."[29]

The aesthetic dimension or "style" of worship, then is closely related to the symbolic nature of worship itself, with each language revealing the symbolic meanings inherent in liturgical enactment. The emphasis on harmony is of great importance here. Worship-centered congregations want their liturgy to express a consistent understanding of God and themselves, even while that expression is complex, paradoxical, and multilayered. They "think of each sensory language as a unique and valuable way in which . . . experience is opened up to us in harmony with all the other languages being used."[30]

The harmonious blending of all the languages of worship seems like an awesome task, and it is! It is a task that requires of worship planners and leaders nothing but their best and most sustained attention. It also requires the articulation of worship's primary orienting purposes and values as its guiding principles for planning, preparation, and evaluation. These purposes and values are primarily theological and pastoral. In addition, however, the enactment of worship displays symbolic, artistic, and liturgical qualities.[31] Whatever symbolic, aesthetic, and liturgical values inform the planning, preparation, and reflection on worship, we do well to remember that they are in service of worship's primary theological and pastoral purposes. Worship begins and ends with God.

Worship begins and ends with God.

Of equal importance is the "full, conscious, active participation" of the assembly in the worship of God. This is worship's primary pastoral principle and grounds all other concerns for taking experience seriously. "The spiritual good [of God's people at prayer] must be the final goal of all our caring for their prayer." In worship-centered congregations, the worship of God is truly the action of the gathered community. People's participation is attentive and receptive to God's presence among them.

The multiple languages of worship invite particular attention as we consider the formative and expressive nature of worship. "Just as the human reality of Jesus mediates God's presence to us, so too our bodily actions and use of human objects in liturgy tangibly express and bring about God's sanctifying presence to us and our worship of God in spirit and truth. Liturgical celebration depends radically on the honest use of the full range of symbolic languages and liturgical symbols. These 'signs perceptible to the human senses' either nourish or destroy faith by the way in which they are performed."[32] Thus these worship-centered congregations give attention to the full variety of liturgical symbols and symbolic languages. They invest considerable care in the way the worship space is arranged. They choose carefully the vestments, paraments, banners, and Communion ware to be used. More and more, people are being encouraged to actively (bodily) participate in worship as they stand for prayers, voice their prayer concerns and the great "Amen," and move out of the pews to come forward for the Lord's Supper. Many of these congregations are noticing the ways the rhythm of sound and silence symbolically orients their worship. They notice how the interplay of speaking and singing and the voice of one in contrast to the voices of all give richness to their enacted praise. "We have more silence now," says pastor Debbie McKinley, "and it is active, participatory silence, not just dead air."[33]

There is growing concern that all the symbolic languages of worship speak with balance and harmony. There is a natural "interplay and redundancy" among the various symbolic languages of worship to which these congregational leaders are giving fuller attention. At Latrobe, where a renovation of the chancel is under consideration, there is strong support for a new arrangement that will put the pulpit, font, and table on the same level of the sanctuary's platform, indicating the primacy of these three liturgical focal points and their inseparable symbolic significance. The people are learning, too, that they cannot change just one element of their worship space. Changes in the arrangement of the primary symbols of the liturgy have required additional changes to seating arrangements, furnishings, and decorative elements in the sanctuary. Proposals for the new design show continuing attention to the ways each of these symbolic languages speaks uniquely and yet respects the other symbols present in worship.

By its very nature every liturgical symbol and action has artistic qualities, qualities which are called upon to serve the community's worship of God. "Liturgy takes its inspiration for symbol and ritual action from the fine arts, both visual arts and performing arts, and welcomes the artistic expressions, both folk and classic, of past ages and of contemporary peoples, when they are able to serve the liturgy beautifully and worthily."[34] Beauty and artistic worth are, of course, notoriously difficult to define, but when objects and performance serve the worship of God, their most necessary qualities include simplicity and honesty. For liturgical objects this means simplicity in design and a clear relationship between form and function. Materials and craftsmanship show artistic care and simple beauty. They invite the congregation's use and enhance the symbolic richness of the entire liturgy. As part of Latrobe's continuing liturgical renewal, the congregation replaced its baptismal font. The new font features a large, clear glass bowl mounted on a wooden stand made from the wood of historic liturgical furnishings of the congregation. Its strikingly simple beauty makes the font a visual focal point, and its weekly use in worship as the place of significant liturgical actions enhances its natural symbolic expression. This congregation "lives into its Baptism" week by week as they gather around "water and the Word."

The performance of liturgical actions, especially by worship leaders, draws its artistic qualities from the performing arts. However, a subtle but important distinction needs to be made. While worship's gestures and actions are "performed" and while these gestures and actions are led by worship leaders, worship is

This congregation "lives into its Baptism" week by week as they gather around "water and the word."

not a performance in the theatrical sense of that word. The performance of worship's actions and gestures by leaders and people is for the sake of the worship of God. In worship-centered congregations musicians, presiders, readers, and other worship leaders are conscious of their roles in the communal performance of worship even while they reject the notion of worship as "their" performance. Within this framework worship leaders strive for a "noble simplicity" in worship where gestures and words enhance one another, where theological intentions are clear, and where all of worship's elements are within the people's power to comprehend and are free of undue explanation.

Music holds a special place in the performance of worship and has received much attention in the midst of the "worship wars." While it may not be possible to avoid conflict over musical tastes, worship-centered congregations are naturally oriented toward a different starting place. Rather than begin with questions of musical genre, style, and appeal, they begin with the requirements for worship itself and invite worshipers to bring nothing but their best to the performance of worship. Congregations discover that when their music (and all of their worship) expresses clear theocentric and artistic commitments, the style of music gains considerable latitude. At Immanuel Presbyterian, organist and choir director Dianne Everson keeps an attentive and discerning eye on the music of the global church. She chooses well-written music and texts from Africa, South America, and Asia that the congregation embrace as their own. In addition, she has introduced the use of African drums and marimbas into worship. On a recent Sunday morning the children and teens of the church led the assembly in worshiping God through music on the marimbas and drums. Their selections were authentic music of Africa and South America, and they conveyed a lively response to the love of God that was entered into by all present. The celebration continued as the postlude was played. No one hurried toward the door but worshipers stayed to participate in the praise expressed in this lively music.

All of worship's intentions are directed toward praise of God and "the spiritual good of the assembled people."[35] Worship should support the people's prayer and spiritual formation, enabling them to know themselves as the people of God. The capacity of worship to communicate these intentions depends on careful attention to all of worship's verbal and nonverbal aspects and continual critical questioning as to what is being communicated. Symbols have a certain transparent quality in this regard. They inhabit space and time in ways that naturally juxtapose them to one another, one layer upon the other, so that the transparency of each naturally enriches the whole. Only careful attention to these spe-

God's promises to be with us when we gather are dependable.

cific juxtapositions can move the assembly toward "seeing through" the symbols. They can just as easily stand in contradiction or competition with one another. Such attention also ensures that the celebration will be suited to the life of the particular congregation. Worship that is "adapted to the culture, way of life, circumstances, and religious development of the people actually assembled" to praise God invites an experience of encounter with God. And while the results depend on God's grace (not on our planning and preparation, no matter how careful), God's promises to be with us when we gather are dependable.

LEADERSHIP FOR WORSHIP

Participation in worship is always unavoidably shaped by the qualities of leadership embodied by those who preside at the community's gatherings. One of the most surprising discoveries is noticing how practices of worship leadership and ritual presiding profoundly affect the spiritual orientation of the congregation. In worship-centered congregations the spiritual participation of worship leaders is always evident. One always had a sense that these pastors and other leaders are sincerely worshiping God as they exercised their role as worship leaders.[36]

In Philadelphia, Deborah McKinley uses abundant silence to support worshipers' reorientation toward God, and in the process one senses that she herself is engaged in the same reorientation. In Tacoma, Paul Galbreath spends many hours over the course of several months practicing ritual gestures until they became his own bodily expression of response to the presence of God in worship. In Bloomsburg, Marjorie Menaul's calm, generous interactions with the acolytes who serve with her bespeaks her own discipline of remaining centered in God through the enactment of the liturgy. Joe Ward and Denise Thorp in Raleigh lead the community in prayer, mentioning by name those whose lives call for celebration and lament before God. In all these ways and more, worship leaders embody a kind of spiritual participation in liturgy that expresses their own response to God and shapes the worship of the people they lead.

What is it that these worship leaders do, or do differently, that gives their worship leadership its spiritual valence? Gilbert Ostdiek offers a helpful starting point when he distinguishes between "planning" for worship and "preparation" for worship. "We easily lose ourselves in the nuts and bolts of 'planning' and begin to think of our task as one of designing the liturgy from scratch, rather than one of making ourselves, the rituals, the space, and the liturgical objects ready for the moment of public prayer."[37] Rather, he says,

In worship-centered congregations the spiritual participation of worship leaders is always evident.

preparation includes planning, but primarily seeks to enable the worshiping assembly, leaders and people, faithfully to enact the worship of God adapted to their particular needs and *spiritual* circumstances.[38] The role of pastors and other leaders in being shaped by the liturgy itself is central to this task. "If our pastoral goal is to adapt the liturgy so that the people can hear God's word and pray in their real life situations, the presider-homilist must be there, to shape and be shaped by what is prepared."[39] Thus spiritual preparation for worship leadership is essential and includes prayer, Scripture study, reflection on the pastoral priorities of the liturgy, along with careful planning, rehearsal, and preparation of the liturgical space, objects, and vestments. The necessity for this kind of preparation cannot be overstated and is given priority in worship-centered congregations.

Worship leadership by laypeople can become an occasion for deep reflection and profound spiritual formation. Laypeople seem to hunger for opportunities to reflect on their experience of leadership in worship. Asking questions that invite these leaders to describe their experiences—a process of telling their own stories back to themselves in the presence of others who are seeking God's presence—is profoundly formative. Central to these conversations are opportunities to discern God's presence in the midst of preparation, planning, and leading worship. So these faithful pastors ask, in one way or another, "Where is God in this?"

CHILDREN AND WORSHIP

Worship that takes experience seriously by giving attention to the physical, sensory, affective, cognitive, social, relational, and imaginative dimensions of human experience is naturally child-friendly. Children meet life holistically as physical, intellectual, affective, and relational beings. Part of what it means to be childlike is the way in which various dimensions of human personhood are inseparable from other dimensions. Children have not yet learned the disciplines of adulthood that enable them to identify and differentiate among the various dimensions of human experience. In a recent issue of a devotional periodical, Jo Ann Staebler gives an account of such a child-friendly church.

> Baptism is a sacrament of abundance in my congregation. . . . Our pastors are careful with babies, gently caressing a baby's head with a wet hand. But anyone over the age of three or four is treated to the gift in abundance. . . . The girl was five years old. Her grandparents had brought her to church regularly, and she always watched intently when the sacrament of Baptism was celebrated. On the day her younger cousin was baptized, she asked, "When am I going to be baptized?" She kept asking. So one Sunday, there she was.
>
> She climbed the chancel steps in excited wonder, and took her place to one side of the font. Her

mother, standing on the opposite side with the grandparents, tried vainly to contain her daughter's exuberance across the distance. But such joyful anticipation was irrepressible. She looked around from the unaccustomed vantage point and moved her body in a tiny dance of pleasure, her face glowing with a smile that could light any darkness.

The pastor managed to get a very ample amount of water into her hands, and it ran down the girl's upturned face and onto her dress. Never have I seen such an enraptured expression. Her face radiated pure delight. She barely flinched as the water flowed across her eyes.

As she stood there with her hair dripping, her face wet and glistening, her dress spattered, I wanted to stand up and dance my own dance.[40]

Congregations like this one have engaged in some of their most serious debates and decision making around the participation of children in worship. Leaders and members know intuitively that worship that is participatory and multidimensional in its enactment is naturally appropriate for children. Most often their conversations deal with issues of adult acceptance of the presence of children in worship and the heightening of worship's naturally child-appropriate aspects. Rarely have they questioned the appropriateness of worship as a place for children. At West Raleigh

Presbyterian the central question for all decisions concerning children, but especially concerning children and worship, is "What do we want children to experience in the church as they enter confirmation class?" The concern is not so much for children's knowledge about Christian faith as it is for children's participation in the worship, prayer, instruction, and mission of a faithful community. And their initiatives begin with including children in worship. They enhance worship's naturally child-friendly aspects—its mood of anticipation and celebration of the presence of God, its inherent story, drama, and enactment of the mighty acts of God, and its call for heartfelt and embodied response from the people of God. Worship's visual, musical, poetic, and dramatic portrayals of the stories of faith constitute a naturally interactive and participatory arena for multidimensional experience.[41] As with ancient Hebrew worshipers, the objects, actions, and interactions of worship naturally invite curiosity and questioning.

In addition to naturally child-friendly patterns of participation in worship, these congregations offer worship times especially suited to the needs of children, opportunities for parents and children to learn about worship and sacraments, and times of reflection on and preparation for worship. Programs similar to "Young Children and Worship,"[42] developed by Jerome Berryman and Sonja Stewart, adapted to the gifts and needs of particular congregations, offer children and adults ways to worship faithfully together. If children are dismissed from worship, several values permeate these congregations' planning. First, they want to include in worship the greatest number of children possible (and dismiss the fewest). Second, they want children to be absent from the worshiping community for the shortest possible time. And third, they want children to continue worshiping in ways that are appropriate for their particular capacities even while they are away from the larger community.

REFLECTION ON WORSHIP

Liturgical theologians say we are all theologians when we engage in communal and personal reflection on the liturgies in which we participate, which they call *secondary liturgical theology*. Reflection on worship occupies a necessary but secondary role in relation to *primary liturgical theology*, mentioned above. Reflection on liturgy serves to deepen our curiosity, insights, and engagement with the church's worship of God. "*Secondary liturgical theology*, then, is written and spoken discourse that attempts to find words for the experience of the liturgy and to illuminate its structures, intending to enable a more profound participation in those structures by the members of the assembly."[43]

This kind of reflection takes place largely outside of worship itself. In

All other activities of congregational life flow from and culminate in participation in worship.

fact, when reflection on worship comes to predominate worship's theocentric intentions, one might ask whether it continues to *be* worship. It is important to keep in mind that the cognitive dimension is integral to holistic participation in worship and that, while it should not dominate to the point of eclipsing other dimensions of holistic participation, it holds a necessary place in the enactment of worship.

If worship is the central orienting activity of the Christian life, then there must naturally exist appropriate relationships with all the other activities of life, particularly congregational life. To say that an activity is "central" implies that other activities occupy particular positions surrounding this "central" activity and that the relationships of these activities are appropriate to the activities themselves and to worship's theocentric commitments. In worship-centered congregations this means that all other activities of congregational life flow from and culminate in participation in worship. Or, as the documents of Vatican II put it, worship is the source and summit of the church's life. To say it another way, all of the activities of the church are, at least in some measure, occasions for implicit and explicit reflection on what the church says and does in worship. While it is certainly true that there is sometimes great dissonance between the church's claims made in worship and the rest of the life of the church, the intention in worship-centered congregations is to reflect on worship and on all their practices of Christian discipleship so that there is coherence and harmony between what the church proclaims and enacts in worship and the rest of its corporate life. For all of these congregations, worship and reflection on worship is of indispensable importance in their life together. In addition to their reflection on worship, these congregations engage in consistent reflection on all other aspects of their congregation's life. Thus the dynamic rhythm of experience and reflection on experience is a natural part of the congregation's culture.

These congregations display patterns of pervasive structures and practices that support the centrality of worship and reflection. Like most congregations they engage in practices of prayer, study and instruction, mission and discipleship, and leadership. Each of these sets of activities offers opportunities to reflect on their life together and to notice ways their practices are (or are not) in harmony with what they do and say in worship. In addition, these sets of practices offer opportunities to give explicit attention to learning the Christian life from their experience of congregational life.

Experiential learning in congregational life depends on several interactive practices that enhance learning and give it a necessary critical edge. As we have noted before, relationships of intimacy, commitment, endurance, and honesty are essential where "deep learning" consistently takes place. These congregations have largely given up patterns of social reserve that inhibit the exploration of their shared life in Christ. They have learned to share openly and appropriately with one another as they continue to center congregational life on the worship of God. These congregations express an inquisitive and courageous intellectual curiosity, marked by a shared vocabulary for the Christian life. They know how to talk about encounters with God with some precision and specificity because they know the language of faith. In addition, they share a unique congregational vocabulary drawn from their shared experiences over months and years of faith-sharing. Within this context of committed relationships and shared vocabulary, members of these congregations engage in mutual questioning, inquiring, and probing in ways that illuminate the details of experience and draw out the many things that can be gleaned from it. They know how to ask the right question at the right time, energizing and propelling the experiential learning cycle and establishing its practice in the culture of the congregation. ∎

Jane Rogers Vann serves as the Associate Professor of Christian Education at Union-PSCE in Richmond, Virginia. The article is adapted from her forthcoming book, *Renewing Congregations: Worship-Centered Renewal,* from Geneva Press later this year.

NOTES

1. Documents of Vatican II.

2. Roy A. Rappaport, *Ritual and Religion in the Making of Humanity* (Cambridge: Cambridge University Press, 1999), 393.

3. Gordon Lathrop, *Holy Things: A Liturgical Theology* (Minneapolis: Augsburg Fortress, 1993), 5. See also Aidan Kavanagh, *On Liturgical Theology* (New York: Pueblo, 1984), 74–75, 89.

4. J. Frederick Holper, "The Promise of Presbyterian Liturgical Renewal," *Praying in Common,* Cynthia M. Campbell and J. Frederick Holper (Louisville, Ky.: Presbyterian Church (U.S.A.), Theology and Worship Occasional Paper no. 6), 22.

5. Robert Bellah, "Liturgy and Experience," in *The Roots of Ritual,* ed. James Shaugnessy (Grand Rapids: Eerdmans, 1973), 233.

6. Ronald P. Byars, *Leading the Lord's Day Service,* forthcoming.

7. Don E. Saliers, "Liturgical Musical Formation," in *Liturgy and Music: Lifetime Learning,* ed. Robin A. Leaver and Joyce Ann Zimmerman (Collegeville, Minn.: Liturgical Press, 1998), 387.

8. Harold M. Daniels, "The Sign of the Cross," *Reformed Liturgy & Music,* 21.1 (1987): 39.

9. Ibid.

10. Ellen T. Charry, "Sacraments for the Christian Life," *The Christian Century,* November 15, 1995, 1076–1079.

11. John Calvin, *Institutes of the Christian Religion* 4.10.19; Library of Christian Classics, ed. John T. McNeill, trans. Ford Lewis Battles (Philadelphia: Westminster Press, 1960).

12. Fred P. Edie, "Liturgy, Emotion, and the Poetics of Being Human," unpublished manuscript, 1998.

13. Ibid.

14. Don E. Saliers, *The Soul in Paraphrase: Prayer and the Religious Affections* (New York: Seabury Press, 1980), 6ff.

15. Ibid., 18.

16. Walter Brueggemann, "Newness Mediated by Worship," *Reformed Liturgy & Music* 20.2 (1986): 58.

17. John H. Westerhoff, *Living in the Community of Faith: The Church That Makes a Difference* (Minneapolis: Winston Press, 1985), 27.

18. Don E. Saliers, *Worship and Spirituality* (Akron: OSL Publications, 1996), 6.

19. Thomas H. Groom, *Christian Religious Education: Sharing Our Story and Vision* (San Francisco: Harper and Row, 1980), 192.

20. James F. White, "Rearranging the Furniture," *Reformed Worship,* no. 64 (June 2002): 18.

21. Benjamin Bloom, ed., *Taxonomy of Educational Objectives, Handbook I: Cognitive Domain* (Boston: Adderson-Wesley Publishing Co., 1984).

22. Thomas Green, *The Activities of Teaching* (Troy, N.Y.: Educators International Press, 1998).

23. Lathrop, 180.

24. Holper, 22.

25. Leland Ryken, *The Liberated Imagination: Thinking Christianly About the Arts* (Wheaton, Ill.: Harold Shaw Publishers, 1989), 98.

26. Ibid.

27. Stanley R. Hall, *The Essential Tenets of Reformed Worship?* (Louisville, Ky.: Presbyterian Church (U.S.A.), 1998), 5–7.

28. Brueggemann, "Newness Mediated by Worship," 57.

29. Gilbert Ostdiek, *Catechesis for Liturgy: A Program for Parish Involvement* (Washington, D.C.: Pastoral Press, 1986), 89.

30. Ibid.

31. These categories and the following discussion are drawn from Ostdiek, *Catechesis for Liturgy,* 41–45.

32. Ibid., 41–42.

33. Ibid., 42.

34. Ibid., 42–43.

35. Ibid., 44.

36. One could contrast this kind of spiritual leadership with a mechanical "going through the motions" or an ego-driven performance that seemed to crave the spotlight.

37. Ostdiek, 27.

38. Emphasis added.

39. Ostdiek, 26.

40. Jo Ann Staebler, "Water of Welcome," *Alive Now* (July–August 2001).

41. Resources include: Joan Halmo, *Celebrating the Church Year with Young Children* (Collegeville, Minn.: Liturgical Press, 1988); Mary Catherine Berglund, *Gather the Children: Celebrate the Word with Ideas, Activities, Prayers and Projects* (Washington, D.C.: Pastoral Press, 1994); Carolyn C. Brown, *Forbid Them Not—Involving Children in Sunday Worship* (Year C) (Nashville: Abingdon, 1994); *Gateways to Worship: A Year of Worship Experiences for Young Children* (Nashville: Abingdon, 1989); *You Can Preach to the Kids Too!* (Nashville: Abingdon, 1997); Sue Lou, Jean Floyd Love, Mickey Meyers, Sylvia Washer, *Get Ready!*

Get Set! Worship: A Resource for Including Children in Worship for Pastors, Educators, Parents, Sessions, and Committees (Louisville, Ky.: Geneva Press, 1999); David Ng and Virginia Thomas, *Children in the Worshipping Community* (Atlanta: John Knox Press, 1981).

42. Jerome Berryman and Sonja Stewart, *Young Children and Worship* (Louisville, Ky.: Westminster John Knox Press, 1990); Jerome Berryman, *Godly Play: An Imaginative Approach to Religious Education* (Minneapolis: Augsburg Fortress, 1995); Jerome Berryman, *Teaching Godly Play* (Nashville: Abingdon Press, 1995); Sonja Stewart, *Following Jesus* (Louisville, Ky.: Geneva Press, 2000).

43. Lathrop, 6–7.

In Spirit and in Truth

Experience and Worship
in the Reformed Tradition

BY JOSEPH D. SMALL

Human experience" and "Reformed worship" do not appear to be natural bedfellows. Reformed churches do not open their doors wide to welcome the rich, sense-laden liturgies of the Orthodox and Catholic traditions, the warm personal engagement of evangelical pietism, or Pentecostalism's experienced immediacy of the Holy Spirit. Reformed worship seems to be dominated by words and fixed on rational discourse to the exclusion of deep contours of personal and communal experience. James White says of Reformed worship that it is "the most cerebral of the western traditions . . . prolix and verbose."[1] Similarly, Brian Gerrish notes that the wordiness of the Reformed tradition can result in "an arid intellectualism that turns the worshiping community into a class of glum schoolchildren."[2] White and Gerrish may paint with too broad a brush, yet their portrait is realistic enough to invite a closer look at the Reformed understanding of human experience generally and the place of human experience in worship particularly.

It is appropriate to begin with the sixteenth-century Swiss Reformation, not because it provides privileged authorities, but because the insights of Zwingli, Calvin, and others—including their reform of worship—have had an enduring effect on churches that trace their heritage to Zurich and Geneva. Common origin is a useful lens through which to view contemporary expressions of Reformed churches' faith and life.

The early reformers found themselves in an unprecedented ecclesial situation. The Great Church, unwilling or incapable of responding positively to reform efforts, had shattered.

Theological ferment throughout Europe gave birth to a wide variety of reform movements and to diverse communities that exhibited different and often disparate forms of community life. The Reformation's centrifugal force was a matter of concern to the reformers themselves, and a cause of sharp rebuke from the Catholic Church. Both the Catholic rebuke and the Reformation defense can be discerned in a remarkable section of the Second Helvetic Confession (circa 1566). The confession acknowledges that "We are reproached because there have been manifold dissensions and strife in our churches since they separated themselves from the Church of Rome, and therefore cannot be true churches."[3] The reformers took seriously the Catholic indictment that disunity signaled defect, mounting a defense on two levels.

The first defense was to point to Rome's own history of conflict and factionalism, and even to strife within the New Testament church, concluding that "there have at all times been great contentions in the Church . . . without meanwhile the Church ceasing to be the Church because of these contentions."[4] It all remained quite confusing, however. It was not sufficient merely to say that disunity was a fact of church life. The increasingly kaleidoscopic spectacle of a multiplying number of disputing churches caused confusion. How could believers make judgments about who was faithful and who was not? What was true and what was false? What communities

claiming to be Christian were true churches? These were not casual questions, but matters of fundamental faithfulness to the gospel.

The reformers' second, and more substantive, response addressed directly the question of the "true church." John Calvin is typical: "Wherever we see the Word of God rightly preached and heard, and the sacraments administered according to Christ's institution, there, it is not to be doubted, a church of God exists."[5] The Word of God rightly proclaimed and heard . . . Baptism and the Lord's Supper celebrated in fidelity to Christ. *These* are the clear indicators of the presence of the one holy catholic and apostolic church. So central are these two marks, Calvin continued, that we must embrace any church that has them, "even if it otherwise swarms with many faults."[6]

Note that Calvin's "two marks of the church" center on worship, on lived faith within congregations. Even then, he does not speak in the first instance about a church's orthodox doctrine or its sacramental theology, but about the faithfulness of proclamation and reception, and the faithfulness of sacramental practice, within worshiping communities. Calvin's marks of the true church point us to congregations, not academies; to assemblies of the faithful,

Calvin's "two marks of the church" center on worship, on lived faith within congregations.

not libraries; to worship, not books. Theological purity and sacramental precision are not the primary issue. Calvin's marks are matters of fundamental ecclesial faithfulness that allows the gospel to be received, believed, and lived by ordinary men and women.

Perhaps it is because Calvin's marks of Word and Sacrament center on the lived faith of actual congregations that they do not work well if they are used only as boundaries to determine who is in and who is out. After all, how could we determine whether the Word is *purely* preached, let alone heard, and whether the sacraments are administered according to *Christ's* institution? Calvin's marks of the true church do not really function as boundaries, however, for they are better understood as directional signs that point to the core of faithful church life. Any community claiming to be a *Christian church* must place proclamation of the gospel of Jesus Christ at the heart of its life, both through proclaiming and hearing the Word and through faithful celebration of Baptism and the Lord's Supper.

Remember Calvin's formulation. A true church is where the Word is purely preached *and heard*. Congregations are active participants in proclamation, for hearing the Word requires discernment, response, and faithful action. A true church is where the sacraments are celebrated in Christ, and members of the congregation are central to the gospel's sacramental enactment. The really interesting question, then, is what it would mean for a congregation to be, truly and fully, a church of the Word and Sacrament. What would it mean for a congregation (or a presbytery or a denomination) to place proclamation and enactment of the gospel at the very heart of its life as the controlling characteristics of all that it says and does?

Calvin placed Word and Sacrament *together* at the core of the church's life because he took it as "a settled principle that the sacraments have the same office as the Word of God: to offer and set forth Christ to us, and in him the treasures of heavenly grace."[7] Calvin's view is remarkable in two ways. First, the purpose of the sacraments is the same as that of the Word. Baptism and Eucharist have the same function as Scripture and preaching: to proclaim the truth of the gospel of Jesus Christ, giving us true knowledge of God. Second, the purpose of both is to communicate the presence of the living Christ to us, uniting us to him in the power of the Holy Spirit. The Word is not for imparting information, and the sacraments are not for imparting feelings; both are occasions for the real presence of Christ in our midst.

Calvin was confident that Word and Sacrament are effective: they give to us precisely what they portray. Preaching God's Word imparts Christ himself to us, maintaining Christ's living presence among us. The sacraments re-present the person and work of Christ, making real among us the very presence of Christ. "I say that Christ is the matter or (if you prefer) the substance of all the sacraments," says Calvin, "for in him they have all their firmness, and they do not promise anything apart from him."[8] Thus, the Lord's Supper and Baptism are not occasions for the Christian community merely to celebrate its own life. The sacraments impart to the community the substance of its life in Christ.

Calvin speaks of nothing less than the *real presence* of Christ in Word and Sacrament. The worshiping community *experiences* the presence of Christ, and thus knows the reality of the triune God—Father, Son, and Holy Spirit. Calvin has no interest in mere intellectual comprehension, "For it now remains to pour into the heart what the mind has absorbed. For the Word of God is not received by faith if it flits about in the top of the brain, but when it takes root in the depth of the heart. . . . The Spirit accordingly serves as a seal, to seal up in our hearts those very promises the certainty of which it has previously impressed upon our minds; and takes the place of a guarantee to confirm and establish them."[9]

This does not appear to be the stuff of arid intellectualism. Can a worshiping congregation that experiences the grace of the Lord Jesus Christ, the love of God, and the communion of the Holy Spirit become a classroom of glum schoolchildren? Yet, in far too many Reformed churches, that is precisely what has happened. A recent consultation on "The Renewal of Reformed Worship," convened by the International Reformed Centre in Geneva, acknowledged this pervasive reality:

Reformed worshiping communities have not always appreciated the fullness of God's presence in their midst, and have not communicated this adequately in their services. . . . The renewal of Reformed worship will involve a deeper understanding and a faithful reclaiming of the reality of God's faithful presence, expressed and experienced in the three persons of the Trinity—*God the Father,* creator of heaven and earth, the author of all blessings and protector of all created things, *Jesus Christ,* the unique Truth and Light of the world, *the Holy Spirit,* the source of true and eternal life.[10]

Does this diagnosis disclose a wrong turn by Reformed churches, a departure from the authentic faith and life of the sixteenth century? Or does it uncover ambiguities within the tradition itself, inherent tensions that have made possible a turn away from the "depth of the heart" toward the "top of the brain"?

The beginning of an answer may be seen in one of the earliest Reformed confessions, the "Ten Theses [or Conclusions] of Berne," adopted by the citizens in 1528 as testimony to the city's intention to be constituted as a community of the reformation. The first three theses set forth convictions that remained characteristic of the Reformed tradition.

The sacraments impart to the community the substance of its life in Christ.

1. The holy Christian Church, whose only Head is Christ, is born of the Word of God, and abides in the same, and listens not to the voice of a stranger.
2. The Church of Christ makes no laws or commandments apart from the Word of God; hence, all human traditions are not binding upon us except so far as they grounded upon or prescribed in the Word of God.
3. Christ is the only wisdom, righteousness, redemption, and satisfaction for the sins of the whole world. For this reason, it is a denial of Christ to confess any other means of salvation or satisfaction for sin.[11]

The church is *creatura verbi*—a creature of the Word—a community called into being by the incarnate Word and shaped by witness to that Word in the word of Scripture. As a creature of the Word, the church's faith, worship, and order should obediently reflect, proclaim, and preserve the Word. Thus, neither true doctrine nor faithful worship nor obedient forms of the church can be shaped by human experiences, needs, desires, or traditions. Christ and Christ alone is the church's only wisdom. Conversely, human experiences, needs, desires, and traditions are the siren voices that call the church to follow the wide and easy way that "leads to destruction" (Matt. 7:13). The true, faithful church heeds Christ

Christ and Christ alone is the church's only wisdom.

alone, and listens not to the voice of a stranger.

Berne's allusion to John 10 makes it clear that the church is born of *Christ* and abides in *Christ*. Yet the Reformed tradition has always asserted, in the strongest possible terms, that the Word of God (Jesus Christ) is heard through the Word of God (Scripture). The church recognizes the rule of its faith and life solely in the Word of God, *and hears that Word of God solely in the Scriptures.* No "Wesleyan Quadrilateral" here, placing tradition, reason, and experience together with Scripture as sources and norms. Positively, the Reformed tradition asserts that it is in Scripture that God's Word is voiced, and so it is in Scripture that the church hears the Source and Norm of its faith and faithfulness. Negatively, the Reformed tradition asserts that apart from or even over against Scripture, no other authority can be trusted to shape faith or faithfulness.

The "Scripture principle" of the Reformed churches is not a sixteenth-century artifact. Contemporary Reformed Confessions express the same exclusive trust in the Word of God in Christ and in Scripture. The Presbyterian Church (U.S.A.)'s Confession of 1967 affirms that

The one sufficient revelation of God is Jesus Christ, the Word of God incarnate, to whom the Holy Spirit bears unique and authoritative witness through the Holy Scriptures, which are received and obeyed as the word of God written. The Scriptures are not a witness among others, but the witness without parallel.[12]

The Confession of 1967, written and adopted at a time of perceived security for the church, confirms the Scripture principle confidently. On the other hand, the Theological Declaration of Barmen (1934) was promulgated at a time when the church was threatened by an alien ideology from without and within. Barmen's first evangelical truth asserts both a powerful "yes" and a firm "no":

> Jesus Christ, as he is attested for us in Holy Scripture, is the one Word of God which we have to hear and which we have to trust and obey in life and in death. We reject the false doctrine, as though the Church could and would have to acknowledge as a source of its proclamation, apart from and besides this one Word of God, still other events and powers, figures or truths, as God's revelation.[13]

The Reformed tradition's attention is consistently riveted on the Word of God. Its recognition that the Word of God is heard through the words of Scripture is a faithful defense against the siren call of a stranger's voice. Nevertheless, Reformed fealty to the Word has been vulnerable to distortion at four crucial points. First, focus on God's Word may lead to neglect of human needs and aspirations. Second, attention to the Word of God may result in minimizing the sacraments. Third,

preoccupation with God's Word may disregard the plenary work of the Holy Spirit. Finally, ambivalence toward human experiences may impede the experience of Christ's grace, God's love, and the communion of the Holy Spirit.

1. For I am God, and not human, the Holy One in your midst

The opening sentence of Calvin's *Institutes* is well known: "Nearly all the wisdom we possess, that is to say, true and sound wisdom, consists of two parts: the knowledge of God and of ourselves."[14] There is no doubt which of the two parts takes precedence, however. Book One, "The Knowledge of God the Creator," and Book Two, "The Knowledge of God the Redeemer," display the typically Reformed priority of God. Everything is related to God and God's giving, commanding, leading, and ordaining, rather than the human person's receiving and having, accomplishing and presenting.

"Knowledge" of God does not mean intellectual comprehension, of course, but full relationship to the self-revealing and self-giving Creator. This knowledge of God is God's gift, not a human attainment, yet the gift is given to *us* and *we* benefit from it. Thus, Calvin understands knowledge of God as "that by which we not only conceive that there is a God but also grasp what befits us and is proper to his glory, in fine, what is to our advantage to know him. Indeed, we shall not say that, properly speaking, God is known where there is no religion or piety."[15]

The Reformed tradition has attempted to hold together God's action and human reception, but always with the clear awareness that it is God who reveals, acts, calls, and sends. Karl Barth characterizes the Reformed tradition well: "It does not begin with human interests, among which emerges finally, ultimately, and as the highest point, the interest in God; rather, it begins with God's interest in the human person. It does not show the way that the human should seek and follow, but rather, the way that God has already found to him."[16]

It is not surprising, then, that Reformed worship has centered on God rather than worshipers. Reformed worship draws attention to the majesty and glory of the triune God, who created all things and by whose power all things are sustained; who for us and our salvation became flesh, suffered, died, and was raised to glory; who is at work in and among us by the power of the Holy Spirit. Reformed worship is theocentric.

There has always been a danger, however, that Reformed worship's proper focus on God can become divorced from human realities, assuming an abstract, remote quality. Centering on God rather than on ourselves and our feelings can lead to repression of ourselves and our feelings. This, in turn, may lead to the objectification of God! Rather than thanking and glorifying God for God's goodness, Reformed worshipers may reduce their response to the bare "conception that there is a God." Once God becomes a remote conception rather than a real presence, a vacuum is created that can be filled by . . . human experience! When God becomes remote, the floodgates open and worship becomes immersed in human aspirations and desires, interests, and caprice.

Many Reformed churches, reacting against objectified worship, have tried to make worship engaging by shaping it to "meet people's needs." Calls to worship, hymns, prayers, and sermons are about ourselves rather than the triune God who creates and sustains all things, who reconciles the world in Jesus Christ, who is at work among us as the Spirit of new life. Such a style that focuses on the worshiper may take the form of reinforcing bourgeois morality—tolerance, sharing, community, and civic responsibility. Its evangelical tone may stress assurance of salvation, God's personal blessings, guidelines for successful living, and bearing witness to the unsaved. In both cases, worship may become technique-driven, relying on proven methods for producing the desired effect upon worshipers. In both cases, God becomes an instrumental means to the fulfillment of human desires.

Clearly, worship should not be reduced to a focus on human needs and aspirations while reducing God to an ally in the achievement of generalized human potential or spiritual advance. Just as clearly, worship

Reformed worship has centered on God rather than worshipers.

should not be confined to God to the exclusion of human realities. Reformed worship must recover its originating vision: worship that is initiated by the call of God and ordered by the work of God *and* that hears the call of God to *us* and knows the work of God for *us*.

Q. What is your only comfort, in life and in death?
A. That I belong—body and soul, in life and in death—not to myself but to my faithful Savior, Jesus Christ, who at the cost of his own blood has fully paid for all my sins and has completely freed me from the dominion of the devil; that he protects me so well that without the will of my Father in heaven not a hair can fall from my head; indeed, that everything must fit his purpose for my salvation. Therefore, by his Holy Spirit, he also assures me of eternal life, and makes me wholeheartedly willing and ready from now on to live for him.[17]

The Heidelberg Catechism's first question is a faithful attempt to articulate the sovereignty of God and God's initiating action, together with the human experience of God and God's Way in the world. The human question of "my comfort" is appropriate, but its answer directs me away from my project to God's self-revelation and self-giving. Christ has redeemed me and the Father protects me, but my salvation is for God's purpose in my life. The Holy Spirit assures me of eternal life, but this assurance makes me ready and willing to serve God. In short, it is not our life with God that is the theme of Reformed faith and life, but rather the certainty of God's glory, God's grace, God's justification and sanctification. And yet, God's glory, grace, justification, and sanctification are *pro nobis,* and therefore engage us at the deepest levels of human experience.

2. Is it not a sharing in the body of Christ?

Calvin believed that "The pure ministry of the Word and the pure mode of celebrating the sacraments are . . . sufficient pledge and guarantee that we may safely embrace as church any society in which both these marks exist."[18] Most Reformed churches, from the sixteenth century on, have not measured up to Calvin's standard. Although we faithfully baptize believers and their children, we have lost a sense that "the benefit it signifies lasts through life and death, so that we have an enduring testimony that Jesus Christ will be our justification and sanctification forever."[19] The Lord's Supper has not been an essential element of the community's Lord's Day gathering. Sacramental minimalism in Reformed churches has pushed Baptism and the Lord's Supper to the periphery of congregational life.

Too often, Reformed practice of Baptism is a mechanical ritual of infant identification. Even in its chummy American version, Baptism is little more than welcome into a gathering of people who are identified, rather arbitrarily, as a baby's new "family." The Lord's Supper, so recently a ritual of quarterly observance, may be on its way to becoming a monthly rite, but an arbitrary designation of the first Sunday of the month as "Communion Sunday" indicates its institutional rather than ecclesial function.

Reformed sacramental practice, long neglected, continues to be marginalized in a tradition that exalts preaching and takes pride in theological precision. Massive pulpits loom over little tables graced with flowers or a Bible rather than bread and wine. Small bowls, often hidden, are usually bone dry. Reformed churches are not churches of the Word and Sacrament; they are churches of the Word alone. When churches cease to be communities of the Word and Sacrament, becoming a church of the Word alone, they are in danger of degenerating into a church of mere *words*. The Reformed obsession with doctrinal purity and penchant for theological disagreement, as well as Reformed worship's tendency to rationalization, grow from our single-minded focus on words. Ironically, when words are exalted and sacraments minimized, the deformation of the Word follows: the Word of God, Jesus Christ, is displaced by the word of God, the Bible; the Bible is then overshadowed by words about the Bible; words about the Bible become

> *When churches cease to be communities of the Word and Sacrament . . . they are in danger of degenerating into a church of mere words.*

quarrels about interpretational control; fights for control result in factions, divisions, and even schism; newly "purified" churches begin the cycle again.

Word and Sacrament are not contrasting aspects of church life: cognitive and affective, abstract and concrete, individual and communal, private and relational, head and heart. Remember, Calvin placed Word and Sacrament together at the core of the church's true life because both offer *Christ* to us. Together with the Word, the sacraments communicate Christ to us and they lead us to real communion with Christ, experienced personally and corporately. In Baptism and Eucharist, Christ is present to the community of faith. In a way that is not dependent on the ability or predilections of preachers and teachers, the sacraments proclaim the gospel, embodying the good news in the lives of the faithful.

Reformed neglect of the sacraments threatens to mute the gospel's proclamation, both by an absence of Christ's sacramental presence and by a sacramental gap in union with Christ. Moreover, reduction of the Word to words can lead to a deformation of the Word as proclamation centers on institutional loyalties and aids to personal growth. The Reformed tradition's proper and necessary focus on the Word of God must be preserved, but it must not be reduced to an emphasis on the words of Scripture and proclamation at the expense of the sacraments. The Word of God, Jesus Christ, becomes present to the gathered community in the word read (Scripture), the word proclaimed (preaching), and the word enacted (Sacraments). In a true church of the Word and Sacrament, worship without the Sacraments would be as unimaginable as worship without Scripture and preaching.

3. Do not grieve the Holy Spirit

Diminution of the sacraments may be a consequence of the Reformed tradition's odd inattention to the person and work of the Holy Spirit. Reformed churches' lack of openness to the Holy Spirit is odd because Calvin himself stressed the work of the Spirit, especially with regard to Word and Sacrament. Perhaps Reformed neglect of the sacraments is a consequence of Reformed inattention to the Holy Spirit.

Calvin aimed to rescue the Sacraments from an institutional use, restoring their capacity to present Christ and his benefits to the community of faith. This intention is not achieved merely by reform of the liturgy, although such reform is crucial in giving free space for the work of the Holy Spirit. It is the presence of the Spirit that brings the sacraments to life. "The sacraments properly fulfill their office only when the Spirit, that inward teacher, comes to them, by whose power alone hearts are penetrated and affections moved and our souls opened for the sacraments to enter in. If the Spirit be lacking, the sacraments can accomplish nothing more in our minds than the splendor of the sun shining upon blind eyes, or a voice sounding in deaf ears."[20]

Calvin believed that the Holy Spirit's chief work is to conceive, sustain, nourish, and establish faith. Faith is not a human achievement, as if our faith appropriates God's grace. Rather, faith is itself the gracious gift of God. Human capacity for faith is so diminished by the fall that we are incapable of belief, trust, and loyalty apart from the grace of God in the particular working of the Holy Spirit. The Word of God alone should be sufficient to engender faith, but human sin cannot perceive the Word of God in Word and Sacrament without the gracious presence of the Holy Spirit. "Our mind has such an inclination to vanity that it can never cleave fast to the truth of God; and it has such a dullness that it is always blind to the light of God's truth," says Calvin with characteristic flourish. "Accordingly, without the illumination of the Holy Spirit, the Word can do nothing."[21] The Word, whether in Scripture or Sacraments, is simply inaccessible to sinful human beings unless the Holy Spirit works in mind, heart, and will.

Mere vestiges of this rich understanding of the Spirit's presence can be found in most Reformed worship. Confidence in the solitary power of the Word has produced word-centered worship that exhibits little need for the Spirit's presence.

Calvin placed Word and Sacrament together at the core of the church's true life because both offer Christ to us.

The Presbyterian Church (U.S.A.)'s *Book of Common Worship* seeks to recover something of Calvin's passion for the Holy Spirit in two small yet telling ways.

First, the *BCW* encourages the use of "prayers for illumination" before the reading of Scripture. These prayers acknowledge that God's help is necessary for the true hearing of the Word. Although most of the prayers are generalized prayers for God's help, some call explicitly for the Spirit's work:

Lord, open our hearts and minds
by the power of your Holy Spirit,
that as the scriptures are read
and your Word is proclaimed,
we may hear with joy what you say
    to us today.[22]

Prayers for illumination that call for the Holy Spirit's inspiration of hearers reflect the traditional Reformed understanding of the Holy Spirit's inspiration of the Scriptures. The Spirit inspired Scripture's authors *and* the Holy Spirit inspires Scripture's hearers and readers. The inspiration of Scripture is a twofold work of the Spirit; an inspired text without inspired hearers/readers is not the Spirit-inspired Word of God.

In far too many Reformed churches, prayers for illumination are omitted or given cursory attention by the congregation. Tellingly, the prayer for illumination is often divorced from the reading of Scripture, inserted as the preacher's own prayer for her preaching. Even when joined to the reading of Scripture, however, the prayers seldom reflect an eager anticipation that the Holy Spirit will open minds and hearts to the reception and confirmation of the Word.

The *BCW* also encourages full eucharistic prayers in the celebration of the Lord's Supper. No fewer than twenty-four Great Thanksgiving prayers exhibit a full Trinitarian structure:

The prayer begins with thankful praise to God for God's work in creation and providence, and in covenant history. . . .

The prayer continues with thankful recalling of the acts of salvation in Jesus Christ. . . .

The Holy Spirit is called upon to lift all who share in the feast into Christ's presence; to make the breaking of the bread and sharing of the cup a participation in the body and blood of Christ; to make us one with the risen Christ and with all God's people; to unite us with all the faithful in heaven and earth; to nourish us with the body of Christ so that we may mature into the fullness of Christ; to keep us faithful as Christ's body, representing Christ in ministry in the world, in anticipation of the fulfillment of the kingdom Christ proclaimed.

There follows an ascription of praise to the triune God.[23]

Similar invocation of the Holy Spirit is included in the baptismal liturgies. The Great Prayers in Eucharist and Baptism acknowledge the necessary presence in power of the Holy Spirit, "without which the sacraments profit not a whit."[24] And yet these prayers are seldom coupled with an eager anticipation of the Spirit's "real presence." The predominance of thanksgiving for God's mighty acts in a history of salvation may even reinforce sacramental *anamnesis* at the expense of *epiclesis*. Sacraments are emptied of their power when hope is buried by memory. Only the vivifying presence of the Spirit can join past and future in the depth of the present.

Calvin did not understand the work of the Holy Spirit in narrowly noetic terms. It is *faith* that is the work of the Holy Spirit: "Now we shall possess a right definition of faith if we call it a firm and certain knowledge of God's benevolence toward us, founded upon the truth of the freely given promise in Christ, both revealed to our minds and sealed upon our hearts through the Holy Spirit."[25] Calvin understood faith as the deep experience of belief, trust, and loyalty—a secure dwelling in the grace of the Lord Jesus Christ, the love of God, and the communion of the Holy Spirit. And yet Calvin's stress on the Spirit's confirmation of faith's certain knowledge has been subject to rationalistic reduction: trust and loyalty become appendices to belief, so that one trusts the doctrine and is loyal to the dogma. The experienced immediacy of being within the household of *God,* the body of *Christ,* and the communion of the *Holy Spirit* fades into the abstraction of rational assent.

It may be that recovery of confidence in the Spirit's power and attention to the Spirit's presence depends upon conscious openness to the Spirit's gifts. The fullness of the gifts of the Holy Spirit, so intimately joined to worship, establish, confirm, enrich, and expand both faith and faithfulness. Yet Reformed worship must retain the integral Trinitarian relationship—the Holy Spirit of God, the Spirit of Christ—so that the Spirit engenders glorification of the Father through the Son.

4. They exchanged the truth about God for a lie

Although Calvin can be eloquent about the experience of faith, it is the experience of *faith's subject,* and not human experience generally, that attracts his approval. The human experience of the grace of Christ, the love of God, and the communion of the Holy Spirit is in the foreground, not generic human experiences such as angst, confidence, emptiness, and fulfillment. For Calvin, knowledge of self is not the introspective knowledge of feelings and dispositions. Rather, truthful and trustworthy self-awareness "requires the kind of knowledge that will strip us of all confidence in our own ability, deprive us of all occasion for boasting, and lead us into submission."[26] The image of God, bestowed on humankind in Creation, has been so defaced that the truth about God and ourselves cannot be known apart from God's gracious redemption and sanctification. Fallen human nature is "a perpetual factory of idols,"[27] the chief of which are gods of our own imagining and selves of our own imagining.

Unredeemed humanity is not destitute, however. Calvin distinguishes between God's natural and supernatural gifts. Supernatural gifts—redemptive knowledge of God and ourselves—are bestowed on the elect. Natural gifts—human arts and sciences—are bestowed indiscriminately upon "pious and impious" alike. Although these natural gifts have been weakened and corrupted through sin, they are genuine gifts given by God for human well-being. Human experience, human knowledge, even human virtue are all "most excellent benefits of the divine Spirit, which he distributes to whomever he wills, for the common good of mankind."[28] Thus, all human experience is not denigrated or dismissed; the "common grace" of God touches the full range of life.

Only the grace of God in Christ . . . is the way to the truth about life.

Yet human experience, apart from Christ, does not lead to knowledge of God or of ourselves. Only the grace of God in Christ—who is the way, the truth, and the life—is the way to the truth about life. In the mercy of God, human experience is redeemed and sanctified, although it is not perfected, for sin is an ever-present reality. It is the keen awareness of the continuing reality of sin that leads to the prominence in Reformed worship of prayers of confession. Calvin's confession liturgy is instructive, however. Unlike the Lutheran pattern—law, confession, forgiveness—the Strasbourg and Geneva liturgies begin with the announcement of the gospel, then proceed to confession, assurance, and finally to the law. It is only on the basis of the gospel's declaration and reception that confession of sin can occur. Knowing forgiveness gives both the insight and the courage to confess. Having heard and believed the gospel, confessed sin, and been assured of pardon, the congregation can then hear the law as God's good gift for shaping the life of a redeemed people. (In Strasbourg, the people *sang* the Decalogue!) Thus, experience of life and God's law for the governance of life is redeemed and continually renewed in the gospel.

The Reformed tradition has tended to maintain Calvin's skepticism about human experience, positing a radical priority to the objective action of God. For Karl Barth, the only truth-giving human experience is the experience of God's Word, and human experience is incapable of leading to God's Word.[29] Resisting any positive valuation of experience as a source for faith's wisdom, Barth asserts that the proper starting point is "to base self-certainty upon God-certainty and to measure it by God-certainty and so to begin with God-certainty without waiting for this beginning to be legitimised by self-certainty."[30] In a treatment of the Apostles' Creed, Barth notes that "apart from this first expression 'I believe,' the Confession is silent upon the subjective fact of faith. Nor was it a good time when this relationship was reversed, when Christians grew eloquent over their action, over the uplift and emotion and experience of this thing, which took place in man, and when they grew speechless as to *what* we may believe. By the silence of the confession on the objective side, by its speaking only of the objective Creed, it also speaks at its best, deepest and completest [*sic*] about what happens to us men, about what we may be, do, and experience."[31]

Barth may be a particularly stark expression of the Reformed depreciation of human experience, but his is not the only word. The tradition contains a subtext within which experience is appreciated both as antecedent and consequence of faith. For Friedrich Schleiermacher, the experience of selfconsciousness opens humankind to the experience of God-consciousness.[32] "To be conscious of oneself as part of the world," says Schleiermacher, "is the same thing as to find oneself in a universal nature-system. . . . we must always be conscious of ourselves in this manner, and this consciousness must also be united to the God-consciousness."[33]

Yet both Barth's stark devaluation of human experience and Schleiermacher's embrace of human experience view experience from the perspective of faith and the life of the church. Neither is much interested in the quotidian experiences that shape personal and group life. Neither is much interested in feelings

and judgments that are engendered by the mundane happenings of human existence. Both Barth's "no" to experience *and* Schleiermacher's "yes" to experience leave empty a vast human space that is susceptible to inundation by a flood of diverse and disparate human experiences. Failure to take account of everyday events and impressions together with their incorporation into the depth of personal and communal life may result in suppression of experience . . . *or* in wholesale embrace of experience!

The mainstream of Reformed theology remains suspicious of experience, perhaps especially of "religious experience." Yet the space will not remain empty. Reformed churches in North America have become enamored of experience as an antidote to "left brain intellectualism." In an often indiscriminate valuation of each and every experience, North American Reformed churches have adopted pluralism as an essential tenet, with "celebrating diversity" as its liturgical component. But this blanket approval of "experiences" leads, ironically, to the emergence of enclaves of privileged experience. The American version of pluralism has tended to transform loose communities of natural affinity into self-contained pockets of experience that are inaccessible to those who do not share the experience.

Spawned by pluralism, clusters of closed experience impose orthodoxies; formed as cohesive communities of experience and conviction, they are mutually exclusive and so lead to fragmentation. Women's experience . . .

born again experience . . . the experience of inherited power . . . black experience . . . the experience of youth . . . new immigrants' experience . . . the experience of the poor . . . gay and lesbian experience . . . the experience of boomers, X-ers, busters, and other sociologists' fantasies . . . all are presented as normative experience *for those who share the experience.* To the extent that these pockets of experience are unavailable to "outsiders," and both advocacy and critique are restricted to "insiders," the church becomes balkanized (and sometimes ideological cleansing becomes the order of the day).

Human experience—both the stream of happenings that comprise life and the incorporation of those happenings in an affective web of thoughts and feelings—is not the stuff of Reformed theology. Reformed worship also has been distrustful of "religious affections." The Reformed tradition focuses on God's Word rather than on human needs and aspirations. Focus on God's Word results in sacramental minimalism and a disregard for the work of the Holy Spirit. Little wonder, then, that the tradition is ambivalent toward human experience.

The very distrust of human experience even leads to an ambivalence toward the experience of redemption—justification and sanctification. But glum schoolchildren will not remain mute forever. Thus, ironically, Reformed worship may be susceptible to the intrusion of experiences that have little to do with deep human responses to God's grace, love, and renewed communion. Reformed worship's necessary appeal to human experience must be, first and always, enriching the experience of the grace of Christ, the love of God, and the communion of the Holy Spirit. Only then will the "common experiences" of living be honored as the gifts of God. ■

JOSEPH D. SMALL serves as the coordinator for the Office of Theology and Worship in the Presbyterian Church (U.S.A.).

NOTES

1. James F. White, *Protestant Worship* (Louisville, Ky.: Westminster/John Knox Press, 1989), 58–78.

2. B. A. Gerrish, *Grace and Gratitude* (Minneapolis: Fortress Press, 1993), 86.

3. *The Constitution of the Presbyterian Church (U.S.A.),* Part I, *Book of Confessions* (Louisville, Ky.: Office of the General Assembly, Presbyterian Church (U.S.A.), 1999), 5.133.

4. Ibid., 127.

5. John Calvin, *Institutes of the Christian Religion* 4.1.9; Library of Christian Classics, ed. John T. McNeill, trans. Ford Lewis Battles (Philadelphia: Westminster Press, 1960).

6. Calvin, *Institutes* 4.1.12.

7. Calvin, *Institutes* 4.14.17.

8. Calvin, *Institutes* 4.14.16.

9. Calvin, *Institutes* 3.2.36.

10. "Common Reflection on the Renewal of Worship in Reformed Churches Today," draft report of a consultation conducted by the International Reformed Centre John Knox in January 2001.

11. "The Ten Conclusions of Berne," in John H. Leith, *Creeds of the Churches* (Garden City: Anchor Books, 1963), 129f.

12. *Book of Confessions* 9.27.

13. *Book of Confessions* 8.11, 8.12.

14. Calvin, *Institutes* 1.1.1.

15. Calvin, *Institutes* 2.1.1.

16. Karl Barth, *The Theology of the Reformed Confessions,* trans. Darrell L. and Judith J. Guder (Louisville, Ky.: Westminster John Knox Press, 2002), 208.

17. *Book of Confessions* 4.001.

18. Calvin, *Institutes* 4.1.12.

19. "The French Confession of 1559," XXXV, trans. Ellen Babinsky and Joseph D. Small (Louisville, Ky.: Presbyterian Church (U.S.A.), 1998), 16.

20. Calvin, *Institutes* 4.14.9.

21. Calvin, *Institutes* 3.2.33.

22. *Book of Common Worship* (Louisville, Ky.: Westminster/John Knox Press, 1993), 60.

23. *Book of Common Worship,* 156, passim.

24. Calvin, *Institutes* 4.14.9.

25. Calvin, *Institutes* 3.2.7.

26. Calvin, *Institutes* 2.1.2.

27. Calvin, *Institutes* 1.11.8.

28. Calvin, *Institutes* 2.2.16.

29. Cf. Karl Barth, *Church Dogmatics,* I/1, ed. G. W. Bromiley and T. F. Torrance, trans. G. W. Bromiley (Edinburgh: T. & T. Clark, 1975), 198–227.

30. Barth, *CD* I/1, 223.

31. Barth, *Dogmatics in Outline,* trans. G. T. Thompson (London: SCM, 1949), 15f.

32. Friedrich Schleiermacher, *The Christian Faith,* ed. H. R. Mackintosh and J. S. Stewart (Edinburgh: T. & T. Clark, 1928), § 32ff., 131–41.

33. Schleiermacher, *Christian Faith,* 138–39.

The Promise for Renewal

BY HAROLD DANIELS

This article originally appeared in Harold Daniels, *To God Alone Be Glory: The Story and Sources of the Book of Common Worship* (Geneva Press, 2003). Reprinted by permission.

How can there be an appreciation of what the liturgy is all about until there is a thirst for God?

A few years ago a Lutheran liturgical scholar and I were discussing the liturgical climate of our churches. I expressed my discouragement with the slowness of liturgical reform. He quickly replied, "It will never happen until the people are converted." I thought, "Yes, he has a point." How can there be an appreciation of what the liturgy is all about until there is a thirst for God (Ps. 63:1–8), and a desire to live in union with the One who alone is the source and giver of life?

While I was serving as a pastor, one of our most faithful members had an experience in which she encountered God in a way that deepened her commitment, and redirected her life. She shared with me how it changed her feelings about the liturgy. Words said and responses sung, repeated Sunday after Sunday, came alive, rising from the depths of her spirit.

LITURGY AS CONVERSION

Such a moment of awakening can produce a leap in one's faith. Such a moment sometimes marks the beginning of one's Christian pilgrimage. However, even when conversion is marked by a dramatic beginning, being formed in the faith is a gradual conversion process that engages us for as long as we live.

As a process, conversion is marked by a maturing in the knowledge and understanding of the faith, by a deepening of our devotion to the One from whom comes the meaning and purpose of life, and by living out the implications of the faith in every aspect of life. Since our knowledge of the ways of God, our devotion to God, and our service of God are all imperfect, the Christian life involves a lifelong venture of growth. Familiar prayers in the *Book of Common Worship* give it voice:

. . . may we know you more
  clearly,
love you more dearly,
and follow you more nearly,
day by day.[1]

And,

> Help us so to know you
> that we may truly love you,
> so to love you
> that we may fully serve you,
> whose service is perfect
>   freedom. . . .[2]

As such, the Christian life is at least as much one of *becoming* Christian as it is of *professing to be* a Christian.

At the core of this life is worship. Our worship forms us in the faith and undergirds every aspect of our discipleship. This is because the offering of ourselves in thankful response to God's grace is the heartbeat of worship. Such offering is expressed in a symbol Calvin cherished at the center of his faith—a hand holding a flaming heart, with the words *prompte et sincere*, which is often represented in English as "My heart I give you, Lord, freely and sincerely." Without such an offering of one's very self to the God "in whom we live and move and have our being,"[3] worship is powerless to transform.

In response to the magnitude of God's glory, Paul implored his readers to fully commit themselves to God:

> O depth of wealth, wisdom and knowledge in God! How unsearchable his judgements, how untraceable his ways! . . . Source, Guide, and Goal of all that is—to him be glory for ever! . . . Therefore, . . . I implore you by God's mercy to offer your very selves to him: a living sacrifice, dedicated and fit for his acceptance, the worship offered by mind and heart. Adapt yourselves no longer to the pattern of this present world, but let your minds be remade and your whole nature thus transformed. Then you will be able to discern the will of God, and to know what is good, acceptable, and perfect. (Rom. 11:33, 36; 12:1–2 NEB)

From ancient times the church's liturgy has been the principal means for conversion. In the waters of Baptism, the proclamation of the Word, and feasting at the Lord's Table, celebrating the mysteries of God in festivals and seasons, and the discipline of daily prayer, Christians are formed in the faith and disciples are made.

In an article appearing in *Reformed Liturgy & Music*, writer Joan Zwagerman Curbow tells how she found the hungers of her spirit fulfilled when she discovered the church's liturgical tradition. Having grown up in a congregation within the Reformed tradition, she describes her journey of discovery and shares the joy of the growth in faith she is experiencing in worship rooted in the liturgical heritage.

Though she early began to hunger for a form of worship that more fully engaged the senses, it was not until attending a Reformed

From ancient times the church's liturgy has been the principal means for conversion.

Church college that she first experienced worship drawn from the liturgical heritage. "I was hooked" she wrote. Later she and her husband moved to a community where there was no Reformed Church, and they worshiped with a rather dispirited Lutheran congregation. She said,

I had expected and yearned for a homecoming on two fronts, one from a common theological and historical background, and the other for my newfound love of formal worship. Instead I was befuddled and set adrift. We mumbled through the music and slogged through the words, as though stuck in a swamp.[4]

In spite of this, the liturgy began to sink in and take hold of her, becoming "an underground spring, whose waters baptized me by stealth."[5]

Her story eloquently describes the experience of those whose earliest Christian experience was within the free church tradition, but who have been led by the Spirit into an ever deepening appreciation of the church's ageless liturgy, finding in it inexhaustible spiritual depth and a source of maturing in the faith:

For some, tradition might seem oppressive or lifeless, but it has given me a sense of solid standing. I am treading an old road, following an ancient path that is marked by words, words that have been crafted and honed to endure "all times" and "all places" in human history. As I say them, I wonder who has said these words before me, and what of their struggles, their own or others? Likewise, such thoughts help me to consider my fellow worshippers and the joys or sorrows that attend them. Repeating the liturgy takes me in and beyond my own worries. So, it is for those words, those same words repeated week after week, that I go to worship. . . .

The liturgy's language respects and maintains God's mystery. Over the years I've come to appreciate that more and more. This is not worship for the intellect alone; this is worship for all of me, worship that sends depth charges into my innermost being. . . .

Gaining a sense of liturgy was a long time in coming. Perhaps I've had a longer catechumenate than most. Maybe I was just an exceedingly dull student. Whatever the case, in the early days, saying the Lutheran liturgy sometimes felt like boring, mindless work, a chore. That may be why love of liturgy is acquired over time and why, in a culture that demands instant gratification, it may be easily passed over, lying like a rare gem in some forgotten field. I don't repeat the liturgy because it lifts my spirits or "gives me a boost"; in truth, that seldom happens. I say the liturgy because it has helped to place me more firmly in the community of faith. I am one of many, journeying to

God on an ancient road, following a well-worn path that, after centuries, still runs true. It's a reality I can point to and hold onto when so much in life fails or falls away. Discovering the liturgy's depths and richness was a slow process, but once it sank in, it left a stubborn residue.

As I've occasionally worshipped in Reformed and Presbyterian congregations over the past decade, I've been stunned to find many of them using liturgy. After attending a chapel service at Calvin College in Grand Rapids, Michigan, I told a friend that I could have sworn I was in a Lutheran church. Liturgy lurked in my tradition all the time, and I did not know it. Coming to see that has been a joke on me, and it is a good one indeed. In the oddest of ways I seem to have rediscovered my roots. . . .

The great beauty of "converting" to liturgy is discovering that it is God's Word and God's presence working in me, converting "me." It matters little what I feel about it, but it does matter that I do it. It matters that I show up and make the effort, but it is God's Spirit that produces the fruit for my labors. And one of those fruits is joy, a joy that continues to sustain me in this long journey. The labor of liturgy is much like a bee gathering pollen. The honey comes after all the work is done.[6]

In reading her article I recalled a paragraph in Marva J. Dawn's excellent book *Reaching Out without Dumbing Down* in which she shares some insights of Jaroslav Pelikan in meeting accusations that the liturgical tradition is dead. She writes:

Many complain that old liturgies are dead, and they're often right. In many places they are dead, for churches have turned them into mere traditionalism, which Jaroslav Pelikan calls "the dead faith of the living." Those who advocate using the Church's historic liturgies are searching instead for what Pelikan calls "the living faith of the dead"—that is, worship within a tradition that enables us to be actively conscious of the Church's past as well as of its eschatological future in Christ. As Pelikan insists, tradition has the capacity to develop while still maintaining its identity and continuity. The tradition serves as a mode for relating to the present through contact with both the practices of the past and our collective hope for the future. It places us into the story of God's people and stirs our sense of belonging to a continuing fellowship that stretches throughout time and space.[7]

Gordon Lathrop in speaking of the *Lutheran Book of Worship*, emphasizes that it is not "just a book," but "the record of a common and lively tradition." What he says of the Lutheran book of services may also be claimed for the *Book of Common Worship*. He writes:

It is better regarded as the fragments and records of the ways many assemblies of Christians have done things, summed up as much as that is possible in print, and passed on as a gift to our present local congregations. The *LBW* is a concrete means of communication and communion between congregations through history. It represents a whole series of actions that cannot be put in print: people gathering, singing, praying, reading the Scriptures, preaching, baptizing, holding the supper, and, in these things, encountering God, coming to faith, going in mission. The gift from the other congregations to our present congregation needs to be put in motion in each place. It needs to be inhabited, experienced, enacted in a lively way with the book as a resource.[8]

SINGING THE LORD'S SONG IN A FOREIGN LAND

Abiding in a Christian discipline is not easy today, and being in ministry in the church is ever more difficult and demanding. Having lost its place of honor, the church labors in a culture that is increasingly indifferent to the church's claims, if not outright unfriendly. We are constantly reminded of the passing of Constantinian Christendom. It is increasingly apparent that we are moving into a time not unlike that of the early Christians.

To maintain integrity, Christians in our time are probing what it means to be *in and of* the world, but *not belonging to* the world (John 17:14–19), all the while remembering that the church's God-given mission is to be *for* the life of the world. We are learning, with increasing clarity, that the Christian faith is a way of being in the world, neither rejecting the world, nor seeking escape from the complex issues facing our common life. While renouncing all of the cultural idols that impact our daily life, we look toward, and labor for, the birth of God's "new creation," enduring the pangs of bearing that attend all birth. This question is crucial. How do we preserve Christian integrity, both in life and ministry, while dwelling in a culture that serves other gods, and where many self-appointed prophets draw attention away from living out what it means to be fully human?

We are beginning to recognize the ways in which the church is counter-cultural, a colony in an alien culture, resident aliens. Philippians 3:20 describes the church as having its "citizenship in heaven." As James Moffatt translated this verse, "we are a colony of heaven." Building on this image from Philippians, Stanley Hauerwas and William H. Willimon, in their book, *Resident Aliens: Life in the Christian Colony,* consider the implications this has for the contemporary church. In the preface they set the context for what they write. It underscores the conviction that, to maintain integrity in the context in which we live and serve today, the vitality of the church's worship is increasingly crucial:

The Jews in Dispersion were well acquainted with what it meant to live as strangers in a strange land, aliens trying to stake out a living on someone else's turf. Jewish Christians had already learned, in their day-to-day life in the synagogue, how important it was for resident aliens to gather to name the name, to tell the story, to sing Zion's songs in a land that didn't know Zion's God.

A colony is a beachhead, an outpost, an island of one culture in the middle of another, a place where the values of home are reiterated and passed on to the young, a place where the distinctive language and life-style of the resident aliens are lovingly nurtured and reinforced.

We believe that the designations of the church as a colony and Christians as resident aliens are not too strong for the modern American church. . . . Perhaps it sounds a bit overly dramatic to describe the actual churches you know as colonies in the middle of an alien culture. But we believe that things have changed for the church residing in America and that faithfulness to Christ demands that *we* either change or else go the way of all compromised forms of the Christian faith.

The church is a colony, an island of one culture in the middle of another. In baptism our citizenship is transferred from one dominion to another, and we become, in whatever culture we find ourselves, resident aliens.[9]

We are beginning to *re-member* ways of being the church that are new to us, though they have roots in the ages when the Christian faith was formed. This is not easy for churches, once considered "mainline churches," that for centuries saw themselves as inseparably linked with culture, shaping and being shaped by the culture. But with the crumbling of Constantinian Christendom, that relationship is changing.

Secularism, which in its self-sufficiency leaves no room for God, is creeping throughout our culture, and a self-centered individualism plagues our common life. Fundamentalism, with its mindless anti-intellectualism, has heightened its aggressiveness, turning thinking people away from the faith because they assume fundamentalism's strident message is what being Christian is all about. Megachurches with their "marketing techniques" to capture "the spiritual market" may be great "successes," but they trivialize Christian faith and life. Popular religion has domesticated God to serve self-centered interests. Main Street Protestantism is atrophying like aging muscles, its great Reformation legacy, both in spirit and in intellect, weakened. Theologically impoverished and spiritually destitute, it is evident in the typical Protestant worship that Protestantism desperately needs a fresh

> *We are beginning to re-member ways of being the church that are new to us.*

infusion of the Spirit touching both mind and heart.

Throughout the centuries the Reformed have stressed integrity in theological discourse and biblical interpretation. Presbyterian historian Lefferts A. Loetscher once declared that "Calvinism at its best is a rather fine balance between reason and feeling, between what is definable human knowledge and what is ineffable divine mystery, between formal and experiential elements."[10] Unfortunately, the Reformed have not always maintained this balance, but it remains a coveted objective in any age, no less in the times in which we live.

We have dared to echo the voice of the prophets and champion unpopular issues of justice. We have cherished a strong sense of connectionalism that emphasizes community, believing that we belong to and are for one another. It is important to us that our life and faith be grounded in the tradition of the church catholic. But with declining membership, some are tempted to surrender the hallmarks of the tradition and embrace the dubious methods of nineteenth-century revivalism warmed over for our time to "grow churches." But to surrender the tradition is to become something other than what we are called to be. Rabbi Abraham J. Heschel once wisely cautioned his fellow Jews:

Only a faith that engages the mind as well as the heart will endure.

Those who, in order to save the Jewish way of life, bring its meaning under the hammer, sell it in the end to the lowest bidder. The highest values are not in demand and are not saleable on the marketplace.[11]

His caution is equally apropos for Christians. We too need to take care lest we sell the Christian faith to the lowest bidder.

But, in spite of this despairing setting, and all that makes ministry difficult today, there is hope. There are signs of a growing awareness that the cultural idols are false, impotent, and cannot fulfill their promise of a truly satisfying life. There is a growing recognition that the tinsel and glitter of popular forms of religion pander to the self and have little to offer when one is suddenly confronted with the inevitable crises of life. Here and there one finds a yearning for a faith that has integrity, a hungering and thirsting for the "solid food" that is missing in the popular religiosity of our time.

This should prompt us to be on our guard about popularizing the faith. For if we surrender what we are called to be, we will miss the opportunity for enduring ministry when those caught up in currently popular religious sentiments become dissatisfied and search for a deeper faith. Only a faith that engages the mind as well as the heart will endure. Only a faith that accepts the realities of history, affirming the findings of science as it embraces the revealed truth of faith, can fully meet the challenge of evangelism in our time. Only a reasoned faith that probes deeply into the meaning and purpose of human existence can guide us through the complexities of life. Recognizing this, theologian Douglas John Hall has noted: "This presents disciplined and serious-minded Protestant Christians . . . with new opportunities; not opportunities for grandeur and certainly not for worldly power and prestige, but for truth and wisdom. And for hope!"[12]

We must never lose hope by giving in to pressures that would weaken our calling. We need the reassurance of Christ's promise, "Remember, I am with you always, to the close of the age" (Matt. 28:20). There is no greater evidence of the truth of this promise than the signs of the Holy Spirit guiding the church in this time of transition. Many of us believe that the liturgical movement is the work of the Holy Spirit equipping and nurturing the church to preserve the integrity of the faith in the midst of a pervasive secularism and a religious climate that distorts Christian faith.

LITURGICAL INTEGRITY

Throughout history, the church's liturgical tradition has been the very core of the life of the Christian community, for it is primarily in its worship that the church's faith is instilled. The critical importance of worship in forming the faith of the people was clearly seen in the earliest centuries when the church endured great persecution and gathered in secret. Its importance was also at the center in the turmoils of the

sixteenth-century Reformation. It is just as important in our time. In the missionary situation into which we are moving, it is crucial that the church begin to understand the critical importance of how it goes about its worship, lest the faithful be ill equipped for witness and service in this age.

Because he understood the formative role of the liturgy, it should not be surprising to learn that Calvin expected the congregations to adhere to prescribed liturgical forms in the turbulent times of the Reformation. Among Calvin's earliest tasks in Geneva was to introduce a reformed liturgy of Word and Sacrament. Adherence to the liturgy, like loyalty to a confessional statement, was meant to ensure that the people were grounded in the faith.

While we would agree that such restrictions are no longer in order, it does underscore that in Calvin's mind, worship—the primary locus of Christian nurture—is not to be taken lightly or done carelessly or recklessly, but to be engaged in with an understanding of the awesomeness of the task that carries the weight of faith formation.

Although offered for voluntary use, there is no better means to convert and to reinforce the faith in the lives of the faithful, than the liturgical heritage embodied in the *Book of Common Worship*. Congregations that have embraced the *Book of Common Worship*, taking it seriously, report that they have experienced a stronger grounding in the faith, more vitality in their worship, and greater intention in their ministry in the world. It is into this discipline that other congregations are invited.

It is expected that congregations, while taking the *Book of Common Worship* seriously, will vary in the way they use it, in keeping with the Reformed liturgical principle of freedom within order. The preface of the *Book of Common Worship* notes that "True freedom does not do away with form. On the contrary, form enables freedom to be truly free. Without structure, freedom can degenerate into license."[13] Consequently, the *Book of Common Worship* provides "for a wide spectrum of styles ranging from free and spontaneous prayer to the use of prayer texts. It is envisioned that while the style of praying will vary from one locale to another, the shape of the service will remain the same."[14] It states further:

> Some will find strength and a sense of unity in the prayers shared in common with the whole church and so will use the liturgical texts as they appear in this book. Others will find it more appropriate to adapt the prayers for use in a particular setting. Others will be prompted to follow the structure of the services as they are outlined and use the texts as models for a free and more spontaneous style of prayer. Each of these styles is appropriate within the provisions of the directories for worship, and it is the intent of the *Book of Common Worship* to provide the necessary resources.[15]

However a congregation may worship, it is critically important to understand the nature of the ordering of worship as set forth in the Directory for Worship and the *Book of Common Worship*. They are to be taken seriously as embodying the wisdom of the church in liturgical matters. Before one begins to tinker with the liturgy, it is essential to know why the church has ordered its worship in the way it has from earliest times, to recognize that it is in worship that we become participants in the grace-filled mysteries of faith, and to have a sensitivity to how the liturgy as a whole and its parts does its work. Not to have this understanding is to play recklessly with the most precious treasure the church has, its worship.

It is not unlike a choir, or an orchestra, offering a masterpiece of great creative beauty. It is important for the conductor to know how to conduct, to be intimately familiar with the musical score, to sense the composer's objective, to be sensitive to the contribution of each voice or instrument to the whole, and to have an ear for balancing and blending the ensemble. It is also essential that singers and instrumentalists have refined skills in reading music, playing their instruments well, or blending their voices.

Such skill and understanding are necessary, for both the conductor and the performers, before any decisions are made about a performance for a given occasion in a specific location. Depending on the occasion, the location, and the musicians, there will be variations in any two performances of the same work, but the musical score of the composer will always set the boundaries.

Yet, more is needed. Musicians must have music in their souls. They must *be* music if the music is to draw those who listen into the music's depths. Playing the notes is not enough. Great music presented by those who live the music touches the soul—mind, emotions, our whole being—and reflects the beauty of the Creator of all things who gave us the gift of music.

So with the liturgy, it is important that one know what the liturgy is all about, know the liturgical heritage and the theology undergirding the liturgy, and know and learn the skills liturgical leadership requires. A firm grounding in the basics is needed before making decisions about variations. Where such an understanding of the nature of Christian liturgy is solidly in place, then variations in keeping with the liturgy's purpose and meaning may be made with integrity.

Just as the musician must have *musical soul*, it is essential for those who lead the people in worship to have *liturgical soul.* Since the essence of the liturgy is prayer, those responsible for preparing and leading worship must *be* prayer, lest worship be merely "playing the notes." Some pastors have said that they cannot pray while leading people in prayer. How unfortunate. How can one expect to engage people in prayer if those who lead in prayer are not themselves engaged in the act of prayer? Prayer needs to be more than words, whether it is free prayer or prayer drawn from a prayer book. It needs to engage the whole person.

Since our abilities and skills will vary, and our understanding will never be complete, no expression of worship will ever be perfect. Nevertheless, the worship of God merits the best we are capable of offering.

THE BUSH THAT BURNS WITHOUT BEING CONSUMED

The burning bush has long been an important symbol in Presbyterian tradition. It is incorporated in the seal of the Church of Scotland as well as Presbyterian churches of other countries. It was prominent in the seals of the Presbyterian Church in the U.S. and the United Presbyterian Church in the U.S.A., the two antecedent churches that formed the Presbyterian Church (U.S.A.). It is presently part of the seal of the Presbyterian Church (U.S.A.), in which the flames of the burning bush share meaning with the tongues of fire at Pentecost. Among other churches within the Reformed tradition, it is part of the seals of The Presbyterian Church in Canada, and of The United Church of Canada, where it signifies the Presbyterian presence in the United Church, formed by a Methodist, Presbyterian, and Congregational merger in 1925.

It is essential for those who lead the people in worship to have liturgical soul.

The symbol of the burning bush is important in the Reformed tradition, for it expresses the sovereignty of God, which is at the heart of Reformed thought and worship, and reminds us of God's call to be God's emissary, engaged in God's work in the world.

The meaning conveyed by the image of the burning bush thus centers on both God's presence and God's call. Presence is implicit in the Voice speaking to Moses from the burning bush. Call is implicit in that Voice sending him to be the means by which God would deliver the Hebrew slaves from Egyptian bondage and form them into God's servant people. To the extent that the flames also signify the flames of Pentecost, we recall the outpouring of the Holy Spirit and the charge to proclaim the good news of God's grace-filled love. Once again, presence and call.

The story surrounding the burning bush (Exod. 3:1–15) undoubtedly comes from a long oral tradition and served a defining role in the life of the Hebrews in relation to their God. The children of Israel were slaves in Egypt. Moses had fled the wrath of the Egyptians for killing an Egyptian who was beating a Hebrew slave. The story relates how one day, Moses was in the desert near Mount Horeb, shepherding the flocks of his father-in-law, the priest of Midian. His attention was drawn to a bush that was burning though not consumed by the flames. When Moses turned to see the spectacle, he heard a Voice calling him from out of the bush. When he acknowledged the summons, the Voice prompted him to remove his shoes, for he was standing on holy ground. The Voice said, "I am the God of Abraham, the God of Isaac, and the God of Jacob." Overwhelmed in this unexpected manifestation of the presence of the Holy, Moses hid his face in fear.

From the flaming bush the Voice called him to return to Egypt and be an instrument to free the people of Israel suffering under the heavy yoke of slavery. Confronted by this unexpected and fearsome spectacle, Moses replied, "But who am I, that I should do this?" The Voice assured him that the appointed mission would not depend upon his abilities, but upon the One who was sending him and who would be with him. After raising every possible objection, Moses finally asked, "Then, who shall I say sent me?" And the Voice replied, "I AM WHO I AM. Say, that I AM has sent you. Say this to the people of Israel, 'The LORD (יהוה), transliterated: YHWH, the God of your fathers, the God of Abraham, the God of Isaac, and the God of Jacob, has sent me to you.' This is my name for ever, and thus I am to be remembered throughout all generations."

The divine name YHWH, the Tetragrammaton (Greek, meaning "having four letters"), appears throughout our English translation of the Hebrew Scriptures as "LORD" and sometimes "GOD." Wherever one of these words is displayed entirely in capital letters, it signifies the divine name YHWH. By the third century B.C., the Name had become so sacred it was never spoken. Only the high priest pronounced the Name, and that only once each year when he entered the holy of holies to pray the ineffable Name of God on the Day of Atonement. After the temple was destroyed in A.D. 70, the Name was never uttered again. To this day the devout avoid the word YHWH, substituting the word "Adonai" (meaning "Lord"), or "Elohim" (meaning "God"). Many Orthodox Jews substitute "ha-Shem" (meaning "the Name").

There is no certainty as to the exact meaning of YHWH. It is a name, yet not a name. It is a verb, rather than a noun or adjective, an archaic form of the verb "to be." It may be interpreted as "I cause to be what I cause to be"; the Creator; the Source of all that is, bringing into being all that is. It may be interpreted as "I am who I am," the Sovereign One, who is beyond every attempt to control, who is present in the midst of events moving toward a divine purpose. Or it may be interpreted as "I will be with you," expressing God's continuing presence in the midst of creation—being there with us, the Beyond in our midst. In the story it is clear that though God is a Presence beyond every attempt to define or describe, God is not aloof from human travail and oppression, but is a Presence in the midst of life and relationships calling all creation to a life that fulfills the purpose and promise for human life, ordained by the Creator. The emphasis is not upon God's being, but upon God's action and presence in human affairs.

Bernhard W. Anderson elaborates this meaning:

Thus the name of God signifies God whose being is turned toward his people, who is present in their midst as deliverer, guide, and judge, and who is accessible in worship. And yet in putting himself at the disposal of his people, so to speak, Yahweh retains his freedom to be present as he will be present, and to show mercy upon whom he will show mercy (Ex. 33:19). As a commandment of the Decalog states (Ex. 20:7), his name cannot be taken in vain—that is, used for human purposes. Perhaps the enigmatic words in 3:14 suggest God's reticence about giving his name. Moses had inquired into the mystery of the divine nature (the name), but his request was handled somewhat evasively, lest by having the name men would hold God himself in their possession and keep him under their (magical) control (see Gen. 32:29 and Judg. 13:17–18). The God who speaks to Moses is the Lord, not the servant of the people; hence the question "Who is God?" would be answered in events that would take place in the future, preeminently the Exodus. "I am Yahweh your God, who brought you out of the land of Egypt, out of the house of bondage" (Ex. 20:2).[16]

Just as the exact meaning of the word is unclear, so also there is no absolute certainty as to how the word is to be pronounced. The ancient Hebrew written language had no vowels. When vowel subscripts were added to Hebrew texts in the Middle Ages, it was unclear how these four consonants were originally pronounced, since they had constituted an unspoken word. Scholars have dismissed the once-popular pronunciation of "Jehovah," still lingering in our hymnody. Nor is there complete assurance that YHWH is to be pronounced "Yahweh," as is the accepted conclusion today. In his book *The Gifts of the Jews,* Thomas Cahill expresses an insightful personal meaning in pronouncing the Name without vowels, "when I attempt to say the consonants without resort to vowels, I find myself just breathing in, then out, with emphasis, in which case God becomes the breath of life."[17]

What the Name seems to convey is that the God we come to know in the Bible is a Presence in our midst that we can never capture and control. The Name given to Moses—a Name that is really not a name—reminds us that God cannot be confined by a name. What we know of God is what God has revealed of God's self.[18] Though we attempt to understand in our theologizing, and in making creeds and confessions, our best thoughts about God are but a shadow of a Presence beyond all we can think or imagine. As such, no creed, confession, or theology is infallible, and properly so, for all our formulations, while formed in response to God's self-revelation, are shaped by the circumstances of a particular time and place. This mystery in the depths of our life will always defy all we can think or imagine. It is as Paul has reminded us, "For now we see in a mirror, dimly, but then we will see face to face. Now I know only in part; then I will know fully, even as I have been fully known" (1 Cor. 13:12). To make absolute any description of God is to serve something less than the God of the Bible.[19]

While full knowledge of God lies beyond our grasp, the theological task will always be important, not only in giving form to our understanding about God and God's grace-filled acts, but in unfolding meaning and purpose for human life. In a very real sense, to speak of God is to speak of the meaning of human existence at its deepest level. Our attempts to explain the truth of God point us toward that Eternal Presence in the depths of existence that is the Source, Guide, and Goal of all that is, the One in whom we live and move and have our being, the Fountain of all that is true and good and beautiful. Though knowledge of the essence of God is denied us, it is enough to know how God has acted and acts toward us, and what God requires of us.[20] As God is toward us, so we are to be in all our relationships. The God who is "full of compassion and mercy" calls us, made in God's image, to acts of compassion and mercy, and thus to be icons of God. Wherever humans engage in acts of compassion and mercy, God's image is shown.

So also, as imperfect as our liturgies may be, the biblical story we celebrate is a progression of God's self-revelation in the midst of human life, giving direction and purpose to our life together as humans. God is revealed as a delivering Presence in the exodus, freeing from all that holds humans in bondage. God is revealed as a just God in the Law given at Sinai, expecting just dealings in all human relationships. In the cries of the prophets, God is revealed as a God of mercy and forgiveness, of justice for the oppressed and compassion for the poor, of infinite love for all creation, a God who calls humans to walk in ways that are just and true.

In Jesus the Christ, God is revealed as in no other—a God of grace who is among us forgiving and offering abundant life, who with compassion brings a healing touch to our deepest need, who shows us what it means to be truly human, who sets before us the command of love, a command that embraces all. And so we confess Jesus the Christ as "Emmanuel, God with us" (Matt. 2:23; Isa. 7:14), as the Word who became flesh and lived among us, full of grace and truth (John 1:14), through whom God was reconciling the world to God's self (2 Cor. 5:19). At Pentecost, God is revealed as a living Presence, beckoning us and all creation into a new creation. In our worship we become participants in this story.

WONDER-FILLED WORSHIP

The bush that burns without being consumed thus becomes a symbol of worship focused unswervingly upon God. It is in worship when, like Moses, we "turn aside to see," that we know we are standing on holy ground. While we may know this Presence in unexpected moments of life, it is in worship that we open ourselves most fully to that Presence. While we may hear that still small Voice in the silent moments of daily life, it is in hearts made still in worship that we listen with greatest care for the Voice of the One who is with us and who calls us into servanthood. In sacrament, Scripture, sermon, prayer, and song—here indeed is our burning bush and holy ground.

While we ask for no spectacular theophanies, our spirits need to encounter the living God. Worship should strip away our callousness to the mystery at the depths of life, opening us to encounter the God of glory who alone is the pathway to true meaning and wisdom. Overburdened with life's cares, we need times when we are moved to exultation, overwhelmed with wonder in the presence of the God who is beyond all we can think or imagine, yet who is as near as the air we breathe. Our hungering spirits need such glimpses of the holy, touching us with wonder.

It is in encountering this Sacred Presence that we are confirmed in the faith, receive the grace of God's loving forgiveness, find our spirits renewed, and are impelled into ministries of

It is in worship that we open ourselves most fully to that Presence.

compassion, peace, and justice. The object of the *Book of Common Worship*, and the reforms it sets forth, is to bring us into such an encounter. And in that encounter our lives are transformed. Here is the promise for renewal. Philip H. Pfatteicher emphasizes the power of the liturgy to transform and renew:

When we are confronted with God's life-giving power, our lives cannot remain the same. Worship does more than simply suggest or teach or urge. Worship in fact requires our renewal because we cannot worship the living God and not be made new. We cannot be washed in God's holy water and cannot eat God's life-giving meal and remain as we were. We are inevitably changed by our encounter with God. Our relationship to God is changed; our relationship to each other is changed; our relationship to the world is changed. We are changed by that encounter precisely because it is an encounter with God.[21]

Liturgical reform holds promise for the renewal of every aspect of the church's life and of our individual lives as Christians. But if that promise is to come to fruition, we must be willing to open ourselves to the Holy Spirit, who alone can touch our hearts through word, ritual, and song.

To God,
from whom comes
all that is true,

all that is good,
all that is beautiful,
soli Deo gloria. ■

HAROLD DANIELS served as the Associate for Liturgical Resources in the Theology and Worship Ministry Unit of the Presbyterian Church (U.S.A.) where his responsibility included work as editor of the *Book of Common Worship*.

NOTES

1. *Book of Common Worship*, prayer [23], p. 23.

2. *Book of Common Worship*, prayer [8], p. 19.

3. See Acts 17:28 and prayer of Augustine of Hippo, *Book of Common Worship*, prayer [2], p. 17.

4. Joan Zwagerman Curbow, "Honey in the Rock: Liturgy as Conversion," *Reformed Liturgy & Music* 33, no. 4 (1999): 18. Originally published in *Perspectives: A Journal of Reformed Thought* (September 1999), a journal of Western Theological Seminary, Holland, Michigan.

5. Ibid.

6. Ibid., 18–20.

7. Marva J. Dawn, *Reaching Out without Dumbing Down: A Theology of Worship for the Turn of the Century* (Grand Rapids: Wm. B. Eerdmans Publishing Co., 1995), 256. The Pelikan reference is to *The Vindication of Tradition* (New Haven, Conn.: Yale University Press, 1984), 65.

8. Gordon W. Lathrop, "How Awesome Is This Place! The Lutheran Book of Worship and the Encounter with God," in Ralph R. Van Loon, ed., *Encountering God . . .* , 44.

9. Stanley Hauerwas and William H. Willimon, *Resident Aliens: Life in the Christian Colony* (Nashville: Abingdon Press, 1989), 11–12.

10. Lefferts A. Loetscher, *The Broadening Church: A Study of Theological Issues in the Presbyterian Church Since 1869* (Philadelphia: University of Pennsylvania Press, 1957), 2.

11. Fritz A. Rothschild, *Between God and Man: An Interpretation of Judaism from the Writings of Abraham Joshua Heschel* (New York: Free Press, 1959), 183. This quotation is taken from an excerpt in Rothschild's book from Heschel's *God*

in Search of Man: A Philosophy of Judaism (New York: Farrar, Straus & Cudahy, 1955).

12. Douglas John Hall, Remembered Voices: Reclaiming the Legacy of Neo-Orthodoxy (Louisville, Ky.: Westminster/John Knox Press, 1998), 144.

13. Book of Common Worship, 9.

14. Ibid., 6.

15. Ibid., 6–7.

16. Bernhard W. Anderson, Understanding the Old Testament 3rd ed. (Englewood Cliffs, N.J.: Prentice-Hall, 1975), 55, 56.

17. Thomas Cahill, The Gifts of the Jews: How a Tribe of Desert Nomads Changed the Way Everyone Thinks and Feels, Hinges of History 2 (New York: Doubleday, Anchor Books, 1998), 110.

18. Aurelia Fule emphasized this in quotations from John Calvin's commentaries, in an address, "The Trinity in Theology and Worship," given at "Sisters in Santa Fe," a conference sponsored by the National Association of Presbyterian Clergy-women and the Women's Ministries Program Area of the Presbyterian Church (U.S.A.), at Plaza Resolana in Santa Fe, New Mexico, September 21–24, 2000:

> "God cannot be comprehended by us except as far as he accommodates himself to our standard" (Calvin, Com. Ezek. 9:3, 4). "For since he is himself incomprehensible, he assumes when he wishes to manifest himself to [women and] men, those works by which he may be known" (Com. Gen. 3:8). "God in his greatness can by no means be fully comprehended by our minds. . . . God accommodates to our measure what he testifies of himself" (Com. Rom. 1:19). "He accommodates himself to our capacity in addressing us" (Com. 1 Cor. 2:17).
>
> Accommodation, the recurring term, refers "to the process by which God reduces or adjusts to human capacities what he wishes to reveal of the infinite mysteries of his being. . . ." (E. Dowey, The Knowledge of God in Calvin's Theology, p. 3).
>
> The essence of God is unknown and inaccessible to us and all speculation is blasphemy, according to our tradition.

We do have knowledge of God, however, in both creation and revelation, as we just heard from Calvin and one of his best interpreters, Professor Dowey.

19. The great Reformed theologian Karl Barth wrote voluminously, expounding every aspect of the faith. His greatest work was his Church Dogmatics, a whole shelf of thick volumes elaborating his theological concepts. Yet he understood the limitations of the theological task in seeking to fathom the unfathomable. Toward the end of his life, he said, "There can only be 'little' theologians." He once commented, "The angels laugh at old Karl. They laugh at him because he tries to grasp the truth about God in a book of Dogmatics. They laugh at the fact that volume follows volume, and each is thicker than the previous one. As they laugh, they say to one another, 'Look! Here he comes now with his little pushcart full of volumes of the Dogmatics!' And they laugh, too, about the men who write so much about Karl Barth instead of writing about the things he is trying to write about. Truly, the angels laugh." This delightful anecdote was shared shortly after his death in 1968. Unfortunately, I have lost the original source.

20. Calvin teaches us that what God has made known about God's self is not God's essence, but "how [God] is toward us." God "consists more in living experience than in vain and high-flown speculation." Toward us, God is known in kindness, goodness, mercy, justice, judgment, and truth. See Calvin, Institutes 1.10.2, pp. 97, 98.

21. Philip H. Pfatteicher, Liturgical Spirituality (Valley Forge, Pa.: Trinity Press, 1997), 251–252. This book is highly recommended, as it probes the spiritual depths of the liturgical heritage. Although it does not always reference the Book of Common Worship in every place it might, it is instructive to all who seek to understand the liturgical tradition. It unfolds the strength and majesty of the liturgy and its power to transform. In my judgment, it merits careful study by all who take the Book of Common Worship seriously, and by those who wish to know what the liturgical heritage is all about. It is a book to read and reread. It was reviewed in Reformed Liturgy & Music 32, no. 2 (1998): 116–117.

Part Two

Resources

Introducing *Holy Is the Lord*

BY MELVA COSTEN

The major goal of the project was to provide a collection of service music that would uplift *and* inspire *while* moving *congregations forward into emerging patterns of life and worship.*

Any task force or committee appointed, or otherwise formed, to prepare a music resource for the Presbyterian Church recognizes immediately the formidable nature of the assignment. The mandate to embrace the diversity of our historical Presbyterian traditions while providing a prophetic vision for the future requires constant prayer, and keen listening ears to the voices in the pew. The task force formed by the Office of Theology and Worship in 1996 "to develop a service music supplement to *The Presbyterian Hymnal* (1990)" enthusiastically accepted the challenge. The major goal of the project was to provide a collection of service music that would *uplift* and *inspire* while *moving* congregations forward into emerging patterns of life and worship. The objectives that we identified from the beginning were clearly defined and equally weighted in terms of importance:

- To utilize texts from the *Book of Common Worship* (1993) for use by congregations in the Presbyterian Church (U.S.A.) and the ecumenical community.
- To provide settings in a wide range of musical styles within the framework of the texts.
- To compile a collection of music that is appropriate for the breadth of membership within the contemporary church, being sensitive to racial, ethnic, social, cultural, and contextual concerns.
- To select music that is accessible to congregations of all sizes and musical abilities.
- To provide a resource that can broaden the understanding of music in worship.[1]

There are indeed numerous ways that this resource can be introduced. The methodology used will be largely determined by the persons gathered to learn of its content. Since complete settings of the Eucharistic Prayer comprise the largest portion of the resource (twenty-two settings), congregations already utilizing musical settings can amplify and enhance their repertoire. In addition to the names of familiar Presbyterian composers such as John Weaver, Hal Hopson, and I-to Loh, choirs and congregations will experience rhythmical settings from African American and Latin American liturgical communities, and a "premier-setting," composed for this resource by Presbyterian pastor/musician Isaiah Jones. As editor David Eicher notes, this resource contains a significant amount of liturgical music from the African American and Hispanic traditions.[2]

Other Presbyterians, whose names will jog some memories, include musicians Michael Morgan and Jay Wilkey. Choirs will be delighted to add to their repertoire "Freedom Mass," based on freedom songs of South Africa, and an adaptation of Schubert's *Deutsche Messe* (*German Mass*).

Three settings for baptism composed in 1997, 1998, and 1999, and a "Prayer over the Water," composed in 1998, are included. Congregations already incorporating music in worship from the global community, and those seeking supplemental ways to do so, will be excited about the variety of musical entries in the Service Music section.

So . . . what about musicians and pastors for whom "singing the Eucharistic Prayer" seems a bit odd and takes too much time? This category of pastors, musicians, and congregations is probably larger than those cited above. Nevertheless, there is good news according to my own introductory and follow-up experiences. First, a local congregation—my own congregation: Church of the Master, Atlanta, Georgia. Upon the request of the task force, I asked Isaiah Jones to consider setting any one of the Eucharistic Prayers. As a pastor and a musician, Isaiah found the task very rewarding, especially since he utilized his own congregation to ascertain the effectiveness of his work. Three weeks later, Isaiah called to thank us for the assignment, and to assure me that he would submit the musical score and a tape recording, which he was preparing. When these were sent, I asked Isaiah's permission to "test" his setting in our congregation, where the pastor was also a singer—and could serve as cantor. Approval was received from the pastor, the session, the worship committee, and the choir director. When the choir and the pastor had learned the setting sufficiently (44–50 in *Holy Is the Lord*), the process was explained *carefully* by the pastor over a period of three Sundays. This not only prepared the congregation for the new procedure for our once-a-month

Congregations already incorporating music in worship from the global community, and those seeking supplemental ways to do so, will be excited about the variety of musical entries in the Service Music section.

Lord's Supper celebration, but it also created excitement. The pastor served as cantor for the first three celebrations, then suggested that a member of the choir carry out this assignment. Very quickly, the congregations learned the melodies and exciting rhythms and have continued with only a two-month interruption.[3]

I introduced this setting to the combined choirs of African American congregations in Atlanta in preparation for the annual meeting of the National Black Presbyterian Caucus (July 2002). Since the Church of the Master pastor was serving as celebrant for the service, and with Isaiah Jones at the piano, the service was exciting! Since this meeting, one additional church has requested assistance in learning this particular setting. There is a further request for an Atlanta area music workshop so that this and other settings and service music can be introduced.

I introduced the entire resource during a workshop session at Providence Presbytery, in September 2002. This session included church choir directors, a few pastors, and members of choirs. Although a lot of interest was engendered, there was not sufficient time to spend in song or dialogue. Perhaps more attention should be given to presbytery workshop settings, with the addition of time slots.

The third introductory approach has to do with the ecumenical body of students at the theological seminary. This process includes:

1. An explanation of the theological meaning of the Eucharistic Prayer. Have the class read through a number of settings that reflect the musical setting to be introduced.

2. Provide the history as cited above, and introduce the names of all African American musicians, as well as musicians of other cultures represented.

3. Over a period of time, introduce several of the settings and all of the service music. ■

Melva Wilson Costen serves as Helmar Nielsen Professor of Worship and Music at the Interdenominational Theological Center in Atlanta, Georgia.

NOTES

1. *Holy Is the Lord: Music for the Lord's Day Worship* (Louisville, Ky.: Geneva Press, 2002), vii.

2. Ibid., x.

3. The interruption occurred when the cantor, a young husband and father, was killed in an automobile accident. The cantor's role is continued by a female in the choir.

The Presbyterian *Psalter* Revisited

BY HAL HOPSON

The year 2003 marks the tenth anniversary of the publication of *The Psalter—Psalms & Canticles for Singing* (Louisville, Ky.: Westminster/John Knox Press, 1993). It is appropriate that we take a fresh look at this significant collection of psalms and canticles, and highlight some of its treasures. The contribution that this book has made to the liturgical life of the whole church is immeasurable. It is fitting that this resource for singing the psalms be made available through a denomination in the Reformed heritage because of that tradition's love for psalm singing. It all began with John Calvin, who engaged the finest poets and musicians of his time to provide metrical settings of the psalms that could be sung by the entire congregation.

"The church reformed, and always being reformed" (*ecclesia reformata semper reformanda*)—we hear this Reformation-era motto quoted often in Presbyterian circles. With reference to psalm singing, this motto suggests that we cherish our Reformed roots in metrical psalmody, and also embrace other ways of experiencing the psalter. The psalms in *The Psalter—Psalms & Canticles for Singing* are basically responsorial, that is, a refrain for the congregation, and verses chanted by a cantor or choir. The challenge has been for Presbyterian pastors, musicians, and congregations to feel comfortable with non-metrical settings of the psalms. This article intends to dispel some apprehensions in this regard and to provide creative ways to adapt these settings to the resources at hand.

The background for many of us, in addition to singing metrical psalms, is for psalms to have been read responsively from an abbreviated version in the back of the hymnal—usually, a minister reading the roman-faced letters, and the congregation reading

> *With reference to psalm singing, the motto "the church reformed, and always being reformed" suggests that we cherish our Reformed roots in metrical psalmody, and also embrace other ways of experiencing the psalter.*

the bold-faced letters. In some Protestant traditions, this became the norm for experiencing the psalter in a responsive/antiphonal format. Some Protestants view chanted psalmody as a non-Protestant activity. In reference to chanted psalms, some mainline Protestants have been heard to say (*Roman Catholic friends, forgive us*): "They sound too Catholic for me." To this, one could add: "Yes, and what a cherished heritage!" A parishioner was heard to say (*Jewish friends, forgive us*): "These chanted psalms sound very Jewish to me." To this, one could add: "As they should."

The following suggestions are made to encourage a more meaningful experience, and an acceptance (or at least a tolerance) for the responsorial singing of the psalms, as found in *The Psalter— Psalms & Canticles for Singing*.

OPENING ESSAYS

Read the enlightening essays at the front of the book. They are as follows by page numbers:

Preface (7–8)—Gives a short history of the development of this collection.
Singing Psalms in Christian Worship (11–16)—Offers valuable information concerning roots of psalm singing, Reformation psalm singing, and the recovery of psalm singing today. Another valuable part of this section is a list that suggests festivals or seasons when use of particular canticles or ancient hymns is especially appropriate.
Responsorial Psalm Singing (17–20)—Some of the topics in this essay are the training of the cantor, an analysis of the structure of psalm tones, the introduction of responsorial psalm singing, and many other aspects of responsorial psalm singing.

THE CREATIVE USE OF SPACE

Not many of us enjoy a worship space such as St. Mark's in Venice, with its many galleries and reverberant acoustics. Regardless of the size of the church, however, we have a front and a back to the worship space. Placing cantors, ensembles, and choirs in antiphonal positions adds greatly to the drama of psalm singing. For example, Psalm 13, page 7, can be effectively sung by two or more cantors alternating the phrases.

THE CREATIVE USE OF CHOIRS

There are forty-five settings in *The Psalter—Psalms & Canticles for Singing* for SATB choir. We would do well to develop an appreciation of psalm verses chanted in harmony by the

Regardless of the size of the church, however, we have a front and a back to the worship space. Placing cantors, ensembles, and choirs in antiphonal positions adds greatly to the drama of psalm singing.

choir, especially those settings to Anglican chant and to the harmonized chants of the Orthodox tradition. Psalms 30, 42, 43, 95, and 145 are set to Anglican chants. Psalms 5, 67, and 90 are set to tones from the Orthodox tradition.

Many psalms, because of their musical settings and texts, provide excellent opportunities for children to chant the verses of some, or all, of the psalm. Psalm 24, page 22, is such an example. Alternating verses between cantor and children's voices is very effective.

THE CREATIVE USE OF INSTRUMENTS

Twenty-one of the psalm settings have instrumental parts included in the score. They include parts for guitar, flute, oboe, brass, strings, double bass, percussion, wind chimes, gong, timpani, Orff instruments, and handbells. For example, Psalm 24, page 21, includes instrumental parts for guitar, soprano recorder (or flute) timpani, and percussion.

Handbells

In addition to the seven psalms that include a handbell part, with imagination, a handbell part may be easily devised for other psalms. For example, a cluster chord may be played before each line of the verses to Psalm 65, page 55, using the following bells: C5, E-flat 5, F5, and B-flat 5. The organ should play only on the refrain.

To create a joyful accompaniment for the refrain to Psalm 96, page 92, handbells could play all the notes in the chords indicated by the chord symbols in addition to the organ.

Trumpet

A trumpet reinforcing the melody on upbeat psalm refrains can be effective. On the last refrain, the "alto" line of the accompaniment may be played an octave higher as an obbligato part.

Percussion

Improvised percussion parts may be added to several of the psalm settings. For example, the addition of the percussion instruments of a trap set could be effectively used in accompanying Psalm 100, page 97.

Psalm 29, page 26, is one of the most dramatic psalms in the entire psalter. It depicts a rainstorm, complete with lightning and loud claps of thunder. Thunderous sound effects may underline the verses with the use of percussion instruments, especially drum rolls.

SPEAKING THE VERSES

With psalm tones provided for the verses, the assumption could easily be made that singing the verses is the only way to use the psalm setting. Consider not having the verses sung

Twenty-one of the psalm settings have instrumental parts included in the score. They include parts for guitar, flute, oboe, brass, strings, double bass, percussion, wind chimes, gong, timpani, Orff instruments, and handbells.

at all, but have them read and the refrain sung as indicated. This may be done in a variety of ways. For example, take Psalm 22, page 15—the refrain may be sung and the verses read with the organist playing the chords on a soft registration, syncing the chords with the spoken part of the reader.

For Psalm 51, page 48, the organ would play only on the refrain, and a handbell could toll E-4 before each phrase is read. This same idea applies to Psalm 13, page 7, with the handbell tolling A-4.

FAMILIAR HYMN PHRASES AS REFRAINS

One of the basic theories of learning is to proceed from the known to the unknown. This theory certainly applies to the choice of refrains in responsorial singing, particularly when responsorial psalms are first introduced. One option is to sing a familiar, appropriate hymn phrase as the psalm refrain. By syncing the key and the thought of a hymn phrase with that of a given psalm text, a refrain is provided that the people will know, and one in which they can sing immediately. Below is a list of psalms from *The*

One of the basic theories of learning is to proceed from the known to the unknown. This theory certainly applies to the choice of refrains in responsorial singing, particularly when responsorial psalms are first introduced.

Psalter—Psalms & Canticles for Singing and an appropriate hymn phrase that can be sung as a refrain. The listing includes the psalm, the page number in *The Psalter,* the name of the suggested hymn to use, the name of the hymn tune, the key, and the phrase of the hymn to be sung as the refrain.

Psalm 22:23–31, page 17
"For the Beauty of the Earth"; DIX, (G)
"Lord of all, to Thee we raise this our hymn of grateful praise."

Psalm 23, page 20
"The Lord's My Shepherd, I'll Not Want," CRIMOND, (F)
"The Lord's my shepherd, I'll not want."

Psalm 30:1–2, 4–5, 11–12, page 27
"Praise, My Soul, the King of Heaven," LAUDA ANIMA, (C)
"Alleluia! Alleluia! Praise the everlasting King."

Psalm 40:1–11, page 36
"Praise to the Lord, the Almighty," LOBE DEN HERREN, (G)
"Praise to the Lord, the Almighty, the King of creation."

Psalm 45, page 39
"For the Beauty of the Earth," DIX, (G)
"Lord of all, to Thee we raise this our hymn of grateful praise."

Psalm 93, page 87
"O Worship the King, All Glorious Above!," LYONS, (A)
"O Worship the King, all glorious above!

O gratefully sing God's power and God's love."

Psalm 96:1–6, 11–13, page 92
"Rejoice, Ye Pure in Heart!," MAR-ION, (F)
"Rejoice! Rejoice! Rejoice, give thanks and sing."

Psalm 104:1–9, page 104
"Praise to the Lord, the Almighty," LOBE DEN HERREN, (G)
"Praise to the Lord, the Almighty, the King of creation."

Psalm 107:1–9, page 109
"God of Our Life," SANDON, (F)
"God of our life, through all the circling years, we trust in Thee."

Psalm 113, page 113
"Ye Servants of God, Your Master Proclaim," HANOVER, (G)
"Ye servants of God, your Master proclaim."

Psalm 118:19–29, page 118
"All Glory, Laud, and Honor," ST. THEODULPH or VALET WILL ICH DIR GEBEN, (C)
"All glory, laud and honor, to Thee Redeemer, King."

Psalm 139:1–5, 7–12, 23–24, page 142
and
Psalm 139:1–5, 13–14, 16–18, page 143
"God of Our Life," SANDON, (F)
"God of our life, through all the circling years, we trust in Thee."

Psalm 150, page 157
"All Creatures of Our God and King," LASST UNS ERFREUEN, (D)

"Alleluia! Alleluia! Alleluia! Alleluia! Alleluia!" (Last phrase)

PRESBYTERIAN PSALM REFRAINS AND TONES

Mention should be made of the eight Presbyterian psalm refrains and tones on pages 342–46. Note the progression of spirit in the refrains, beginning with the joyful, upbeat "Alleluia" in No. 1 and moving to the lament "Lord, you are my strength, hasten to help me" in No. 8. You can find a description of the use of these refrains and tones on pages 341 and 345. The simplicity of structure of the psalm tones provides an opportunity for the musician to point any psalm text at hand with a corresponding refrain in the same key. With the varying texts of the refrains, settings are provided for all major themes found in the psalter, be they praise, lament, wisdom, trust, God's kingship, God's law, or salvation history.

COMMENTS IN THE WORSHIP BULLETIN

It is certainly true that psalms express our deepest emotions and our attempt to make sense of life before

The simplicity of structure of the psalm tones provides an opportunity for the musician to point any psalm text at hand with a corresponding refrain in the same key.

God in both lament and praise. These expressions were originally in a cultic setting, reflecting the life, myths, metaphors, and poetic patterns of the people of Israel and their neighbors.

Without having some understanding and background of the psalms, individuals in the pew are often puzzled by some of the psalms they hear in church. An example of this is found in Psalm 91, verse 2: "The young lion and the serpent you will trample under foot." Another example is found in Psalm 22, verse 12: "Many bulls encircle me, strong bulls of Bashan surround me." Unless we have some context for understanding, we are baffled when we hear "Do not harden your hearts, as at Meribah, as on the day at Massah in the wilderness" (Ps. 95:8). The challenge is to find ways to educate the congregation to the subtle meanings and background of such obscure passages so that when they are heard in worship, there is a context for understanding.

For those who follow the three-year *Revised Common Lectionary,* the psalm after the first lesson usually relates to it. A short paragraph in the worship bulletin can help the congregation appreciate and understand this correlation. For example, the Hebrew Scripture lesson for the Baptism of the Lord, Year B, is Genesis 1:1–5. This passage is followed by Psalm 29, which describes a fierce rainstorm. To help the congregation understand the correlation, the following paragraph could be printed in the church bulletin:

The Genesis passage in today's service describes the writer's concept of the first day of creation, in which God "swept over the face of the waters." Psalm 29 picks up the same theme of God's might over the waters of a thunderstorm. These two passages thus reinforce the powerful image of God over all waters, especially in the waters of baptism as we celebrate Christ's baptism in the River Jordan.

THE PSALM PRAYERS

Mention should be made of the psalm prayers in the *Book of Common Worship,* which follow each psalm in that resource beginning on page 611. When the psalm is sung as a part of the lections for the day, the prayer may be read immediately afterward. These psalm prayers are effective summaries or reflections of the psalm just sung. They are in the form of a petition, which provides an application of the psalm for the worshiper.

CANTICLES AND SERVICE MUSIC

A revisit of *The Psalter—Psalms & Canticles for Singing* would not be complete without some comments regarding the canticles and service music included in the second portion of this resource. There are musical settings for all the traditional New and Old Testament canticles and other scriptural passages, plus the following: "O Antiphons," "Hymn to Christ as Light" (*Phos Hilaron*), *Te Deum, Gloria in Excelsis,* "The

Beatitudes," "The Lord's Prayer," and "The Easter Proclamation" (the Exsultet).

The four settings of "The Lord's Prayer" represent various musical genres. The setting on page 194, from an unknown source, can be taught easily to the congregation. After the congregation knows the melody well (the larger note in the middle), the other cue-size notes may be added by both bass and treble clef voices of the choir. This rich harmonic overlay, with hints of Russian chant, adds greatly to the beauty of this setting.

Mention should be made of a setting by John Rutter—"A Canticle of Praise" (Song of the Three Young Men), on page 182. It can be sung easily as an anthem for unison voices alternating between men's and women's voices.

Other settings that deserve a closer scrutiny are "Canticle of Zechariah," on page 158, set to a Byzantine chant, and Jack Noble White's setting of "Canticle of the Redeemed," on page 184.

VARIETY OF
MUSICAL STYLES

Several aspects of *The Psalter—Psalms & Canticles for Singing* make it one of the most significant resources of its kind in publication. Except for a few settings, the entire book is in inclusive language both toward God and toward humankind. Another strength of the collection is the variety of musical styles and composers that it represents. All major traditions of chant are

included: Anglican Chant, Gregorian tones, Orthodox tones, Gelineau, Lutheran, and Presbyterian psalm tones. Thirty-two composers are represented, whose creative output stretches well over four centuries. Some of the settings were commissioned by the task force and appeared first in this book.

Pastors and musicians are encouraged to become better acquainted with the riches of this valuable collection and are encouraged to be creative in the use of the settings. Responsorial psalm singing provides a unique musical expression that draws on a variety of musical skills at appropriate levels, be it cantor, choir, organist, instrumentalists, or congregation. It is a form that reaches far back into the worship of ancient Israel. Even to the present day it has not lost its timeless value. Responsorial singing of the psalms may fall on the ears of many mainline Protestants as a new musical form. It is helpful to remember that its roots are deep in the hearts of the faithful, who for centuries used chanted verses of the psalter to express their deepest emotions and needs to a listening God.

INDEX OF CANTICLES
AND OTHER
MUSICAL SETTINGS

The following index is provided to help planners of worship access specific settings in the book and to make this valuable collection a more user-friendly resource. It is suggested that this index be cut out and pasted on the empty pages in the back of the book.

New Testament Canticles

158 "Canticle of Zechariah" (Byzantine Chant)

159 "Canticle of Zechariah" (John Weaver)

160 "Canticle of Zechariah" (Howard Hughes)

161 "Canticle of Mary" (Joseph Gelineau)

162 "Canticle of Mary" (John Weaver)

163 "Canticle of Mary" (*"Tonus peregrinus"*)

164 "Canticle of Simeon" (Gregorian)

165 "Canticle of Simeon" (John Weaver)

166 "Canticle of Simeon" (Hal H. Hopson)

Old Testament Canticles

172 "Canticle of Hannah" (John Weaver)

174 "Canticle of Miriam and Moses" (John Weaver)

175 "Canticle of Thanksgiving" [First Canticle of Isaiah] (Norman Mealy)

176 "Seek the Lord" [Second Canticle of Isaiah] (Gregorian)

177 "The New Jerusalem" [Third Canticle of Isaiah] (John Weaver)

178 "A Canticle of David" (Stigall/Gelineau)

179 "Canticle from Lamentations" (John Weaver)

180 "Canticle of Creation" [Song of the Three Young Men 35–65, 34] (Hal H. Hopson)

181 "Canticle of Creation" [Song of the Three Young Men 35–63] (A. Gregory Murray)

182 "A Canticle of Praise" [Song of the Three Young Men 29–34] (John Rutter)

183 "A Canticle of Penitence" [Prayer of Manasseh] (Hal H. Hopson)

The Lord's Prayer

192 "The Lord's Prayer" (Rimsky-Korsakov/Hopson)

193 "The Lord's Prayer" (Plainsong Chant)

194 "The Lord's Prayer" (Source unknown)

195 "The Lord's Prayer" (John Weaver)

Various Other Settings

167 "Hymn to Christ as Light" [*Phos Hilaron*] (David Clark Isele)

168 "Hymn to Christ as Light" [*Phos Hilaron*] (St. Meinrad Mode 5)

169 "Hymn to Christ as Light" [*Phos Hilaron*] (Gregorian)

170 "We Praise You, O God" [*Te Deum Laudamus*] (John Weaver)

173 *Gloria in Excelsis* (Old Scottish Chant)

184 "A Canticle of the Redeemed" (Jack Noble White)

185 "Christ, the Head of All Creation" (Howard Hughes)

186 "Jesus Christ Is Lord" (Howard Hughes)

187 "A Canticle of Love" (Jacques Berthier) [Taizé]

188 "The Beatitudes" (Jacques Berthier) [Taizé]

189 "Christ the Servant" (Richard Proulx)

190 "Christ Our Passover" (Stewart/Hopson)

191 "Canticle to the Lamb" (David Clark Isele)

196 "The Easter Proclamation" [the Exsultet] (the Roman Missal)

197 "The Easter Proclamation" [the Exsultet] (John Weaver)

162I—"O Antiphons" (John Weaver) ■

HAL H. HOPSON serves as a full-time composer/conductor residing in Dallas, Texas.

Music Review

Requiem

REVIEWED BY JANET LOMAN

Requiem, by Bradley Ellingboe. San Diego, Calif.: Neil A. Kjos Music Co., 2002. ISBN 0–8497-4198-X. 80 pages. $9.95 (Organ edition VM3). Sextet and orchestra editions available by rental.

The Presbyterian Association of Musicians' Albuquerque 2002 Conference on Worship and Music was the venue for the premiere of Bradley Ellingboe's *Requiem* for SATB chorus and instrumental sextet. A lovely and evocative work, *Requiem* was warmly received by both the audience and the conference choir. According to the composer, his intention was to create a piece that is uplifting to the human spirit in general, and comforting to those who are grieving while assuring them that there is nothing to fear in death and that, indeed, death is the arrival to a better place. The result is a singable, meaningful work whose text and melody are easily accessible to today's audiences.

Requiem is written in ten movements; performance time is approximately forty-five minutes. Based on liturgical models of the traditional requiem form, this work is true to the overall structure but with some innovations. Since the Dies Irae is no longer a required text for the funeral mass in the Catholic Church, and as Ellingboe disagrees with its dark message, he therefore has excluded it. He has, however, added a psalm (Psalm 22: "Why Have You Forsaken Me?"), the Lord's Prayer, and two poetical texts. The movements from the Mass may be sung in Latin or English; remaining texts are in English. Central to the piece is an alto solo, a Quasi Tarantella in 8/8 meter, on John Donne's hopeful poem, "Death Be Not Proud," of which the opening lines are mentioned here:

Death be not proud, though some
     have called thee
   Mighty and dreadful, for thou art
     not so.
For, those, whom thou think'st, thou
     dost overthrow,
   Die not, poor death, nor yet canst
     thou kill me.

A beautiful cello solo emerges in the introit, and is paired with a plaintive Norse folk tune in the graduale and Agnus Dei. George Herbert's illuminating poem "Evensong" is sung during the Communion, followed by the closing words of Lux Aeterna.

The choral writing is expressed in simple terms, is quite effective, and reflects the text well. The organ accompaniment is not difficult, and can be successfully registered on an instrument of moderate size. The cello and alto solo parts, especially, require competent musicians. There are lovely countermelodies offered by the flute and oboe, and well-placed percussive effects. Choral directors will find this composition rehearsal friendly and adaptable to many uses, as each movement stands on its own. It is a memorable work, and a welcome addition to the church and concert repertoire.

Bradley Ellingboe is professor of music at the University of New Mexico and winner of three consecutive ASCAP Plus awards for his body of work, which includes over sixty choral octavos. *Requiem* is available in three accompaniment versions: organ only; instrumental sextet (including organ, flute, oboe, cello, harp, and timpani); or small orchestra (with optional organ). Neil A. Kjos Music Company of San Diego publishes it. Permission is granted to reproduce the words, which are printed in the score. ■

JANET LOMAN serves on the music faculty at New Mexico State University in Las Cruces, New Mexico.

Errata for *Call to Worship* 36, no. 3: The review by Chip Andrus of the book *Facing the Music: Faith and Meaning in Popular Songs* was originally published in Volume 15:4, Winter 2001 of the journal *Family Ministry: Empowering Through Faith.* This quarterly journal is published by Louisville Seminary. Subscription inquiries can be directed to Family Ministry at (502) 895-3411, ext. 437 or www.fmef.org.

Editor's note: It has come to our attention that lectionary aids suggestions for piano pieces in the year 2000 and re-run again in vol. 37, no. 1 were taken in the most part from *Prepare,* published and copyrighted by Abingdon Press, Nashville, TN.

Book Review

Interchurch Families: Resources for Ecumenical Hope

Edited by John C. Bush
Patrick R. Cooney

REVIEWED BY CHARLES WILEY

Interchurch Families: Resources for Ecumenical Hope. Edited by John C. Bush and Patrick R. Cooney. Louisville, Ky.: Westminster John Knox Press, 2002. ISBN 0–664-22562–4. 104 pages, $10.95.

Oh, and while my son is a Presbyterian, his bride is a devout Roman Catholic. Will that be a problem for you in doing the wedding?"

My introduction to interchurch families began as a favor for a departing pastor, making good on her agreement to conduct a wedding. After months of negotiating the intricacies of a wedding in a Presbyterian Church that would be considered valid in the eyes of the Roman Catholic Church, I was exhausted, questioning the wisdom of ever agreeing to such a thing.

Interchurch Families is a gift to all those who have encountered the growing phenomenon of families in which one spouse is Roman Catholic and the other a member of a Reformed Church. The product of the sixth round of Catholic/Reformed dialogues—published jointly by Westminster John Knox Press and

the United States Conference of Catholic Bishops—*Interchurch Families* explores issues related to marriage and family in Roman Catholic/Reformed families, focusing on issues such as shared worship, Baptism, marriage, and Eucharist.

While I experienced my first interchurch wedding as a problem to be solved (that is, how can we honor the bride's sincere hope that the Eucharist be celebrated), the writers of *Interchurch Families* see such unions as signs of ecumenical hope: "Interchurch families are a gift both for our churches and for the whole Church of Jesus Christ. The creativity and longing for a unity that can be visibly manifest, often expressed by members of such families, can serve as a witness to the whole Church" (p. 1).

For each of the main issues, the writers develop case studies to invite the reader into the situation. When addressing the question, "How does an interchurch family worship?" the authors introduce us to Bernard, a Presbyterian, and Sandra, a Catholic. In this narrative we see the richness and difficulty of family ecumenism as we see Bernard coming to grips with why he must not commune at Sandra's Catholic Church and Sandra's difficulty accepting the new female minister at Bernard's Presbyterian Church. In the chapter on marriage, Catherine and Mark's wedding planning gives hope to those who are in similar situations. This case study approach is helpful in making the issues concrete, even when the descriptions seem to be forced.

The book's approach stresses commonality, but divergences are clearly addressed. In the chapter on marriage the writers describe what Roman Catholics and Reformed Christians hold in common on marriage (the uniting of two Christians in marriage on the basis of their common Baptism), they explain where the churches diverge (a sacramental in contrast to a covenantal basis for marriage), and they offer a practical guide for working out questions (where the ceremony might take place, who might officiate, and how to work it out so the marriage is recognized by both ecclesiastical bodies). Both the theological and practical sections are concise and well done.

The case study on Eucharist/ Lord's Supper is especially poignant, since there remains no satisfying solution to the problem of sharing at the Table in a Roman Catholic/Reformed marriage. In real life we know that individuals, ministers, and churches sometimes work through the issues involved so that interchurch families do share the sacrament together, but out of respect for the traditions of both churches, such practices are not acknowledged.

For each situation one story of a family is told with one resolution. This works well except for the chapter on Baptism. In that chapter the parents decide to have the child baptized in the mother's Roman Catholic Church, with a celebration of that Baptism held in the father's United Church of Christ congregation the following week. According to the case study, this decision was made because of the mother's strong commitment to the vow she made at marriage to raise her children in the nurture of the Roman Catholic Church. I would have liked a second scenario where the child was baptized in the Reformed Church. From the logic laid out in the book, the Baptism in the Roman Catholic Church made sense because "Bernadette felt bound to the promise about the religious upbringing of children she had made to her church at the time of their wedding. David felt great commitment to his church, but he was not required to make a comparable promise" (p. 29). Although the text suggests that "other people make different decisions," it is not clear to me how an interchurch family could do otherwise if both spouses take their church commitment seriously. A Roman Catholic spouse makes a promise at marriage to raise the child in the Roman Catholic Church. Thus a child of this union could not be baptized in a Reformed Church without the breaking of a promise by the Roman Catholic parent. Is there a situation where an interchurch couple could legitimately baptize their child in a Reformed Church? I would appreciate more guidance here, but I am confident that such a scenario remains beyond the consensus of this product of Catholic/Reformed dialogue.

It is difficult for a Reformed person to read about restrictions at the Table or in Baptism and not blame the Catholics for the problem. But in *Interchurch Families* special care is taken to avoid blaming either the Catholic Church or the Reformed Churches for the tensions that exist. For this the authors should be commended.

I have only one criticism of the book. In a section called "The Counter Demands of Culture," the authors sharply criticize the consumerist individualism of contemporary American culture and its deleterious effects on Christian identity. In an ethos where "members become consumers," church unity is obscured and notions of voluntary association replace incorporation into the Body of Christ. The book states that this consumerist model has a "corrosive effect" on interchurch families, casting the relationship between the churches of the respective spouses in competitive terms. This analysis is correct as far as it goes. What the authors fail to acknowledge, however, is that voluntary association is the underpinning for so many interchurch families. Because many American Christians reject the church's authority to have a say in whom they shall marry, "ecumenical families" proliferate. While such unions may indeed give all of us ecumenical hope, the increase in interchurch families is made possible largely because of this ethos.

The two appendixes in the book are extremely helpful. The first contains practical helps on marriage preparation, family planning, canon law, and annulments. The second is a glossary of terms with everything from the *Book of Order* to the difference in understanding of "local church" in Roman Catholic and Reformed usage to the definition of a valid marriage in the Roman Catholic Church. In a book of this length (69 pages plus 15 pages of appendixes), it is pointless to criticize topics left out or not elaborated at length. An enormous amount is packed into this brief volume, and it will be invaluable to pastors and those entering into or already a part of an interchurch family. ■

CHARLES WILEY serves as an associate for theology in the Office of Theology and Worship, Presbyterian Church (U.S.A.).

Part Three

Aids for the
Revised Common Lectionary

Year C—Advent 2003 through Reign of Christ 2004

Introduction to Lectionary Aids

BY CHIP ANDRUS, DON ARMITAGE, JASON ASBURY, ALAN BARTHEL, KEN CARTER, PAUL GALBREATH, SALLY GANT, MICHAEL MORGAN, AND DAVID VANDERMEER

LECTIONARY AIDS

The following aids are based on the *Revised Common Lectionary* prepared by the Consultation on Common Texts. This ecumenical forum provides readings for each Sunday and feast day in a three-year cycle. Hymn suggestions are coordinated with the fourfold pattern of worship in the *Book of Common Worship*:

Gathering
The Word
The Eucharist
Sending

In addition, hymns are coordinated with particular biblical readings for each Sunday and feast day:

O = Old Testament/Hebrew Scripture
A = Acts of the Apostles
E = Epistle
G = Gospel

The proliferation of hymnals in recent years provides a wealth of materials to enrich worship. Extensive suggestions are offered from these resources in coordination with Scripture readings, the psalm for the day, and occasionally the particular liturgical day.

In addition to the calls to worship and prayers of confession offered in the *Book of Common Worship*, suggestions are made for these elements of the gathering movement for each Sunday and feast day. It is recommended that the calls to worship are preceded by one of the greetings suggested in the *Book of Common Worship* (p. 48). Prayers of Confession are provided for each day. The prayers for feast days are taken from the *Book of Common Worship*.

A KEY TO FREQUENTLY CITED SOURCES

SUGGESTED HYMNS

HB   *The Hymnbook* (Philadelphia: Presbyterian Church in the U.S.A., 1955)

LBW   *Lutheran Book of Worship* (Minneapolis: Augsburg Publishing House, 1978)

NCH   *The New Century Hymnal* (Cleveland: Pilgrim Press, 1995)

PH   *The Presbyterian Hymnal: Hymns, Psalms, and Spiritual Songs* (Louisville, Ky.: Westminster/John Knox Press, 1990)

RL   *Rejoice in the Lord* (Grand Rapids: Wm. B. Eerdmans Publishing Co., 1985)

TFF   *This Far by Faith: An African American Resource for Worship* (Minneapolis: Augsburg-Fortress, 1999)

WOV   *With One Voice* (Minneapolis: Augburg-Fortress, 1995)

PSALM RESOURCES

HP 1 and 2   *A Hymntune Psalter, Books One and Two.* Carl P. Daw Jr. and Kevin R. Hackett (New York: Church Publishing Inc., 1998)

NMP   *A New Metrical Psalter.* Christopher L. Webber (New York: Church Hymnal Corporation, 1986)

P   *The Psalter: Psalms & Canticles for Singing.* Hal H. Hopson (Louisville, Ky.: Westminster/John Knox Press, 1993)

PH   *The Presbyterian Hymnal: Hymns, Psalms, and Spiritual Songs* (Louisville, Ky.: Westminster/John Knox Press, 1990)

PCW   *Psalter for Christian Worship.* Michael Morgan (Louisville, Ky.: Witherspoon Press, 1999)

PsH   *Psalter Hymnal* (Grand Rapids: CRC Publications, 1988)

SP   *The Selah Psalter.* Richard Leach and David P. Schaap (Kingston, N.Y.: Selah Publishing Co., 2001)

SOURCES FOR MULTICULTURAL/ CONTEMPORARY RECOMMENDATIONS

Multicultural and contemporary selections are organized based on the usual pattern of lectionary readings and the psalm of the day from the *BCW*: Old Testament (or Acts), Psalm setting, Epistle, and Gospel readings are presented in chronological order. Some Sundays also include other selections for gathering, Communion, sending, or music appropriate to that particular day.

AAHH   *African American Heritage Hymnal* (Chicago: GIA Publications, 2001)

CG   *Common Ground: A Song Book for All the Churches* (Edinburgh: St. Andrew's Press, 1998)

CLUW   *Come Let Us Worship: The Korean-English Presbyterian Hymnal and Service Book* (Louisville, Ky.: Geneva Press, 2001)

El Himn *El Himnario Presbiteriano* (Louisville, Ky.: Geneva Press, 1999)

GP   *Global Praise 2* (New York: General Board of Global Ministries, 2000)

GS   *Global Songs—Local Voices* (Minneapolis: Bread for the Journey, 1995)

HFTG   *Hymns for the Gospels* (Chicago: GIA Publications, 2001)

TFF   *This Far by Faith: An African American Resource for Worship* (Minneapolis: Augsburg-Fortress, 1999)

LUYH   *Lift Up Your Hearts* (Louisville, Ky.: Geneva Press, 1999)

Mar   *Praise: Hymns and Choruses Book 4* (Nashville: Maranatha! Music, a division of Word, Inc., 1997)

PH   *The Presbyterian Hymnal: Hymns, Psalms, and Spiritual Songs* (Louisville, Ky.: Westminster/John Knox Press, 1990)

Renew   *Renew! Songs and Hymns for Blended Worship* (Carol Stream, Ill.: Hope Publishing Co., 1995)

SNC   *Sing! A New Creation* (Grand Rapids: Calvin Institute of Christian Worship, 2001)

W&P   *Worship & Praise* (Minneapolis: Augsburg-Fortress, 1999)

WOV   *With One Voice* (Minneapolis: Augsburg-Fortress, 1995)

ORGAN NOTES AND ABBREVIATIONS

Organ selections are designated by degree of difficulty:

(E) = Easy   (M) = Moderate   (D) = Difficult

LITURGICAL NOTES

Advent

To mark Advent as unique from the rest of the church year, the following gathering rite may be used in place of the prelude, or following the prelude. The rite is marked by considerable silence and quiet.

The church is dimly lit as the people gather; the presider and others in the chancel party are in their places in an attitude of prayer.

After a period of time a soloist begins to sing: "Be Still and Know That I Am God" (Wild Goose Publications, John Bell). More voices gradually join in the singing until the whole congregation is participating. During the singing, the appropriate candle(s) in Advent is lit (with no explanation!).

All stand for the Advent Greeting (*Book of Common Worship*)
Silence

Prayer of Confession and Litany (*This Far by Faith,* Augsburg-Fortress)
Prayer of the Day
All are seated for the Service of the Word

Lent

During Lent it is customary not to sing settings of the *Gloria* or the *Gloria Patria,* hymns containing "alleluias." The music in general should be more subdued and reflective and less ornamented (no descants, or organ variations on the hymn). Consider the use of more a cappella singing of the hymns and choral music. If it is your custom to sing "alleluias" at the gospel reading, you might consider using the hymn by Carol Doran, "O Praise the Gracious Power," in a responsorial manner to introduce the gospel. Use one stanza for each of the five Sundays in Lent like this: Choir or cantor (soloist) sings refrain, all repeat. Choir sings one stanza, all sing refrain. This would be an excellent place to use a children's choir liturgically.

Follow the prelude on each of the five Lenten Sundays with a penitential rite taken from the *Book of Common Worship.* Use the Litany for Lent in conjunction with the prayer of Confession for the Lenten season. One of the simple settings of the *Kyrie* from *Holy Is the Lord* would be an appropriate response in the litany.

The Great Fifty Days

The period from Easter until the eve of Pentecost is known as the Great Fifty Days. Alleluias abound; the liturgy should be extravagant. It is a time for mystagogical preaching and focusing on the post-resurrection stories. The themes of the Sunday lections should take precedence over all other influences. This is no ordinary time.

Pentecost

This is a great day to begin and end worship outside, weather permitting. Using the Presbyterian *Book of Common Worship* or *The New Handbook for Christian Worship,* create a gathering rite to be used outdoors. Greeting, opening prayer, Litany for Pentecost, and a processional hymn accompanied by brass or handbell choir. (With the handbell choir you may wish to use a more repetitious piece of music such as a chant from *Taizé, Veni Sancti Spiritus: Music from Taizé, Vol. 1* [GIA SATB (Cong) Solo, Instrumentalists].) One possible hymn would be the Pentecost version of "Hail Thee, Festival Day" with the congregation, brass, handbells, singing, and playing on the refrain and a soloist or choir singing the stanzas. Use festive banners, Processional Cross, and so forth to lead the procession into the sanctuary. After Easter, this is the second most important day for baptisms.

Summer Months

Beginning this Sunday through Labor Day weekend, if your church choir does not provide musical leadership, introduce a hymn choir, made up of anyone who wants to show up forty-five minutes before worship to learn the hymns and other service music, to provide substantial leadership during the summer.

PUBLISHER ABBREVIATIONS

AB	Abingdon	HIN	Hinshaw
ABS	Anton Böhm and Sons	HL	Hal Leonard
AF	Augsburg-Fortress	HP	Hope
AGP	Agape Press	HTF	H. T. FitzSimons Co.
AL	Alphonse Leduc	HWG	H. W. Gray
AM	Alliance Music	IC	Iona Community
AP	Alfred Publishing Co.	IM	Integrity Music
APG	Alan Publishing Group	JFB	J. Fischer Bros.
BB	Bote and Bock	KAL	Kalmus
BE	Boremann Editions	KM	Kindred Music
BAR	Bärenreiter	LG	Lawson-Gould
BH	Boosey and Hawkes	LLB	Lloyd Larson-Brookfield
BLP	Broadman/Lindsborg Press	LAP	Laurel Press
		LP	Lindsborg Press
BM	Belwin-Mills	LY	Lyche
BOM	Boston Music	MER	Mercury
BOU	Bourne Co.	MCA	McAfee
BP	Beckenhorst Press	MCAM	MCA Music
BR	Basil Ramsey	MF	Mark Foster
BRM	Brodt Music	MS	MorningStar
BSS	B. Schotts Söhne	NK	Neil A. Kjos
C	Concordia	OCP	OCP Publications
CF	Carl Fischer	ODC	Oliver Diston Co.
CFP	C. F. Peters	OLF	Organ Literature Foundation
GC	Choristers Guild		
CHM	Chapel Hill Music	OS	Organized Sound
CP	Coronet Press	OXU	Oxford University Press
CRC	CRC Publications	PEM	Peer Music
DUR	Durand	PM	Plymouth Music
EA	Edwin Ashdown	PP	Paraclete Press
EBM	Edward B. Marks	RKM	Robert King Music
ECS	E.C. Schirmer	SAL	Salabert
ECSP	ECS Publishing	S&B	Stainer and Bell
ES	Earthsongs	SB	Summy Birchard
EWE	Ernest White Editions	SE	Salabert Editions
EV	Elgan Vogel	SEL	Selah
FBM	Fred Brock Music	SJM	St. James Music Press
FP	Fortress Press	SMP	Sacred Music Press
GIA	Gregorian Institute of America	SP	Shawnee Press
		TP	Theodore Presser
GLS	Glory Sound	WAM	Walton Music
GM	Galaxy Music	WJK	Westminster John Knox
GP	Gallean Press	WL	World Library
GS	G. Schirmer	WM	Willy Muller
HF	Harold Flammer, Inc.	WMP	Woodland Music Press

November 30, 2003

LECTIONARY READINGS

Jeremiah 33:14–16
1 Thessalonians 3:9–13
Luke 21:25–36

Psalm 25:1–10

CALL TO WORSHIP

Give thanks to the Lord of hosts,
  for the Lord is good,
for God's steadfast love endures forever!
God leads the humble in what is right,
  and teaches the humble God's way.
**All the paths of the Lord
  are steadfast love and faithfulness.**

PRAYER OF CONFESSION

Most holy God,
signs everywhere are pointing
to your coming day of reckoning.
Yet we continue in the sins of youth,
as though your day were far off;
we chart our course by worldly wisdom,
as though our destiny lies in our own hands.

Remember your steadfast love,
and look upon us with mercy.
Quicken our hearts by your Spirit
to lift up our heads in trust,
looking eagerly and gladly
for the coming of our Savior,
Jesus Christ, the Lord.

HYMNS FOR THE DAY

GATHERING	HB	LBW	NCH	PH	RIL	TFF	WOV
Lift Up Your Heads, Ye Mighty Gates	152	2	11	8	185	4	631
THE WORD							
O—O Come, O Come, Emmanuel	147	34	116	9	184	—	—
Lo, How a Rose E'er Blooming	162	58	127	48	204	—	—
O Word of God Incarnate	251	231	315	327	387	—	—
E—We All Are One in Mission	—	—	—	435	—	—	755
Blest Be the Tie That Binds	473	370	393	438	407–8	—	—
G—Jesus Comes with Clouds Descending	234	27	—	6	605	—	—
"Sleepers, Wake!" A Voice Astounds Us	—	31	112	17	606	—	—
O Day of God, Draw Nigh	—	—	611	452	178	—	—
THE EUCHARIST							
Savior of the Nations, Come	—	28	—	14	189	—	—
Now to Your Table Spread	—	—	—	515	—	—	—
SENDING							
Rejoice! Rejoice, Believers	231	25	—	15	—	—	—

First Sunday of Advent

Color: Purple/Blue

PSALM SETTINGS

METRICAL

"Lord, to You My Soul Is Lifted," PH 178, CM, Wiersma

RESPONSORIAL

"Lord, You Are My Strength," P 23 (Presbyterian 8)

MULTICULTURAL/CONTEMPORARY

O—"Come Now, O Prince of Peace," CLUW 148/GS II, p. 50/SNC 209, Geonyong Lee

"Come to Be Our Hope, O Jesus," *Global Songs 2*, p. 18, GIA

"He Came Down," SNC 92/AAHH 200, Cameroon traditional

"Come, Lord Jesus," GP II, p. 58, SNC 103, Carey Landry

"Emmanuel/Emmanuel," AAHH 189, Bob McGee

"We Bring the Sacrifice of Praise," W&P 150/SNC 12/AAHH 529, Kirk Dearman

Psalm—"A ti, Senor," El Himn 415

"Lead Me, Lord," AAHH 145, Samuel Sebastian Wesley

E—"What Shall I Render?" TFF 239/AAHH 389, Margaret Pleasant Douroux

"Awake! Awake and Greet the New Morn," SNC 91/WOV 633, Marty Haugen

G—"Wait for the Lord," *Taizé: Songs for Prayer*, GIA #30/SNC 96, Jacques Berthier

"All the Earth Is Waiting," SNC 93, Albert Taule

"While We Are Waiting, Come," AAHH 190, Don Cason

"When the Lord in Glory Comes," HFTG 100

ANTHEMS

"O Come, O Come, Emmanuel," Robert Shaw/Alice Parker, LG 727, SATB

"O Come, O Come Emmanuel," John Ferguson, MS MSM-50–0015, SSATBB

MUSIC FOR THE SMALL CHURCH

"O Come, O Come, Emmanuel," John Bell, in *Two Advent Hymns* (solo, SATB), GIA G5493

"Come, Emmanuel," Don Besig (SATB), HF A6499

"Let Us Light a Candle in the Darkness," Richard Shephard in *Canons & Crotchets: The York Minister Two-Part Anthem Book*, SJM, 58

OTHER VOCAL MUSIC

"Come, Thou Dear Redeemer," Cesar Franck in *Solos for the Church Year*, LG/GS

"Come, Thou and with Us Dwell," William Byrd in *Solos for the Church Year*, LG/GS, edited by Lloyd Pfautsch

ORGAN

Prelude or postlude on the hymn tune HELMSLEY ("Jesus Comes with Clouds Descending")

Charles Callahan, "Lo! He Comes . . . ," *Advent Music for Manuals*, MS (E)

Kenneth Leighten, *Six Fantasies on Hymn Tunes*, BR (D)

Alan Ridout, *Chorale Preludes on English Tunes*, OXU (M)

Wilbur Held, *Four Advent Hymns Set 1*, MS (M)

"Savior of the Nations Come" (NUN KOMM, DER HEIDEN HEILAND) [If your congregation is unfamiliar with this tune, have an instrumentalist play the choral melody, and alternate organ pieces with the choir singing stanzas of the hymn.]

J. S. Bach, several settings of various levels of difficulty

Paul Manz, *Ten Chorale Improvisations*, vols. 1, 3, 7, C (M)

Postlude on the chorale WACHET AUF ("Sleepers, Wake!")

Jan Bender, *Kleine Choralvorspiele*, AF (M)

J. S. Bach, "Schübler Chorales," various editions (use a trombone, or have the men of the choir sing the chorale melody) (M)

Felix Mendelssohn, complete works, GS (M-E)

Alexander Schreiner, *Organ Voluntaries*, JFB (E)

Alec Wyton, *A Little Christian Year*, CF (E)

THE CONFESSION OF 1967

For today's selection, see p. 221.

December 7, 2003

LECTIONARY READINGS

Malachi 3:1–4
Philippians 1:3–11
Luke 3:1–6

Luke 1:68–79

CALL TO WORSHIP

Blessed be the Lord God of Israel,
   for the Lord has come to the Lord's people to set
    them free.
By the tender mercy of our God,
  the dawn from on high shall break upon us,
To give light to those who sit in darkness
   and the shadow of death,
and to guide our feet in the way of peace.

PRAYER OF CONFESSION

Holy Savior,
you are coming in power
to bring all nations under your rule.
But who can endure the day of your coming?
We confess you as Lord,
yet our paths remain crooked,
our ways, rough.

Show us the tender mercy of our God;
break in upon us from your holy heights.
Refine us with the fire of your Spirit,
that we may live as people of light,
and walk in ways of peace,
to your glory and praise.

HYMNS FOR THE DAY

GATHERING	HB	LBW	NCH	PH	RL	TFF	WOV
O Worship the King, All Glorious Above!	26	548	26	476	2	—	—
THE WORD							
O—O Lord, How Shall I Meet You?	—	23	102	11	368	—	—
As a Chalice Cast of Gold	—	—	—	336	—	—	—
Soon and Very Soon	—	—	—	—	—	38	744
E—With Joy I Heard My Friends Exclaim	439	—	—	235	132	—	—
More Love to Thee, O Christ	397	—	456	359	—	—	—
G—Comfort, Comfort You My People	—	29	101	3	169	—	—
On Jordan's Banks the Baptist's Cry	—	36	—	10	187	—	—
Wild and Lone the Prophet's Voice	—	—	409	—	—	—	—
THE EUCHARIST							
Deck Yourself, My Soul, with Gladness	—	224	334	506	536	—	—
SENDING							
Song of Zechariah	—	—	733	601–2	—	—	725

Second Sunday of Advent

Color: Purple/Blue

PSALM SETTINGS

METRICAL
"Song of Zechariah," PH 602
RESPONSORIAL
"Canticle of Zechariah," P 158 (Byzantine Chant setting)

MULTICULTURAL/CONTEMPORARY

O—"Refiner's Fire," LUYH 66, Brian Doerksen
"It's in My Heart," AAHH 416, Arthur Slater
Psalm—"Bendito el Senor y Dios," El Himn 485
"Blessed Be the Lord God of Israel," W&P 20/SNC 104, Ralph C. Sappington
"Guide My Feet," AAHH 131, arr. by Valeria A. Foster
E—"La cruz excelsa al contemplar," El Himn 145
"He Who Began a Good Work," W&P 56, Jon Mohr
"More About Jesus," AAHH 565, John R. Sweney
"It's My Desire," SATB, GIA, Freda Bagley/Horace Clarence Boyer
G—"Prepare Ye the Way of the Lord," CLUW 141/SNC 105, Jacques Berthier
"Make Way," SNC 98, Graham Kendrick
"Come Out the Wilderness," AAHH 367, arr. by Evelyn Simpson-Curenton
"Preparen el camino del Senor," El Himn 69

ANTHEMS

"Comfort All Ye My People," Gabriel Faure, CF CM8017, SATB
"Comfort, Comfort," arr. by John Ferguson, AF 11-2381, SATB

MUSIC FOR THE SMALL CHURCH

"Herald, Sound the Note of Gladness!" Sally Ann Morris (SATB or unison), in *Giving Thanks in Song and Prayer*, GIA G-4930, 55

OTHER VOCAL MUSIC

"Comfort Ye," from *Messiah*, G. F. Handel
"Every Valley Shall Be Exalted," from *Messiah*, G. F. Handel
"Come, Thou Long-Expected Jesus," Glenn L. Rudolph, OXU 96.800
"Come, Thou Long-Expected Jesus," Timothy E. Kimbrough in *Sweet Sing (Hymns of Charles Wesley)*, CHM
"Prepare Thyself, Zion," J. S. Bach
"Rejoice Now My Spirit," K. Lee Scott, AF 11-10228

ORGAN

"Comfort, Comfort You My People" (FREU DICH SEHR, Psalm 42)
Paul Manz, *Ten Chorale Improvisations*, C (M)
Marcel Dupré, *Two Chorales*, GP (M)
Johann Pachelbel, any edition of his complete organ works (M) [Suggestion: As an introit follow the prelude with the choral arrangement of this hymn as in the one by John Ferguson arranged for SATB, snare drum, and fife (or flute and clarinet/oboe) by John Ferguson, AF]
"On Jordan's Banks the Baptist's Cry" (WINCHESTER NEW)
Flor Peeters, WINCHESTER NEW, *Thirty Short Preludes*, CFP (E)
C. S. Lang, WINCHESTER NEW, *Festal Voluntaries—Advent*, (MD)
"O Lord, How Shall I Meet You?" (VALET WILL ICH DIR GEBEN)

THE CONFESSION OF 1967

For today's selection, see p. 221.

December 14, 2003

LECTIONARY READINGS

Zephaniah 3:14–20
Philippians 4:4–7
Luke 3:7–18

Isaiah 12:2–6

CALL TO WORSHIP

Sing aloud, O daughter Zion;
   shout, O Israel!
Rejoice and exult with all your heart,
   O daughter Jerusalem!
Shout aloud and sing for joy!
For great in our midst is the Holy One of Israel.

PRAYER OF CONFESSION

God of strength and might,
we proclaim, "The Lord is near!"
Yet we fret over our destiny,
clutching your good gifts anxiously,
afraid to share those gifts with others.

Forgive us for living
as though you were not among us,
and your good promises meant nothing.
Renew us with your Spirit's fire,
that we may bear good fruit
of justice, mercy, peace, and gladness—
embodying your Good News to all
through our Savior, Christ the Lord.

HYMNS FOR THE DAY

	HB	LBW	NCH	PH	RL	TFF	WOV
GATHERING							
Come, Thou Long-Expected Jesus	151	30	122	1, 2	183	—	—
THE WORD							
O—Prepare the Way, O Zion	—	26	—	13	—	—	—
New Songs of Celebration Render	—	—	—	218	119	—	—
E—Rejoice! Rejoice, Believers	231	25	—	15	—	—	—
Rejoice, the Lord Is King	140	171	303	155	596–97	—	—
G—Baptized in Water	—	—	—	492	—	—	693
Come, Ye Thankful People, Come	525	407	422	551	18	—	—
Somebody's Knockin' at Your Door	—	—	—	—	44	—	—
Wild and Lone the Prophet's Voice	—	—	409	—	—	—	—
THE EUCHARIST							
Let All Mortal Flesh Keep Silence	148	198	345	5	188	—	—
Creator of the Stars of Night	—	—	—	4	—	—	—
SENDING							
My Lord! What a Morning	—	—	—	449	—	40	627

Third Sunday of Advent

Color: Purple/Blue

PSALM SETTINGS

METRICAL

"Surely It Is God Who Saves Me," *The Alfred Fredak Hymnary*, SEL

RESPONSORIAL

"Canticle of Thanksgiving," P 175

MULTICULTURAL/CONTEMPORARY

O—"Songs with My Whole Heart," LUYH 60, Danny Chambers

"God Brings the Kingdom," CLUW 149

"Soon and Very Soon," W&P/SNC 106/AAHH 193, Andraé Crouch

"Be My Home," W&P 16, Handt Hanson and Paul Murakami

Psalm—"Surely It Is God," LUYH 81, Jack Noble White

"Lord, My Strength," W&P 93, Dean Krippaehne

E—"Awake! Awake, and Greet the New Morn," WOV 633/SNC 91, Marty Haugen

"Give Thanks," W&P 41/CLUW 247 LUYH 114/SNC 216, Henry Smith

"Rejoice in the Mission," W&P 120, Dori Erwin Collins

"I Must Tell Jesus," AAHH 375, Elisha A. Hoffman

"Suelta la alegria," El Himn 213

G—"A Story for All People," W&P 2, Dori Erwin Collins

"Hail to the Lord's Anointed," AAHH 187, Sheffield

ANTHEMS

"Rejoice in the Lord Always," M. Thomas Cousins, BRM 591, SSATBB

"O Thou That Tellest Good Tidings to Zion," No. 9 from Handel's *Messiah*, GS, SATB and alto solo

MUSIC FOR THE SMALL CHURCH

"Lift Up Your Heads," John Bell (SATB, organ), GIA G-5494

"Rejoice in the Lord Always," Richard W. Gieseke (unison/keyboard), MS MSM-50-0003

OTHER VOCAL MUSIC

"Rejoice Greatly, O Daughter of Zion," from Handel's *Messiah*

ORGAN

Using the hymn tune FREU DICH SEHR ("Comfort, Comfort")

Paul Manz, *Ten Chorale Improvisations*, C (E)

Marcel Dupré, *Two Chorales*, GP (M-E)

Johann Pachelbel, any edition of his organ works (M) [Suggestion: Use the anthem version of this hymn following the prelude arranged for SATB, snare drum and fife (or flute and clarinet/oboe), by John Ferguson, AF (E)]

J. S. Bach, KOMMST DU NUN, JESU, VOM HIMMEL HERUNTER ("Comest Thou, Jesu, from Heaven to Earth Now Descending?"), "Schübler Chorales," various editions (M-D) [Choir sings the choral (it is also known by the tune name LOBET DEN HERREN), followed by the organ setting. Alternate setting: have the men (or a bassoon) perform the pedal part.]

Postlude on the tune VENI, EMMANUEL ("O Come, O Come, Emmanuel")

G. Winston Cassler, VENI, EMMANUEL, *Organ Music for the Church Year*, AF (E)

Wilbur Held, VENI, EMMANUEL, *Nativity Suite*, C (E)

Kenneth Leighton, VENI, EMMANUEL, *Six Fantasies on Hymn Tunes*, BR (D)

Walter MacNutt, *Choral Fantasy on Veni, Emmanuel*, HWG (D)

Paul Manz, VENI, EMMANUEL, *Ten Chorale Improvisations*, C (M)

THE CONFESSION OF 1967

For today's selection, see p. 222.

December 21, 2003

LECTIONARY READINGS

Micah 5:2–5a
Hebrews 10:5–10
Luke 1:39–45 (46–55)

Luke 1:47–55 or Psalm 80:1–7

CALL TO WORSHIP

From Bethlehem there is to come
   the one who is to rule in Israel,
whose origin is from of old,
   from ancient days.
And we shall live secure, for his name
   Shall be great to the ends of the earth;
and he shall be the one of peace.

PRAYER OF CONFESSION

God of all hope,
We rejoice in your sure promise
to send us a Ruler and Shepherd.
He lifts up the lowly and fills the hungry;
yet we strive to promote ourselves
and guarantee our own welfare.
We have denied his power,
and disbelieved your promise.

In mercy, do not scatter us in our pride;
do not send us away empty.
Teach us to embrace your way with us,
your will for us,
your Spirit in us,
for the sake of Jesus Christ, our Lord.

HYMNS FOR THE DAY

GATHERING	HB	LBW	NCH	PH	RL	TFF	WOV
People, Look East	—	—	12	—	—	—	626
THE WORD							
O—O Little Town of Bethlehem	171	41	133	43–4	193–4	—	—
See Amid the Winter's Snow	—	—	51	219	—	—	—
All Hail to God's Anointed	146	87	205	232	—	—	—
E—O Lord of Every Shining Constellation	—	—	297	31	—	—	—
What Does the Lord Require?	—	—	—	405	176	—	—
G—Song of Mary	596	180	119	600	—	168	—
The Angel Gabriel from Heaven Came	—	—	—	16	—	—	632
That Boy-Child of Mary	—	—	—	55	—	54	—
THE EUCHARIST							
Love Divine, All Loves Excelling	399	315	43	376	464	—	—
SENDING							
Prepare the Way, O Zion	—	26	—	13	—	—	—

Fourth Sunday of Advent

Color: Purple/Blue

PSALM SETTINGS

METRICAL
"O Hear Our Cry, O Lord," PH 206, SM with
refrain, Anderson
RESPONSORIAL
"Restore Us, O God of Hosts," HP 1, p. 59,
Daw/Hackett

MULTICULTURAL/CONTEMPORARY

Psalm—"Mi alma glorifica al Senor mi Dios," El
Himn 483
"Canticle of the Turning," W&P 26/GS II, p. 46,
Kelly Willard
"A Story for All People," W&P 2, Dori Erwin Collins
"Bless His Holy Name," W&P 19, Renew, Andraé
Crouch
"Song of Mary," SNC 102, German tune
G—"To a Maid Engaged to Joseph," CLUW 151
"When to Mary, the Word," HFTG 144
Additional Songs—"Awake! Awake and Greet the
New Morn," WOV 633/SNC 91, Marty Haugen

ANTHEMS

"O Magnum Mysterium," Morten Lauridsen, PEM
01–098779-121, SSAATTBB
"Mid-Winter," Bob Chilcott, OXU X389, SATB

MUSIC FOR THE SMALL CHURCH

"My Soul Proclaims with Wonder," Sally Ann Morris
(unison, choir/congregation), in *Giving Thanks in
Song and Prayer*, GIA G-4930, 56 (Luke)

OTHER VOCAL MUSIC

"He Shall Feed His Flock Like a Shepherd," from
Handel's *Messiah*

ORGAN

"O Come, O Come, Emmanuel" (VENI, EMMANUEL)
Austin Lovelace, *Fantasy, Trio and Toccata on
"O come . . . ,"* C
G. Winston Cassler, *Organ Music for the Church
Year*, AF
Wilbur Held, *Nativity Suite*, C
Kenneth Leighton, *Six Fantasies on Hymn Tunes*,
BR
Walter MacNutt, *Choral Fantasy on Veni,
Emmanuel*, HWG
Paul Manz, VENI, EMMANUEL, *Ten Chorale
Improvisations*, C
Using the Magnificat as a basis for the prelude:
Have the choir alternate verses of the Magnificat
(plainsong version) with pieces for organ by
Pachelbel, J. S. Bach, Guillmant, Dandrieu
"All Hail to God's Anointed," Rockport

THE CONFESSION OF 1967

For today's selection, see p. 222.

December 24, 2003

LECTIONARY READINGS

Isaiah 9:2–7
Titus 2:11–14
Luke 2:1–14 (15–20)

Psalm 96

CALL TO WORSHIP

The people who walked in darkness
  have seen a great light;
**those who lived in the land of deep darkness
  on them light has shined.**
For a child has been born for us,
  a son given to us.
**Let the heavens be glad,
  let all the earth rejoice!**

PRAYER OF CONFESSION

**Glorious Lord,
You send us a Savior—
heaven's light breaking into human night.
Yet we close our doors to your light,
afraid to give you room in our midst.
Still, your light shines;
your mercy refuses to let our rejection
quench the light of your love.**

**Forgive us for denying your due honor.
Lift us by your Spirit
to join angelic hosts
in anthems of joy and peace,
brought to us in the holy advent
of Jesus Christ, our Lord.**

HYMNS FOR THE DAY

	HB	LBW	NCH	PH	RIL	TFF	WOV
GATHERING							
Once in Royal David's City	462	—	145	49	201	—	643
THE WORD							
O—Break forth, O Beauteous Heavenly Light	—	—	140	26	—	—	—
It Came upon a Midnight Clear	160	54	131	38	—	—	—
E—Good Christian Friends, Rejoice	6	55	129	28	218	—	—
Silent Night, Holy Night	154	65	134	60	216	—	—
G—Born in the Night	—	—	152	30	—	—	—
Infant Holy, Infant Lowly	164	44	—	37	221	—	—
Hush, Little Jesus Boy	—	—	—	—	—	56	—
Gentle Mary Laid Her Child	167	—	—	27	210	—	—
While Shepherds Watched Their Flocks	169	—	—	589	1990	—	—
THE EUCHARIST							
From Heaven Above to Earth I Come	—	51	130	54	207	—	—
In Bethlehem a Babe Was Born	—	—	—	34	—	—	—
Away in a Manger	157	67	124	245	2134	—	644
SENDING							
Joy to the World!	161	39	132	40	198	—	—

Christmas Eve

PSALM SETTINGS

METRICAL
Psalm 96, "O Sing New Songs unto the Lord," PCW, CMD, Morgan
RESPONSORIAL
"O Sing a New Song to the Lord," PH 217, Wright/Hopson

MULTICULTURAL/CONTEMPORARY

O—"King of Kings," W&P 80, Naomi Baty and Sophie Conty
Psalm—"Great Is The Lord," W&P 53, Michael W. Smith
"Sing unto the Lord," LUYH 53, Tom Fettke
"Shout to the Lord," W&P 124, Darlene Zschech
E—"Night of Silence," W&P 101, Daniel Kantor
G—"Hear the Angels," W&P 57, Robin Cain
"That Boy-Child of Mary," TFF 54, Tom Colvin
"Mary Had a Baby," SNC 107, Kenneth Fenton
"Still as Dew Falls on the Meadow," HTFG 107

ANTHEMS

"Infant Holy, Infant Lowly," John Rutter, CF CM8123, SSATBB and baritone solo
"Sing We Noel," Chesnorov/Hirt, HIN HMC-219, SSAATTBB

MUSIC FOR THE SMALL CHURCH

"Song of the Stable," David Haas (solo, SATB/keyboard/guitar/c instrument), GIA G-5218
"Were You There?" Natalie Sleeth (SAB), HP C 5032

OTHER VOCAL MUSIC

"The Holy Boy," John Ireland, *Christmas Song Album,* vol. 2, BH
"Christmas Joy," C. P. E. Bach, *Solos for the Church Year,* LG/GS
"O Jesus So Gentle, Jesus So Sweet," J. S. Bach

ORGAN

Jean Langlais, *La Nativité,* vol. 2 of *Poemes Evangeliques*
Joel Martinson, "Salvation Unto Us Has Come Prelude," PP
Olivier Messiaen, "Les Anges," *La Nativité,* AL
Jeremy Young, "Behold the Marvel of This Night," from *Pianoforte Christmas*
"From Heaven on High to Earth I Come" (VOM HIMMEL HOCH)
  J. S. Bach: "Chorale Prelude on VOM HIMMEL HOCH," several editions available
  Healey Willan, *Six Preludes,* C
  Marcel Dupré, *Seventy-nine Chorales,* HWG (E)
  Hugo Distler, *Neue Weinachtsmusik für klavier,* BAR (M-D)
"Silent Night"
  Samuel Barber, *Chorale Prelude,* GS
  Wilbur Held, *A Nativity Sweet,* CPH [Suggestion: The prelude could be a carol sing employing a mix of well-known carols interspersed with some recently composed ones, such as "Behold the Marvel of This Night." As introductions to each carol, have the organist play a "noel" based on that carol.]

December 25, 2003

LECTIONARY READINGS

Isaiah 52:7–10
Hebrews 1:1–4 (5–12)
John 1:1–14

Psalm 98

CALL TO WORSHIP

Make a joyful noise to the Lord,
   all the earth;
Break forth into joyous song
   and sing praises.
For God's Word became flesh and lived among us.
And we have seen his glory,
   the glory of God's only son,
   full of grace and truth.

PRAYER OF CONFESSION (*BCW*)

God of grace and truth,
in Jesus Christ you came among us
as light shining in darkness.
We confess that we have not welcomed the light,
or trusted good news to be good.
We have closed our eyes to glory in our midst,
expecting little, and hoping for less.

Forgive our doubt, and renew our hope,
so that we may receive the fullness of your grace,
and live in the truth of Christ the Lord.

HYMNS FOR THE DAY

	HB	LBW	NCH	PH	RIL	TFF	WOV
GATHERING							
O Come, All Ye Faithful	170	45	135	41–42	195	—	—
On This Day Earth Shall Ring	—	—	—	46	—	—	—
THE WORD							
O—Hark! The Herald Angels Sing	163	60	160	31–32	196	—	—
People, Clap Your Hands	—	—	—	194	—	—	—
E—Angels from the Realms of Glory	168	50	126	22	229	—	—
Of the Father's Love Begotten	7	42	118	309	190	—	—
G—What Child Is This	159	40	148	53	217	—	—
He Came Down That We May Have Love	—	—	—	—	—	37	—
THE EUCHARIST							
Joyful Christmas Day Is Here	—	—	—	39	—	—	—
In the Bleak Midwinter	—	—	128	36	—	—	—
SENDING							
Go, Tell It on the Mountain	70	154	29	—	—	—	—

Christmas Day

Color: White/Gold

PSALM SETTINGS

METRICAL
Psalm 97, "God Reigns! Let Earth Rejoice!" PCW,
   SMD, Morgan
RESPONSORIAL
"To Us a Child Is Born," HP 1, p. 84, Daw/Hackett
METRICAL
Psalm 98, "Sing New Songs to God Almighty," PCW,
   8.7.8.7.D, Morgan
METRICAL
"New Songs of Celebration Render," PH 218,
   9.8.9.8.D, Routley
RESPONSORIAL
"All the Ends of the Earth," HP 1, p. 85, Daw/Hackett

MULTICULTURAL/CONTEMPORARY

O—"Our God Reigns," LUYH 84, Lenny Smith, arr.
   by Stephen A. Beddia
"The King of Glory," W&P 136, Israeli traditional
"A Stable Lamp Is Lighted," AAHH 198, tune: andu-
   jar, text: Richard Willard
"Fuera con nuestro temor," El Himn 305
Psalm 98—"Sing unto the Lord," LUYH 53, arr. by
   Tom Fettke
"Sing a New Song to the Lord," SNC 112, David G.
   Wilson
"Sing to the Lord," SATB, GIA, Melvin Bryant Jr.
E—"Majesty," W&P 94, Jack Hayford
"Florece una rosa," El Himn 57
G—"Jesus, Name Above All Names," LUYH 39/SNC
   114, Naida Hearn
"Glory," LUYH 148, Danny Daniels
"Messiah Now Has Come," AAHH 203, Nolan
   Williams Jr.
"Rise Up, Shepherd and Follow," STB, OS, Phillip Orr
"Good News, the Savior Is Born," GIA, Glenn Jones
"Mary, Did You Know?" SATB, HP, arr. by Jack Schrader
"A La Ru/O Sleep, Dear Holy Baby," PH 45/WOV 639
"Hitsuji Wa/Sheep Fast Asleep," PH 52
"Go Tell It on the Mountain," PH 29/El Himn
   87/AAHH 202
"Gloria, Gloria," SNC 115/PH 576/CLUW 353/El
   Himn 491
"Word of God When All Was Silent," HTFG 82

ANTHEMS

"Christmas Bells with Joy Are Ringing," Hal H.
   Hopson, SMP 5-190, SATB
OPTIONAL HANDBELLS
"Shepherd's Pipe Carol," John Rutter, OXU X167, SATB

MUSIC FOR THE SMALL CHURCH

"Voces Angelorum," John Bell (solo, SATB), GIA G-
   5496
Gloria a Dios ("Glory to God"), traditional Peruvian
   (unison/choir or congregation), in C. Michael
   Hawn, *Halle Halle: We Sing the World Round,* CG
   CGC42, 31

OTHER VOCAL MUSIC

"In the Bleak Midwinter," Gustav Holst
"Winter Carol (In the Bleak Midwinter)," Sherri
   Porterfield
"Christmas for Solo Singers," AP
"Sweet Little Jesus Boy," Robert MacGimsey, CF

ORGAN

Olivier Messaien, DIEU PARMIS NOUS, *La Nativité,* AL (D)
Or prelude on the hymn tune ADESTE FIDELES ("O
   Come All Ye Faithful")
   Thomas Adams, ADESTE FIDELES, *Graveyard Gems,*
      EWE (E)
   Marcel Dupré, *Variations on Adeste Fideles,* HWG (D)
   Eugene Gigout, *Dix Pièces,* AL (M)
   Bruce Neswick, *Fantasia on Adeste Fideles . . .* (M-E)
   Charles Ives, *Prelude on "Adeste Fideles,"* MER (M)
or
Prelude on the hymn tune DIVINUM MYSTERIUM ("Of
   the Father's Love Begotten")
   G. Winston Cassler, *Organ Music for the Church
      Year,* AF (E)
   Wilbur Held, from *Six Carol Settings,* CPH (M)
   David Johnson, *Of the Father's Love Begotten,* AF (M)
   Richard Purvis, *Eleven Pieces for the Church
      Organist,* MCA (M)

December 28, 2003

LECTIONARY READINGS

1 Samuel 2:18–20, 26
Colossians 3:12–17
Luke 2:41–52

Psalm 148

CALL TO WORSHIP

Praise the Lord, all the earth!
Praise God, sun and moon;
praise God, all you shining stars!
Let all creation praise the name of the Lord;
for God's glory is above earth and heaven.
All people; young men and women alike,
old and young together,
praise the Lord!

PRAYER OF CONFESSION

Loving Father,
you nurture us from our mothers' wombs
with blessings of divine and human favor.
Yet we have withheld our favor
from those whom we deem unlovely.
Forgiven by you,
we have refused to forgive others.

In your love, show us mercy.
Give us a heart to love as we have been loved,
to show favor as we have been shown favor.
Enable us always to act in Jesus' name,
with thanksgiving for your unchanging love
revealed to us in his coming to us,
and abiding with us.

HYMNS FOR THE DAY

GATHERING	HB	LBW	NCH	PH	RIL	TFF	WOV
Good Christian Friends, Rejoice	165	55	129	28	218	—	—
THE WORD							
O—How Happy Is Each Child of God	—	—	—	239	—	—	—
O Hear Our Cry, O Lord	—	—	—	206	—	—	—
E—Christ, You Are the Fullness	—	—	—	346	—	—	—
O Master, Let Me Walk with Thee	304	492	503	357	428	—	—
Father, We Praise Thee	43	267	90	459	515	—	—
G—Amen, Amen	—	—	161	299	—	—	—
O Sing a Song of Bethlehem	—	—	51	308	356	—	—
Come and Go with Me to My Father's House	—	—	—	—	—	141	—
THE EUCHARIST							
Lo, How a Rose E'er Blooming	162	58	127	48	204	—	—
SENDING							
See Amid the Winter's Snow	—	—	—	51	—	—	—

First Sunday after Christmas

Color: White/Gold

PSALM SETTINGS

METRICAL
Psalm 148 "Praise God in the Highest Heaven,"
    PCW, 8.7.8.7.8.7, Morgan
RESPONSORIAL
"Alleluia!" P 155, Hopson

MULTICULTURAL/CONTEMPORARY

O—"God Has Done Marvelous Things," W&P 51,
    David Haas
Psalm—"Psalm 148," CLUW 531 and 532
"Psalm 148," SNC 31, Robert Williams
"Al caer la lluvia/As the Rain Is Falling," El Himn 23
"Sing the Lord a New Song," GP II 13, Indonesian
"Shout to the Lord," SATB, IM 09707, arr. by Daniel
    Smith
"He Is Exalted," W&P 55/SNC 41, Twila Paris
"Shout to the Lord," W&P 124/SNC 223, Darlene
    Zschech
"Lift Every Voice and Sing," AAHH 540
E—"You Are the Rock of My Salvation," W&P 161,
    Teresa Muller
"Give Thanks," W&P 41/CLUW 247/LUYH
    114/SNC 216, Henry Smith
"Let Me Have My Way Among You," LUYH 91,
    Graham Kendrick
"Do It All in the Name of the Lord," AAHH 621,
    Donna Jones
G—"Within the Father's House," HTFG 42

ANTHEMS

"Christmas-Tide," Bob Chilcott, OXU X412, SATB
"Love Came Down at Christmas," John Rutter, OXU
    84.224, SATB

MUSIC FOR THE SMALL CHURCH

"Like a Child," Dan Damon, arr. by David Cherwien
    (two-part mixed/optional flute), HP C 5013

OTHER VOCAL MUSIC

"O God of Love, Our Rest and Hope," Austin C.
    Lovelace, *Three Solos for Medium Voice*, AF
    11-9478

ORGAN

Olivier Messaien, Les Bergers, *La Nativité*, AL (M)
Or prelude on the chorale IN DULCI JUBILO ("Good
    Christian Friends")
    J. S. Bach, numbers setting, various editions (E-D)
    Herbert Gotsch, *The Concordia Hymn Prelude
        Series,* vol. 3, C (E)
    Wilbur Held, *Six Carol Settings*, C (E)
    Flor Peeters, *Thirty Chorale Preludes,* vol. 3, CFP (M)
    Ernst Pepping, *Zwölf Choralvorspiele*, BV (M)
    Alec Wyton, *A Little Church Year*, CF (M)

Or have the congregation participate in the prelude by
singing carols interspersed with organ variations on
those carols.

Or several carols trace the story of Jesus from birth to
resurrection; these would be particularly appropriate.
"Tomorrow Shall Be My Dancing Day" is one example. Have a soloist sing the stanzas (telling the story)
and the congregation sing the refrain, with organ (or
other instruments) providing variations on the tune.
This would provide an interesting time for the gathering of the community.

Or if you have a very faithful choir, you might consider performing a cantata for a prelude such as "Where
Is the Newborn King?" by Hammerschmidt, C, SATB
with instruments.

THE CONFESSION OF 1967

For today's selection, see p. 222.

January 4, 2004

LECTIONARY READINGS

Jeremiah 31:7–14
Ephesians 1:3–14
John 1:(1–9) 10–18

Psalm 147:12–20

CALL TO WORSHIP

Great is the Lord, gracious and understanding!
How good it is to sing praises to our God.
Great is our God and greatly to be praised!
   For God's mercy and understanding are beyond
     measure.
Let us sing to God with thanksgiving;
   and put all our hope in God's steadfast love.

PRAYER OF CONFESSION

God of the oppressed,
we enjoy the privilege of worshiping you openly,
while forgetting our brothers and sisters
who face persecution for being Christ's disciples.
We enjoy the blessings of a good inheritance,
while others of your beloved children
are denied that which is their right.

Forgive our self-centeredness.
Stir us by your Spirit
to prayer and to action,
that we will not rest until all your children
enjoy your justice and peace,
living in the good news of great joy to all,
that in Christ we are set free.

HYMNS FOR THE DAY

	HB	LBW	NCH	PH	RIL	TFF	WOV
GATHERING							
Angels from the Realms of Glory	168	50	126	22	229	—	—
THE WORD							
O—Joy to the World!	161	39	132	40	198	—	—
Let the Whole Creation Cry	—	242	—	256	12	—	—
E—All Glory Be to God on High	—	166	—	133	620	—	—
Here, O Lord, Your Servants Gather	—	—	72	465	—	—	—
G—O Word of God Incarnate	251	231	315	327	387	—	—
O Splendor of God's Glory Bright	—	—	87	474	76	—	—
Mary Had a Baby	—	—	—	—	55	—	—
THE EUCHARIST							
I Come with Joy to Meet My Lord	—	—	349	507	534	—	—
SENDING							
Go with Us, Lord	—	—	—	535	—	—	—

Second Sunday after Christmas

Color: White/Gold

PSALM SETTINGS

METRICAL
"Now Praise the Lord," PH 255, CM, Anderson
RESPONSORIAL
"The Word Was Made Flesh," HP 1, p. 86,
   Daw/Hackett

MULTICULTURAL/CONTEMPORARY

O—"Carol at the Manger," WOV 638
"Mourning into Dancing," W&P 99, Tommy Walker
Psalm—"Psalm 147: Sing to God, with Joy," SNC
   29, John Bell
"Sing, Praise and Bless the Lord," SNC 30/*Taizé:*
   Songs for Prayer, p. 12/CLUW 121/SNC 30,
   Jacques Berthier
E—"Look Forward in Faith," p. 73, CG, Andrew
   Scobie
"Holy Love, Holy Light," Mar 118, Bill Batstone
G—"Jesus, Name Above All Names," SNC 114,
   Naida Hearn
"Emmanuel," W&P 36/TFF 45/CLUW 211/SNC
   117, Bob McGee
"Word of God When All Was Silent," HFTG 82

ANTHEMS

"Jesus, Word of God Incarnate," W. A. Mozart,
   Novello No. 190, SATB
"Mary Had a Baby," Sam Batt Owens, MS MSM-
   50-1060, SATB and solo

MUSIC FOR THE SMALL CHURCH

"Now Greet the Swiftly Changing Year," Alfred Fedak
   (mixed voices), C 98-2691

OTHER VOCAL MUSIC

"Angel Carol Duet on Infant Holy, Infant Lowly,"
   Anna Laura Page, *Carols for Two*, AP 11536
"Watchman, Tell Us of the Night," John Ness
   Beck/transcribed by Craig Courtney in *Hymn*
   Settings of John Ness Beck, BP VC4

ORGAN

Prelude on the hymn tune ALLIEN GOTT ("All Glory
   Be to God on High")
   Andreas Armstorff, *Graveyard Gems* (M)
   J. S. Bach, several settings, various editions (M-D)
   Paul Manz, *Ten Chorale Improvisations*, vols. 1 and
   5, C (M)
   Johann Pachelbel, *The Parish Organist*, vol. 1, C (E)
   Friedrich Zachau, *The Organist's Companion*, MCA
   (E-M)
Postlude on VOM HIMMEL HOCH ("From Heaven on
   High")
   Joseph Ahrens, *Das Heilige Jahr*, WM (D)
   Walter Pelz, *Variations on From Heaven Above*,
   AFP (M)
   Ernst Pepping, *Kleines Orgelbuch*, BSS (M-D)
   David Johnson, *Music for Manuals*, AFP (E)

THE CONFESSION OF 1967

For today's selection, see p. 222.

January 6, 2004

LECTIONARY READINGS

Isaiah 60:1–6
Ephesians 3:1–12
Matthew 2:1–12

Psalm 72:1–7, 10–14

CALL TO WORSHIP

Arise, shine; for your light has come,
   and the glory of the Lord has risen upon you.
We have seen the darkness cover the earth,
   and thick darkness cover the people;
The Lord will rise upon you,
   and God's glory will appear over you.
Let every nation rejoice,
   for God has come to deliver us.

PRAYER OF CONFESSION *(BCW)*

God of glory,
you sent Jesus among us as the light of the world,
to reveal your love for all people.
We confess that our sin and pride
hide the brightness of your light.
We turn away from the poor;
we ignore cries for justice;
we do not strive for peace.

In your mercy, cleanse us of our sin,
and baptize us once again with your Spirit,
that, forgiven and renewed, we may show forth
   your glory
shining in the face of Jesus Christ.

HYMNS FOR THE DAY

GATHERING	HB	LBW	NCH	PH	RIL	TFF	WOV
The First Nowell	156	56	139	56	223	—	—
THE WORD							
O—Fairest Lord Jesus	135	518	44	306	370	—	—
Arise, Your Light Is Come!	—	—	164	411	418	—	652
E—All Hail to God's Anointed	146	87	104	205	232	—	—
Ye Servants of God, Your Master Proclaim	27	252	305	477	598	—	—
G—We Three Kings of Orient Are	176	—	—	66	225	—	646
Brightest and Best of the Sons of the Morning	175	84	156–57	67	230	—	—
Sister Mary Had but One Child	—	—	—	—	—	60	—
THE EUCHARIST							
Be Known to Us in Breaking Bread	446	—	342	505	—	—	—
O Morning Star, How Fair and Bright	415	76	158	69	367	—	—
SENDING							
As with Gladness Men of Old	174	82	159	63	228	—	—

Epiphany

Color: White/Gold

PSALM SETTINGS

METRICAL
"All Hail to God's Anointed," PH 205, 7.6.7.6.D,
  Montgomery
RESPONSORIAL
Psalm 72, PH 204, Bevenot/Schiavone

MULTICULTURAL/CONTEMPORARY

O—"Siyahamba/We Are Marching in the Light Of
  God," WOV 650 SNC 293/El Himn 317/W&P
  148/CG 139/AAHH 164, South African
"God Almighty, Ruling the World," CLUW 164
"Shine, Jesus Shine," arr. by Mark Hayes Alfred,
  18934 SATB M-D
Psalm—"Estan en tu mano, Senor," El Himn 427
"Psalm 72," SNC 120, German tune, text: James
  Montgomery
"O God, with Holy Righteousness," John Bell, *Psalms
  of Patience, Protest and Praise*, GIA
"We Bow Down," Twila Paris, W&P 149
E—"Our Confidence Is in the Lord," Noel Richards
  and Tricia Richards, W&P 114
"Sizohamba naye," GS II, p. 10
G—"Los majos/The magi," El Himn 113, SNC 118,
  Puerto Rican traditional
"De Tierra Lejana Venimos/From a Distant Home,"
  PH 64
"Alleluia," Jerry Sinclair, W&P 6
"Behold the Star," AAHH 216
"Famed Though the World's Great Cities Be," HFTG
  119

ANTHEMS

"Nativity Carol," John Rutter, OXU 84-169, SATB
"Arise, Shine, for Your Light Has Come," Allen Pote,
  CP 392-41548, SATB

MUSIC FOR THE SMALL CHURCH

"A Star Not Mapped on Human Charts," Carol
  Doran (unison), *New Hymns for the Lectionary*,
  OXU, 23
"Brightest and Best," Richard Shephard (two-
  part/organ), in *Canons & Crotchets: The York
  Minister Two-Part Anthem Book*, SJM, 11

OTHER VOCAL MUSIC

"Song of the Camels," Ralph Blane, CF V2351
"Alleluia," Antonio Vivaldi in *Sacred Songs for the
  Soloist*, David Patrick, BH
"The Kings," Peter Cornelius and Philipp Nicolai in
  Rejoice Now My Spirit, K. Lee Scott, AF 11-10228

ORGAN

Prelude on the chorale WIE SCHÖN LEUCHTET ("O
  Morning Star How Fair and Bright")
  Joseph Ahrens, *Das Heilig Jahe*, WM (D)
  J. S. Bach, several settings, various editions (M-D)
  Dietrich Buxtehude, several settings, various edi-
    tions (E-D)
  Hugo Distler, *Kleine Orgelchoral*, BAR (M)
  Sigfrid Karg-Elert, *Choral Improvisations,* vols. 4
    and 6, EBM (M)
For the postlude: During the singing of the closing
  hymn, pass a light from a main sanctuary candle
  to each member of the congregation who was
  given a taper at the beginning of the worship.
  Invite them to sit for a period of meditation fol-
  lowing the blessing and sending forth, and then
  send them into the world as Christ's light.
  Jan Bender, *Wie Schön leuchtet*, MS (M-E)
  Paul Manz, *Ten Chorale Improvisations,* vol. 2,
    C (M)
  Max Reger, *Wie Schön leuchtet*, KAL (M)
  Flor Peeters, *Wie Schön leuchtet*, CFP (M)

January 11, 2004

LECTIONARY READINGS

Isaiah 43:1–7
Acts 8:14–17
Luke 3:15–17, 21–22

Psalm 29

CALL TO WORSHIP

God, who created you, says, "Do not fear,
    for I have redeemed you; I have called you by name,
    you are mine.
For I am the Lord your God,
    the Holy one of Israel, your savior.
Do not fear, for I am with you;
    I will bring your offspring from the east,
    and from the west I will gather you.
Let all the nations gather together,
    and let all the people assemble.
    May the Lord bless the people with peace."

PRAYER OF CONFESSION *(BCW)*

Merciful God,
in baptism you promise forgiveness and new life,
making us part of the body of Christ.
We confess that we remain preoccupied with
    ourselves,
separated from sisters and brothers in Christ.
We cling to destructive habits, hold grudges,
and show reluctance to welcome one another;
we allow the past to hold us hostage.

In your loving kindness, have mercy on us,
and free us from sin.
Remind us of the promises you make in baptism
so that we may rise to new life,
and live together in grace.

HYMNS FOR THE DAY

GATHERING	HB	LBW	NCH	PH	RIL	TFF	WOV
From All That Dwell Below the Skies	33	550	27	229	126	—	—
THE WORD							
O—God, Who Stretched the Spangled Heavens	—	—	463	556	268	29	—
In Christ There Is No East or West	479	359	394–5	440	410	214	—
How Firm a Foundation	369	507	407	361	172	—	—
A—Come, O Spirit	—	—	—	127	—	—	—
Like the Murmur of the Dove's Song	—	—	270	314	—	—	685
Holy Ghost, Dispel Our Sadness	—	—	—	—	317	—	—
G—Christ, When for Us You Were Baptized	—	—	—	70	241	—	—
When Jesus Came to Jordan	—	—	—	72	—	—	647
Baptized in Water	—	—	—	492	—	—	693
Wash, O God, Our Sons and Daughters	—	—	—	—	—	112	697
THE EUCHARIST							
Spirit of God, Descend Upon My Heart	236	486	290	326	445	—	—
SENDING							
God Be with You Till We Meet Again	78	—	81	540	—	—	—

Baptism of the Lord

Color: White

PSALM SETTINGS

METRICAL
Psalm 29 "All on Earth, and All in Heaven," PCW, 8.7.8.7.D, Morgan
RESPONSORIAL
"Praise the Lord," P 26, Hopson

MULTICULTURAL/CONTEMPORARY

Gathering—"Praise and Thanksgiving Be to God," CLUW 230
O—"You Are Mine," W&P 158, David Haas
"Through the Love of God," CG 131, M. Peters
"Stand by Me," GIA SATB, arr. by Jewel Taylor Thompson
Psalm—"Psalm 29," CLUW 418/SNC 127, Walter Greatorex
A—"Loving Spirit," SNC 235, I-to Loh
"With Thy Spirit Fill Me," AAHH 322, tune: fill me
G—"Wash Me Through and Through," SNC 239, Sam Batt Owens
"Wash, O God, Our Sons and Daughters," AAHH 674

ANTHEMS

"Let Thy Holy Spirit Come Upon Us," P. Tschesnokoff, LG 660, SATB
"Spirit of God," John Carter, HIN HMC-268, SATB

MUSIC FOR THE SMALL CHURCH

"The Baptism of Jesus," Austin C. Lovelace (SATB/keyboard), GIA G-5313
"Jesus Went to Jordan's Stream," Johanne Plag, ed. Richard Proulx (two-part mixed), AF 11-10649

OTHER VOCAL MUSIC

"Wade in the Water," Mark Hayes, in *Spirituals for Solo Singers*, Jay Althouse, AP

"Come, Thou Fount of Every Blessing," Robert Robinson, in *Ten Hymns and Gospel Songs for Solo Voice*, arr. by Mark Hayes, AP
"Come, Thou Fount of Every Blessing," Richard Walters, in *Hymn Classics*, HL
"This Is De Healin' Water," Hall Johnson, in *Thirty Spirituals*, GS
"Deep River," Hall Johnson, in *Your Favorite Spirituals*, SP HE-13
"Deep River," Moses Hogan in *The Deep River Collection Volume I - Low/High Voice*, HL
"Shall We Gather at the River?" Robert Lowry in *Five American Gospel Songs*, Luigi Zaninelli, HF

ORGAN

Prelude on the chorale CHRIST UNSER HERR ZUM JORDAN KAM ("When Jesus to the Jordan Came")
    J. S. Bach, CHRIST UNSER HERR ZUM JORDAN KAM, several settings, various editions (E-M)
    Marcel Dupré, CHRIST UNSER HERR ZUM JORDAN KAM, *Seventy-Nine Chorales*, HWG (E)
    Ernst Pepping, *Gorsses Orgelbuch*, vol. 1, BAR (M)
    Johann Walther, *The Church Organist's Golden Treasury*, ODC (M)
Postlude on the chorale GOTTES SOHN IST KOMMEN ("Once He Came in Blessing")
    J. S. Bach, various editions, several settings (E-M)
    Paul Manz, *Ten Chorale Improvisations*, vols. 1 and 10, C (M)
    Johannes Petzold, *The Concordia Hymn Prelude Series*, vol. 1, C (E)
    Helmut Walcha, *Choralvorspiele*, CFP (M)

THE CONFESSION OF 1967

For today's selection, see p. 223.

January 18, 2004

LECTIONARY READINGS

Isaiah 62:1–5
1 Corinthians 12:1–11
John 2:1–11

Psalm 36:5–10

CALL TO WORSHIP

How precious is your steadfast love, O God!
 All people may take refuge in the shadow of your
  wings.
They feast on the abundance of your house,
 and you give them drink from the river of your
  delights.
For with you is the fountain of life;
 in your light we see light.
Your steadfast love, O God, extends to the heavens,
 Your faithfulness to the clouds.

PRAYER OF CONFESSION

God of steadfast love,
you unite us as members of Christ's one body,
through the work of the Spirit.
Yet we disown one another.
We reject those whom you accept;
cutting ourselves off
from those whom we need,
and who need us.

Lord, have mercy on us.
Forgive and heal our warring madness;
grant us grace to embrace one another
and work together as your one body,
to your honor and glory.

HYMNS FOR THE DAY

GATHERING	HB	LBW	NCH	PH	RIL	TFF	WOV
Christ, Whose Glory Fills the Skies	47	265	—	462	463	—	—
All Creatures of Our God and King	100	527	17	455	4	—	—
THE WORD							
O—"Sleepers, Wake!" A Voice Astounds Us	—	31	112	17	606	—	—
I Love Thy Kingdom, Lord	435	368	312	441	409	—	—
E—Come, Holy Spirit, Our Souls Inspire	237	472–3	—	125	385	—	—
Open My Eyes That I May See	390	—	—	324	—	—	—
Lord, Speak to Me That I May Speak	298	403	531	426	436	—	—
We All Are One in Mission	—	—	—	435	—	—	755
One Bread, One Body	—	—	—	—	122	—	—
G—Thy Mercy and Thy Truth, O Lord	82	—	—	186	—	—	—
The Church's One Foundation	437	369	386	442	394	—	—
THE EUCHARIST							
Deck Yourself, My Soul, with Gladness	—	224	334	560	536	—	—
SENDING							
God, Whose Giving Knows No Ending	—	408	565	422	—	—	—

Second Sunday in Ordinary Time

Color: Green

PSALM SETTINGS

METRICAL
"Your Love and Faithfulness, O Lord," NMP 86, LM, Webber
RESPONSORIAL
"Your Love, Lord, Reaches to Heaven," P 34, Gelineau

MULTICULTURAL/CONTEMPORARY

O—"My Lord, What a Morning," AAHH 195
Psalm—"These Things Are True of You," Mar 248, Tommy Walker
E—"Christ, from Whom All Blessings Flow," CLUW 250
"Veni Santo Espiritu creador," El Himn 184
"That Christ Be Known," W&P 133, Marty Schaefer
"We Are One," AAHH 323, arr. by Valeria A. Foster
G—"The Trumpets Sound, the Angels Sing," W&P 139, Graham Kendrick
"Lord, I Have Seen Thy Salvation," AAHH 679
Other—"One Bread, One Body," LUYH 130, John Foley
"Come, Join in Cana's Feast," HFTG 52

ANTHEMS

"As the Bridegroom to His Chosen," Peter Cutts/Jane Marshall, HIN HMC-448, SATB
"Many Gifts, One Spirit," Allen Pote, CP 392-41388, SATB

MUSIC FOR THE SMALL CHURCH

"Come, Join in Cana's Feast," Sally Ann Morris (unison or SATB), in *Giving Thanks in Song and Prayer*, GIA G-4930, 19

OTHER VOCAL MUSIC

"Lord, Who at Cana's Wedding Feast," Wilbur Held in *Three Solos for Medium Voice*, AF 11-9478

ORGAN

Prelude on the hymn tune SALZBURG ("Songs of Thankfulness and Praise")
    Gerald Near, *Choraleworks*, PP (M)
    Johann Pachelbel, *Complete Works*, K (M)
    Ralph C. Schultz, *The Parish Organist*, C (E)
Postlude on the chorale JESU MEINE FREUDE ("Jesus, Priceless Treasure")
    Joseph Ahrens, *Choral Partita*, last movement, ABS (D)
    J. S. Bach, several settings, various editions (M)
    Jan Bender, *Klein Choralvorspiele Barenreiter* (E)
    Paul Manz, *Ten Chorale Improvisations*, C (M)

THE CONFESSION OF 1967

For today's selection, see p. 223.

January 25, 2004

LECTIONARY READINGS

Nehemiah 8:1–3, 5–6, 8–10
1 Corinthians 12:12–31a
Luke 4:14–21

Psalm 19

CALL TO WORSHIP

The heavens proclaim the glory of God;
   and the firmament proclaims God's handiwork.
Day by day pours forth speech,
   and night to night declares knowledge.
Good news to the poor, release to the captives
   and recovery of sight to the blind.
The oppressed shall go free
   and proclaim the year of the Lord's favor.

PRAYER OF CONFESSION

Judge of all,
we have strayed from your good law,
both in what we have done,
and what we have left undone.
We have cast aside your counsel,
and departed from your ways.

Show us your tender mercy;
forgive us and restore us.
Heal our blindness to our sins,
release us from captivity to selfish desires.
Empower us by your Spirit,
that our words, thoughts, and intentions
will truly glorify you, O Lord,
our Rock and Redeemer.

HYMNS FOR THE DAY

GATHERING	HB	LBW	NCH	PH	RIL	TFF	WOV
Jesus Shall Reign Where'er the Sun	496	530	300	423	233	—	—
In Christ There Is No East or West	479	359	394–5	439–0	410	214	—
THE WORD							
O—Open My Eyes That I May See	390	—	—	324	—	—	—
O Word of God Incarnate	251	231	315	327	387	—	—
Thanks to God Whose Word Was Written	—	—	—	331	390	—	—
E—With Joy I Heard My Friends Exclaim	—	—	—	235	132	—	—
We Know That Christ Is Raised	—	189	—	495	528	—	—
I Come with Joy to Meet My Lord	—	—	349	507	534	—	—
G—Live into Hope	—	—	—	332	—	—	—
THE EUCHARIST							
Break Thou the Bread of Life	250	235	321	329	—	—	—
SENDING							
O for a Thousand Tongues to Sing	141	559	42	466	362–3	—	—
Today We All Are Called to Be Disciples	—	—	—	434	—	—	—

Third Sunday in Ordinary Time

Color: Green

PSALM SETTINGS

METRICAL

"The Heav'ns Unfold Your Glory, Lord," PCW, CMD, Morgan

RESPONSORIAL

"Heaven and Earth Tell Your Glory," P 12, Monks of Saint Meinrad/Weber

RESPONSORIAL

"The Statutes of the Lord Rejoice the Heart," HP 2, p. 56, Daw/Hackett

MULTICULTURAL/CONTEMPORARY

Gathering—"Come into God's Presence," SNC 3, anonymous

O—"I Will Celebrate," Mar 43, Paul Baloche

"The Joy of the Lord," AAHH 612, Alliene G. Vale

"Amen, Siakudumisa," AAHH 122, South African traditional, arr. by John Bell

E—"Come Now, O Prince of Peace," CG 25

"There's No Me, There's No You," AAHH 619

"One Bread, One Body," TFF 132/W&P 111, John Foley

"Children of God," AP, SATB, arr. by Benjamin Harlan

G—"Thy Word," TFF 132/W&P 144, Amy Grant

Psalm—"Let's Sing unto the Lord," CLUW 67

"Salmo 19: Los cielos cuentan las obras," El Himn 409

"Let the Words of My Mouth," AAHH 665, C. E. Leslie

"A Year of God's Favor," HFTG 50

ANTHEMS

"The Heavens Are Telling," Ludwig van Beethoven, TP 312-10398, SATB

"Lord Speak to Me," Hal H. Hopson, HWG, GCMR9701, SATB

MUSIC FOR THE SMALL CHURCH

"Jesus, When You Walked This Earth," Sally Ann Morris (unison or SATB), in *Giving Thanks in Song and Prayer*, GIA G-4930, 36

OTHER VOCAL MUSIC

"Sing Ye a Joyful Song," Antonín Dvořák

"I Will Sing New Songs," Antonín Dvořák in *Dvořák Biblical Songs*, GS #1824 (High Voice) or #1825 (Low Voice)

"I Will Sing of Thy Great Mercies," Felix Mendelssohn

"Sing a Song of Joy," in *Vocal Solos for Worship*, K. Lee Scott, AF 11-8195

ORGAN

On the hymn "Once He Came in Blessing" (GOTTES SOHN IST KOMMEN) [Suggestion: Have the choir sing the SATB chorale arrangement by J. S. Bach as part of the prelude. Include the words on the order of worship for people's meditations.]

Postlude: Based on the hymn GOTTES SOHN IS KOMMEN

Ernst Pepping, various editions and settings (M-D)

Johann Walther, *The Organist's Golden Treasury*, ODC (or collected works) (M)

THE CONFESSION OF 1967

For today's selection, see p. 223.

February 1, 2004

LECTIONARY READINGS

Jeremiah 1:4–10
1 Corinthians 13:1–13
Luke 4:21–30

Psalm 71:1–6

CALL TO WORSHIP

O Lord, in you I take refuge;
   let me never be put to shame.
In your righteousness deliver me and rescue me;
   incline your ear to me and save me.
Be to me a rock of refuge,
   a strong fortress
to save me,
   for you are our rock and our fortress.

PRAYER OF CONFESSION

God of love,
we delight in well-chosen words,
in manifestations of wisdom and faith,
and in self-sacrificial generosity.
But we have sought more
to be successful and admired
than to serve and suffer in love.

Forgive us for neglecting
the greatest gift of all.
Quicken our faith by the Spirit,
stir up our hope in Christ;
and, in all things,
help us to love
as we have been loved
to the honor of your holy name.

HYMNS FOR THE DAY

	HB	LBW	NCH	PH	RIL	TFF	WOV
GATHERING							
God of Grace and God of Glory	358	415	436	420	416	—	—
THE WORD							
O—Fill My Cup	—	—	350	—	—	—	—
Take My Life and Let It Be	310	406	448	391	475	—	—
E—Gracious Spirit, Holy Ghost	—	—	61	318	—	—	—
Though I May Speak	—	—	—	335	—	—	—
Not for Tongues of Heaven's Angels	—	—	—	531	—	—	—
G—I'm Gonna Live So God Can Use Me	—	—	—	369	—	—	—
Lord, Speak to Me That I May Speak	298	403	531	426	436	—	—
God Has Spoken by His Prophets	—	238	—	—	—	—	—
THE EUCHARIST							
Great Is Thy Faithfulness	—	—	423	276	155	283	771
SENDING							
Joyful, Joyful, We Adore Thee	21	551	4	464	521	—	—

Fourth Sunday in Ordinary Time

Color: Green

PSALM SETTINGS

METRICAL
"In You, O Lord, I Put My Trust," PsH 71, LM,
Walhout/Wischmeier
RESPONSORIAL
"My Tongue Will Proclaim Your Righteousness,"
HP 1, p. 63, Daw/Hackett

MULTICULTURAL/CONTEMPORARY

Psalm—"You Are the Rock of My Salvation," W&P
161, Teresa Muller
"Never Failed Me Yet," SATB, HL, Robert Ray
"Leaning on the Everlasting Arms," AAHH 371
E—"Though I May Speak with Bravest Fire,"
CLUW 341
"El amor," El Himn 279
"Believe in God's Word," GP II 29
"We'll Understand It Better By and By," AAHH 418
"No Greater Love," Mar 54, Tommy Walker
G—"Jesus, I Believe," Mar 130, Bill Batstone

ANTHEMS

"Love Never Ends," Elizabeth Volk, AM AMP0180,
SATB
"Hear Me, O Lord," Franz Schubert/Maynard Klein,
NK 5480, SATB

MUSIC FOR THE SMALL CHURCH

"The Gift of Love," Hal H. Hopson, two-part/
keyboard, HP

OTHER VOCAL MUSIC

"The Greatest of These Is Love," from *A New
Creation*, René Clausen, MF 2047
"The Gift of Love," Hal H. Hopson, HP 371

ORGAN

On the chorale LIEBSTER JESU ("Blessed Jesus, at Your
Word")
  Unaccompanied solo voice (or all women, or
  children's choir) one stanza
  LIEBSTER JESU, J. S. Bach, several settings
  SATB choir sing one or two or more stanzas
  unaccompanied
On the hymn tune CWM RHONDDA ("God of Grace
and God of Glory")
  David Cherwien, *Interpretations,* vol. 6, AMSI (M)
  Paul Manz, *Ten Chorale Improvisations,* vol. 5,
  C (M)
  Jan Bender, *Preludes for the Hymn in Worship
  Supplement,* C (E)
Or J. S. Bach, "Prelude and Fugue in A," various
editions (M)

THE CONFESSION OF 1967

For today's selection, see p. 223.

February 8, 2004

LECTIONARY READINGS

Isaiah 6:1–8 (9–13)
1 Corinthians 15:1–11
Luke 5:1–11

Psalm 138

CALL TO WORSHIP

All the kings of the earth shall praise you, O Lord,
   for they have heard the words of your mouth.
**They shall sing the ways of the Lord,
   for great is the glory of the Lord.**
For though the Lord is high, God regards the lowly;
   but the arrogant the Lord perceives from far away.
**Your steadfast love, O Lord, endures forever;
   do not forsake the work of your hands.**

PRAYER OF CONFESSION

Holy Lord,
you call us to follow you,
to bear witness in speech and deed
to the good news of the Gospel.
But we resist your call,
persistently pursuing our own desires,
fearful of your claims upon us.

Forgive us for seeking to justify
our refusal to heed your call.
Stir us up by your Spirit
to embrace the mission of Jesus Christ—
healing the broken,
feeding the hungry,
and proclaiming the good news
that God is indeed with us.

HYMNS FOR THE DAY

	HB	LBW	NCH	PH	RIL	TFF	WOV
GATHERING							
Let the Whole Creation Cry	—	242	—	256	12	—	—
THE WORD							
O—Holy, Holy, Holy! Lord God Almighty!	11	165	277	138	611	—	—
Here I Am, Lord	—	—	—	525	—	230	752
Isaiah in a Vision Did of Old	—	528	—	—	—	—	—
E—Amazing Grace, How Sweet the Sound	275	448	547–8	280	456	—	—
Hear the Good News of Salvation	—	—	—	355	—	—	—
G—Lord, You Have Come to the Lakeshore	—	—	377	—	—	—	784
THE EUCHARIST							
Jesus, Thou Joy of Loving Hearts	215	356	329	510	273	—	—
SENDING							
How Clear Is Our Vocation, Lord	—	—	—	419	433	—	—
The Spirit Sends Us Forth to Serve	—	—	—	—	—	—	723

Fifth Sunday in Ordinary Time

Color: Green

PSALM SETTINGS

METRICAL
"I Will Give Thanks with My Whole Heart," PH 247, LM, Webber
RESPONSORIAL
"When I Called, You Answered Me," HP 2, p. 80, Daw/Hackett

MULTICULTURAL/CONTEMPORARY

O—"The Voice of God Is Calling," CLUW 139
"Dios nos hizo mayordomos," El Himn 372
"Will You Come and Follow Me?" GIA, arr. by John Bell
"Here I Am Lord," HP, SATB/handbells, arr. by Arnold B. Sherman
"Holy Lord," LUYH 32, Claire Cloniger and Don Moen
"Thuma Mina," CG 129, South African traditional
"We See the Lord," W&P 153, arr. by Betty Pulkingham
Psalm—"Everything Is Yours, Lord," LUYH 115, Zambian offertory, arr. by Geoff Weaver
"For He Alone Is Worthy," TFF 284, traditional
E—"Wotanin Waste Nahon Po" ("Hear the Good News of Salvation"), PH 355
"That We May Be Filled," W&P 134, Handt Hansonand Paul Murakami
G—"Lord, You Have Come," CG 79, Cesareo Gabarain
"I Have Decided to Follow Jesus," AAHH 400, Indian folk music
Other—"We Will Glorify," Renew/AAHH 286, Twila Paris
"When Jesus Walked Beside the Shore," HFTG 148

ANTHEMS

"O God Beyond All Praising," Gustav Holst/Richard Proulx, GIA G-3190, SATB, brass and timpani

"In the Year That King Uzziah Died," HWG, GCMR, SATB

MUSIC FOR THE SMALL CHURCH

"You Walk Along Our Shoreline," Sally Ann Morris (unison or SATB), in *Giving Thanks in Song and Prayer*, 50

OTHER VOCAL MUSIC

"Amazing Grace," John Ness Back in *Hymn Settings*, BP, VC 4
"Amazing Grace," Ovid Young, LP L0404

ORGAN

Prelude on the tune GROSSER GOTT ("Holy God We Praise Your Name")
  Wilbur Held, *Hymn Preludes for the Pentecost Season*, C (M)
  Flor Peeters, *Little Organ Book*, SB (E)
  Flor Peeters, *Thirty Choral Preludes,* vol. 3, CFP (D)
  Alec Wyton, *A Little Christian Year*, CF (E) [The prelude might lead directly into, or be surrounded by, the choral setting of "Holy God, We Praise Your Name," by John Ferguson, GIA. This setting incorporates quotations from the Gregorian setting of the TE DEUM and employs handbells and brass.]
Postlude: On the tune REPTON ("How Clear Is Our Vocation, Lord")
  Charles Callahan, *Six Meditations on English Hymn Tunes*, OLF (E)
  Peters Pindar Stearns, *Twelve Hymn Preludes for General Use*, HF (M)
Or Charles Tournimere, *The Mystic Organ, Epiphany 5*, final movement

THE CONFESSION OF 1967

For today's selection, see p. 223.

February 15, 2004

LECTIONARY READINGS

Jeremiah 17:5–10
1 Corinthians 15:12–20
Luke 6:17–26

Psalm 1

CALL TO WORSHIP

Blessed are those who trust in God,
> who put their trust in the Lord.
They shall be like a tree planted by water,
> **sending out its roots by the stream.**
It shall not fear when heat comes;
> and its leaves shall stay green;
in the year of drought it is not anxious,
> **and it does not cease to bear fruit.**

PRAYER OF CONFESSION

God of all blessing,
We seek to gain blessing
through accumulation of riches,
satisfaction of appetites,
and embrace of pleasures.
We have rejected the way of Jesus,
who teaches the true blessings
of forsaking such pursuits,
and embracing generosity toward others.

In mercy, forgive our waywardness.
Teach us and guide us by your Spirit
to live in the way of true blessing,
the way of Jesus our Savior,
who laid down his life for us,
to your honor and glory.

HYMNS FOR THE DAY

	HB	LBW	NCH	PH	RIL	TFF	WOV
GATHERING							
God Is Here!	—	—	70	461	—	—	719
THE WORD							
O—My Soul in Silence Waits for God	—	—	—	197	—	—	—
Open Now Thy Gates of Beauty	40	250	67	489	502	—	—
E—Lord, Enthroned in Heavenly Splendor	—	172	—	154	537	—	—
G—Jesus, the Very Thought of Thee	401	316	507	310	—	—	—
Blessed Assurance	139	—	473	341	453	118	699
Your Ways Are Not Our Own	—	—	170	—	—	—	—
THE EUCHARIST							
Great God, Your Love Has Called Us Here	—	—	353	—	—	666	—
SENDING							
O Praise the Gracious Power	—	—	54	471	—	—	750

Sixth Sunday in Ordinary Time

Color: Green

PSALM SETTINGS

METRICAL
"The One Is Blest," PH 158, CM, *The Psalter* (1912)
RESPONSORIAL
"Happy Are They Who Delight in the Law of God,"
P 1, Hopson

MULTICULTURAL/CONTEMPORARY

O—"I Will Trust in the Lord," AAHH 391
Psalm—"Psalm 1," CLUW 394
"I Will Delight," W&P 72, Walt Harrah and John
Schreimer
"Salmo 1: Es como el arbol de ausubo," El Himn 405
E—"We Are Called," W&P 147, David Haas
"He Is Exalted," W&P 55, Twila Paris
G—"Speak to My Heart," GIA, SATB, arr. by Eric
Brown

ANTHEMS

"Blessed Is the Man," Jane Marshall, HIN HMC-627,
SATB
"I'll Praise My Maker," Lloyd Pfautsch, AB APM-110,
SATB

MUSIC FOR THE SMALL CHURCH

"Blessed Are You Poor," John L. Bell (SATB), in *An
Iona Sampler*, GIA G-3995, 6

OTHER VOCAL MUSIC

"Assurance," John Ness Beck/transcribed by Craig
Courtney in *Hymn Settings of John Ness Beck* VC4,
BP

ORGAN

Prelude and Introit on the hymn tune DONNE SEC-
OURS ("Hope of the World")
Naji Hakim, *Variation on Two Themes* (commis-
sioned by First Presbyterian, Evansville, Ind.); con-
tact Naji Hakim at www.najihakim.com (M-D)
Introit: Concertato on "Hope of the World" for
brass, choir, and congregation, HOP (M)
Or David Ashley White, "Aria," SEL (E)

Postlude on the hymn tune WOJIKIEWIECZ ("Rise,
Shine, You People!")
David Cherwien, *Toccata and Fugue for Organ*,
AF (M-D)
Larry Cook, "Rise, Shine, You People," organ,
brass (M)
Or Gordon Lawson, *Tuba Mirum*, SEL (M-D)

THE CONFESSION OF 1967

For today's selection, see p. 224.

February 22, 2004

LECTIONARY READINGS

Exodus 34:29–35
2 Corinthians 3:12–4:2
Luke 9:28–36 (37–43)

Psalm 99

CALL TO WORSHIP

The Lord is our ruler; let the peoples tremble!
　God sits enthroned upon the cherubim; let the
　　earth quake!
The Lord is great in Zion;
God is exalted over all the peoples.
　Let them praise your great and awesome name.
　Holy is God!
Let us praise God's holy name!

PRAYER OF CONFESSION *(BCW)*

God of compassion,
in Jesus Christ you reveal the light of your glory,
but we turn away, distracted by our own plans.
We confess that we speak when we should listen,
and act when we should wait.

Forgive our aimless enthusiasms.
Grant us wisdom to live in your light
and to follow in the way of your beloved Son,
Jesus Christ, our Lord and Savior.

HYMNS FOR THE DAY

GATHERING	HB	LBW	NCH	PH	RIL	TFF	WOV
Love Divine, All Loves Excelling	399	315	43	376	464	—	—
THE WORD							
O—Immortal, Invisible, God Only Wise	85	526	1	263	7	—	—
E—Thee We Adore	—	199	339	519	—	—	—
G—Swiftly Pass the Clouds of Glory	—	—	—	73	—	—	—
Jesus on the Mountain Peak	—	—	—	74	—	—	653
Shine, Jesus, Shine	—	—	—	—	—	64	651
Jesus, Take Us to the Mountain	—	—	183	—	—	—	—
THE EUCHARIST							
For the Bread Which You Have Broken	—	200	—	508–9	547	—	—
SENDING							
O Wondrous Sight, O Vision Fair	182	80	184	75	256	—	—

Transfiguration of the Lord

Color: White

PSALM SETTINGS

METRICAL
"God Is King," *Psalm Praise*, GIA, 113, 8.8.8.6, Saward
RESPONSORIAL
"Proclaim the Greatness of the Lord Our God," HP 1, p. 69, Daw/Hackett
RESPONSORIAL
"Alleluia! Holy Is the Lord," P 96, Hopson

MULTICULTURAL/CONTEMPORARY

O—"Holy Ground," W&P 59, AAHH 183, Geron Davis
Psalm—"God the Creator," LUYH 27, Gaelic Melody Words, arr. by The Iona Community
"I Exalt Thee," Mar 123, Pete Sanchez Jr.
"Commune With Me," Mar 20, Kirk Dearman
E—"Shine, Jesus Shine," WOV 651/W&P 123/TFF 64/LUYH 50/CLUW 264/SNC 128, Graham Kendrick
"Let It Be Said of Us," Mar 217, Steve Fry
"There's a Sweet, Sweet Spirit in This Place," TFF 102/AAHH 326, Doris Akers
G—"O Wondrous Sight! O Vision Fair," CLUW 169/El Himn 118
"Stand Up," Mar 240, Milton Carroll
"Shine on Me," AAHH 527, arr. by Jimmie Abbington
Sending—"Canto de Esperanza," ("Song of Hope"), PH 432/El Himn 314
Other—"Come to the Mountain," W&P 32, Scott Tunseth, music by Kathy Donlan Tunseth

ANTHEMS

"Heavenly Light," A. Kopylow, CF CM497, SATB
"Transfiguration," Alec Wyton, HF A-5724, SATB & soprano solo

MUSIC FOR THE SMALL CHURCH

"Into the Image of God," Howard G. White (two-part mixed voices/keyboard) AB 50371X

"This is My Beloved Son," Knut Nystedt (SAB), C 98-1805

OTHER VOCAL MUSIC

"Praise to the Lord Who Reigns Above," Glen L. Rudolph in *Wesley Songs* 96.800, OXU
"Be Thou My Vision," Craig Courtney in *Music for the Master*, BP, VC1

ORGAN

Prelude on the hymn tune SCHÖNSTER HERR JESU *or* CRUSADER'S HYMN *or* ST. ELIZABETH ("Fairest Lord Jesus / Beautiful Saviour")
Joseph Ahrens, Das Heilige Jahr, Willy Müller (M)
Jan Bender, *The Organist's Companion*, vol. 3, #2 MCA (E)
David Cherwien, *Crusaders Hymn*, MS MSM 10701 (M)
Gerre Hancock, a Paraphrase of ST. ELIZABETH, OXU (M)
Gerhard Krapf, *Historia Nativitatis*, JFB (M)
Flor Peeters, *Hymn Preludes for the Liturgical Year*, vol. 6, CFP (M)
Hermann Schroeder, *Six Organ Chorales*, B. Schotts, Söhne (M)
Postlude: During the closing of the hymn you might want to "strip" the church of festive things. For example, remove flowers in preparation for the lenten "Desert Garden" and remove banners with "Alleluia" on them.
Olivier Messaien, *Transports de joi*, AL (D)
Simon Preston, *Serene Alleluyas*, OXU (M) D
Charles Tournimere, *The Mystic Organ*, transfiguration, final movement (D)
Or based on the chorale WEDER MUNTER
Paul Manz, *Ten Chorale Improvisation*, C (M)
Johann Pachelbel, any edition of his collected works (E-D)

THE CONFESSION OF 1967

For today's selection, see p. 224.

February 25, 2004

LECTIONARY READINGS

Joel 2:1–2, 12–17 or
Isaiah 58:1–12
2 Corinthians 5:20b–6:10
Matthew 6:1–6, 16–21

Psalm 51:1–17

CALL TO WORSHIP

The Lord is our ruler; let the peoples tremble!
  God sits enthroned upon the cherubim; let the
    earth quake!
The Lord is great in Zion;
  God is exalted over all the peoples.
Let them praise your great and awesome name.
  Holy is God!
Let us praise God's holy name!

PRAYER OF CONFESSION

(See *BCW* 225–26)

HYMNS FOR THE DAY

GATHERING	HB	LBW	NCH	PH	RIL	TFF	WOV
Have Mercy on Us, Living Lord	—	—	—	195	—	—	—
THE WORD							
O—Wild and Lone the Prophet's Voice	—	—	—	409	—	—	—
Kind Maker of the World	—	—	—	79	—	—	—
E—Alas! And Did My Savior Bleed	199	98	199–0	78	—	—	—
Out of the Depths	—	295	483	240	134	—	—
G—O Savior, in This Quiet Place	—	—	555	390	—	—	—
Be Thou My Vision	303	—	451	339	67	—	776
Again We Keep This Solemn Fast	—	—	187	—	—	—	—
THE EUCHARIST							
My Song Is Love Unknown	—	94	222	76	284	—	—

Ash Wednesday

Color: Purple

PSALM SETTINGS

METRICAL
"Have Mercy, Lord," PCW, CM, Morgan
RESPONSORIAL
Psalm 51, PH 196 ("The Grail"/Isele)
RESPONSORIAL
"Have Mercy on Me, O God," HP 1, p. 16,
    Daw/Hackett

MULTICULTURAL/CONTEMPORARY

O—"Let Justice Roll Like a River," W&P 85, Marty
    Haugen
"Morning Has Broken," W&P 98, Gaelic
    traditional/Farjeon
Psalm—"Change My Heart O God," W&P 28/SNC
    56, Eddie Espinoza
"Fall, Slow Tears," CF, SAB, Ruth Elaine Schram
"Give Me a Clean Heart," AAHH 461, Margaret
    Pleasant Douroux
E—"Dios santisimo que en Gloria," El Himn 326
G—"Beauty for Brokenness," W&P 17, Graham
    Kendrick
"Is There Any Room in Your Heart for Jesus?" AAHH
    353, Wyatt Tee Walker
"Jesus Walked This Lonesome Valley," CLUW 180
"O for a Faith," GIA, SATB, arr. by Nathan Carter

ANTHEMS

"Be Thou My Vision," John Rutter, HIN HMC-
    1035, SATB
"Create in Me, O God," Johannes Brahms, GS 7504,
    SATBB

MUSIC FOR THE SMALL CHURCH

"A Song for Lent," Marie Pooler (unison or two-part,
    keyboard), AF 11-10361

OTHER VOCAL MUSIC

"Wondrous Love," Wilbur Held in *Vocal Solos for
    Funeral and Memorial Services*, AF 11-10226
"A Contrite Heart," Ludwig van Beethoven in *Sing a
    Song of Joy*, K. Lee Scott, AF 11-8195
"Create in Me a Clean Heart," Carl Mueller in *Twelve
    Sacred Songs*, GS/HL

ORGAN

The *Book of Common Worship*, WJK, 1993, has an
    excellent example of an Ash Wednesday liturgy on
    pages 221–34. Music should be reflective, and may
    include, in addition to hymnody and psalmody,
    meditative songs—particularly during the imposi-
    tion of ashes and at the receiving of Communion.
Prelude: Gather in silence, prayer, and meditation. No
    music. You might consider how to make your wor-
    ship space more conducive to prayer, quiet, and
    meditation with the use of artwork that depicts the
    themes of five Sundays in Lent.
Postlude: Based on the hymn tune ST. FLAVIAN ("Lord
    Who Throughout These Forty Days")
    Healey Willan, *Ten Hymn Preludes*, CFP (M)

February 29, 2004

LECTIONARY READINGS

Deuteronomy 26:1–11
Romans 10:8b–13
Luke 4:1–13

Psalm 91:1–2, 9–16

CALL TO WORSHIP

You who live in the shelter of the Most High,
   who abide in the shadow of the Almighty, will say
     to the Lord,
my refuge and my fortress;
  my God, in whom I trust.
For God brought us out of Egypt with a mighty hand
   and an outstretched arm.
Therefore we come before God
   with our offerings, celebrating all God has done
     for us.

PRAYER OF CONFESSION

Almighty protector and provider,
we have sought security
in shelters of our own making.
Instead of trusting your Word,
we have relied upon our own will
to overcome evil within and around us.
Our will has not been strong enough;
when tempted, we have fallen.

Forgive us for turning away
from the sustaining Bread
you have so generously provided us.
Indwell us by your Spirit,
that we would entrust ourselves wholly
to the power of your saving Word,
Jesus Christ, our Lord.

HYMNS FOR THE DAY

	HB	LBW	NCH	PH	RIL	TFF	WOV
GATHERING							
The Glory of These Forty Days	—	—	—	87	242	—	—
THE WORD							
O—Come, Sing a Song of Harvest	—	—	—	558	—	—	—
Now Thank We All Our God	9	53–4	419	555	61	—	—
E—Here, O Lord, Your Servants Gather	—	—	—	465	—	—	—
I Want Jesus to Walk with Me	—	—	490	363	—	66	660
G—Lord, who Throughout These Forty Days	181	99	211	81	—	—	—
Forty Days and Forty Nights	—	—	205	77	—	—	—
THE EUCHARIST							
Be Known to Us in Breaking Bread	446	—	342	505	—	—	—
SENDING							
As Those of Old Their Firstfruits Brought	—	—	—	—	414	—	—

First Sunday in Lent

Color: Purple

PSALM SETTINGS

METRICAL
"Deep in the Shelter of the Lord I Dwell," PCW,
    10.10.10.10, Morgan
RESPONSORIAL
"God Is Our Refuge," P 85 (Presbyterian 6)

MULTICULTURAL/CONTEMPORARY

O—"He Brought Me Out," AAHH 509, Henry L.
    Gilmour
Psalm—"On Eagle's Wings," LUYH 87/W&P 110/El
    Himn 350, SNC 185, Michael Joncas
"On Eagle's Wings," AP, SATB, Michael Joncas/arr. by
    Mark Hayes
E—"Jesus, I Believe," Mar 130, Bill Batstone
"He Is Lord," AAHH 285
G—"Lord, Who Throughout These Forty Days,"
    CLUW 181
"Out in the Wilderness," W&P 115, Jay Beech
"From the River to the Desert," HFTG 54

ANTHEMS

"First-Fruits," Austin Lovelace, AGP HAS 103, SATB
    with flute and trumpet
"Offertory," John Ness Beck, BP BP1280, SATB

MUSIC FOR THE SMALL CHURCH

"A Lenten Prayer," Robert J. Powell (unison/
    keyboard/flute), CG CGA-159 (Lent)

OTHER VOCAL MUSIC

"Now Thank We All Our God," Richard Walters in
    Hymn Classics, HL
"Humbly I Adore Thee," 13th c. Plainsong in *Solos
    for the Church Year*, LG/GS

ORGAN

Based on the hymn "From the River to the Desert,"
    by Sylvia Dunstan in *In Search of Hope and Grace*,
    and *Hymns for the Gospel*, GIA, using the tune
    RHUDDLAN. This hymn could be made into a sim-
    ple chancel drama and encounter between Satan
    and Jesus, with one of the choirs singing the text
    to the stanzas while the "action" occurs. Surround
    this with two organ pieces based on RHUDDLAN.
    Raymond Haan, *Welsh Hymn Tune Preludes*,
        SMP (E)
    Donald Johns, *The Concordia Hymn Prelude Series*,
        vol. 36, C (E)
Postlude on the chorale EIN FESTE BURG
    Charles Callahan, MS (M)
    Wilbur Held, *Hymn Preludes for Autumn Festivals*,
        C (E)
    J. S. Bach, complete works, several settings (M-D)
    Johann Pachelbel, complete works, KAL (M)

THE CONFESSION OF 1967

For today's selection, see p. 224.

March 7, 2004

LECTIONARY READINGS

Genesis 15:1–12, 17–18
Philippians 3:17–4:1
Luke 13:31–35

Psalm 27

CALL TO WORSHIP

The Lord is my light and my salvation;
  whom shall I fear?
The Lord is the stronghold of my life;
  of whom shall I be afraid?
I believe that I shall see the goodness of the Lord
  in the land of the living.
Wait for the Lord; be strong,
  and let your heart take courage; wait for the
  Lord!

PRAYER OF CONFESSION

Eternal Ruler of all,
you have made us citizens
of your glorious realm,
led us into a land of milk and honey,
and given us a place in your house.
Yet we have lived as though your table were bare,
and your promises empty.

Quicken us to believe your words of promise;
open our eyes to see the goodness and bounty
of our inheritance in Christ.
Teach us to live as children of heaven,
trusting fully the goodness of your rule,
the greatness of your power,
and the extravagance of your love.

HYMNS FOR THE DAY

	HB	LBW	NCH	PH	RIL	TFF	WOV
GATHERING							
If Thou but Trust in God to Guide Thee	344	453	410	282	151	—	—
THE WORD							
O—The God of Abraham Praise	89	544	24	488	595	—	—
Great Is Thy Faithfulness	—	—	423	276	155	283	771
E—Christ Is Made the Sure Foundation	433	367	400	416–7	392	—	—
G—Lord Christ, When First You Came to Earth	—	421	—	7	608	—	—
O Jesus Christ, May Grateful Hymns Be Rising	—	427	212	424	—	—	—
THE EUCHARIST							
Now to Your Table Spread	—	—	—	515	—	—	—
SENDING							
Guide Me, O Thou Great Jehovah	339	343	18–9	281	50	—	—

Second Sunday in Lent

Color: Purple

PSALM SETTINGS

METRICAL
Psalm 27, "God, My Light and My Salvation," PCW,
8.7.8.7.D, Morgan
RESPONSORIAL
"The Lord Is My Light," HP 1, p. 10, Daw/Hackett
TAIZÉ CHANT
"The Lord Is My Light," P 25, Berthier/Hopson

MULTICULTURAL/CONTEMPORARY

O— "Step by Step," W P 132, arr. by Nylea Butler-
Moores
Psalm—"Psalm 27:1–9," CLUW 416
"Salmo 27: El Senor es mi luz," El Himn 416
"The Lord Is My Light," SNC 192, Iona Community,
music: Czechoslovakian hymn tune
"We Are Singing," LUYH 56, Zulu text, arr. by Hal
H. Hopson
"Steal Away to Jesus," AAHH 546
G— "Come and See," spiritual song, W&P 29, Lenny
LeBlanc
"Just a Closer Walk with Thee," AAHH 455
Other—"Open Our Eyes Lord," W&P 113/SNC
80/Renew 91, Bob Cull
"What Shall We Pray?" CG 141, John Bell
"Welcome, All You Noble Saints," HFTG 88

ANTHEMS

"Open Thou Mine Eyes," John Rutter, HIN HMC-
467, SATB
"Christ Is Made the Sure Foundation," Milburn Price,
CF CM7926, SATB and brass ensemble

MUSIC FOR THE SMALL CHURCH

"The Lord Is My Light," Michael Bedford
(unison/two-part/keyboard), CG, CGA

OTHER VOCAL MUSIC

"O Rest in the Lord (Elijah)," Mendelssohn

ORGAN

Prelude and postlude based on the chorale WER NUR
DEN LIEBEN GOTT ("If Thou but Suffer God to
Guide Thee")
  J. S. Bach, complete works, several settings (M-D)
  Sigfrid Karg-Elert, *Chorale Improvisations,* vol. 6,
  MCAM (M)
  Johann Kirnberger, *Chorale Preludes for Organ or
  Keyboard,* AF (M)
  Loyd Pfautsch, "If Thou but Suffer God to Guide
  Thee," with brass, RKM (M)
  Ernest Pepping, *Fündundzwanzig Orgelchoräle,*
  BSS (E)
  Johann Walther, complete works (M)

THE CONFESSION OF 1967

For today's selection, see p. 224.

March 14, 2004

LECTIONARY READINGS

Isaiah 55:1–9
1 Corinthians 10:1–13
Luke 13:1–9

Psalm 63:1–8

CALL TO WORSHIP

O God, you are my God, I seek you,
   my soul thirsts for you;
my flesh faints for you,
   and in a dry and weary land where there is no
      water.
So I have looked upon you in the sanctuary,
   beholding your power and glory.
Because your steadfast love is better than life
   I will lift up my hands and call upon your name.

PRAYER OF CONFESSION

Fountain of life, we have drunk
from dusty wells of our own making.
Bread of heaven, we have set our table
with the meager fruits of our own labors.
Treasure of all, we have sought riches
in bankrupt storehouses of our own building.

Forgive us for turning away from your generous
      grace.
Satisfy our hunger with your bounty,
that we may praise you joyfully,
cling to you only,
seek you wholly,
and tell of your goodness gladly.

HYMNS FOR THE DAY

GATHERING	HB	LBW	NCH	PH	RIL	TFF	WOV
O God, What You Ordain Is Right	366	446	415	284	153	—	—
THE WORD							
O—Seek Ye First	—	—	—	333	—	149	—
O Lord, You Are My God and King	—	—	—	252	—	—	—
Stand Up and Bless the Lord	—	—	—	491	499	—	—
E—O God, Our Faithful God	—	—	513	277	69	—	—
G—O for a Closer Walk with God	319	—	450	396–7	437	—	—
Kind Maker of the World	—	—	—	79	—	—	—
THE EUCHARIST							
You Satisfy the Hungry Heart	—	—	—	521	—	711	—
SENDING							
O Lamb of God Most Holy!	—	111	—	82	—	—	—

Third Sunday in Lent

Color: Purple

PSALM SETTINGS

METRICAL

"O God Eternal, You Are My God," *Psalm Praise*, GIA 100, 9.9.9.8, Idle

RESPONSORIAL

"O God, You Are My God," HP 1, p. 33, Daw/Hackett

MULTICULTURAL/CONTEMPORARY

Gathering—"Here, O Lord, Your Servants Gather," CLUW 251

O—"Busquen a Dios," El Himn 124

"Most Holy One," Mar 223, Kelly Willard and Paul Baloche

Psalm—"Resting in You," LUYH 93, Ed Beaty and Lenny Smith

"Change My Heart, O God," Renew 143, Eddie Espinoza

"Make Me a Channel of Your Peace," W&P 95, Sebastian Temple

"Lord, Make Me an Instrument," GIA, SATB, M. Roger Holland II

E—"Lord, My Strength," W&P 93, Dean Krippaehne

"The Solid Rock," AAHH 385

G—"Change My Heart, Oh God," W&P 28, Eddie Espinoza

"Sovereign Maker of All Things," HFTG 136

ANTHEMS

"Comfort All Ye My People" ("Seek Ye" alternate text), G. Faure and Hal H. Hopson, CF CM8017, SATB

"In the Shadow of Your Wings," John Leavitt, GIA G-3345, SATB and oboe

MUSIC FOR THE SMALL CHURCH

"O, My Savior," J. S. Bach, ed. Douglas E. Wagner (unison), GIA G-2354

OTHER VOCAL MUSIC

"O Lamb of God," W. A. Mozart, in *Solos for the Church Year*, Lloyd Pfautsch, LG/GS

ORGAN

On the hymn "O Holy Spirit, by Whose Breath," VENI SANCTI SPIRITUS
  Jan Bender, *The Organist's Companion*, MCA (M)
  Maurice Duruflé, *Variations on Veni Creator*, DUR (M-D)
  Nicholas de Grigny, *Organ Book*, EWE (M)
  Flor Peeters, *The Little Organ Book*, CFP (E)

Postlude on the hymn tune AUSTRIA ("Glorious Things of Thee Are Spoken")
  Richard Purvis, *Seven Chorale Preludes*, CF (M)

Or on the hymn tune NEW BRITAIN ("Amazing Grace")
  Alec Wyton, *Preludes for Christian Praise*, SMP (M)
  Wilbur Held, *Preludes and Postludes*, AF (E)

THE CONFESSION OF 1967

For today's selection, see p. 225.

March 21, 2004

LECTIONARY READINGS

Joshua 5:9–12
2 Corinthians 5:16–21
Luke 15:1–3, 11b—32

Psalm 32

CALL TO WORSHIP

Let all the faithful offer prayers to God!
  In times of distress, trouble shall not overtake us.
You are a hiding place for us, O God,
  You preserve us and show us your way.
Be glad in the Lord and rejoice,
  O righteous,
and shout for joy, all you upright in heart,
  for steadfast love surrounds those who trust in
    God.

PRAYER OF CONFESSION

God of steadfast mercy,
we have kept silence
when we should have confessed our sin.
We have hidden ourselves,
when we should have acknowledged our shame.
Even as we have denied our weakness,
our strength has shriveled to nothing.

Still you receive us as we call upon you,
forgive us as we confess to you,
and renew us as we trust in you.
Be our hiding place,
our secure refuge in times of distress,
and we will praise you
with glad songs of deliverance.

HYMNS FOR THE DAY

GATHERING	HB	LBW	NCH	PH	RIL	TFF	WOV
O Love, How Deep, How Broad, How High	—	88	209	83	342–3	—	—
THE WORD							
O—Come, Ye Thankful People, Come	525	407	422	551	18	—	—
Let All Things Now Living	—	557	—	554	—	—	—
E—O God the Creator	—	—	291	273	—	—	—
God, You Spin the Whirling Planets	—	—	—	285	—	—	—
Walk on, O People of God	—	—	—	296	—	—	—
G—What Wondrous Love Is This	—	385	223	85	—	—	—
There's a Wideness in God's Mercy	110	290	23	298	349	—	—
Jesus, Keep Me Near the Cross	—	—	—	—	—	73	—
THE EUCHARIST							
We Come as Guests Invited	—	—	—	517	—	—	—
SENDING							
When We Are Tempted to Deny Your Son	—	—	—	86	—	—	—

Fourth Sunday in Lent

Color: Purple

PSALM SETTINGS

METRICAL
Psalm 32, "How Blest Those Whose Transgressions,"
    PCW, 7.6.7.6.D, Morgan
RESPONSORIAL
"You Are My Hiding Place, O Lord," P 29,
    Isele/Hopson

MULTICULTURAL/CONTEMPORARY

O—"God Is So Good," TFF 275/AAHH 156
Psalm—"You Are My Hiding Place," W&P 160,
    Michael Ledner
E— "Dios santisimo que en Gloria," El Himn 326
"Jesus, I Believe," Mar 130, Bill Batstone
"There's No Me, There's No You," AAHH 619
G—"Come Back Quickly to the Lord," CLUW 272
"Come, Ye Disconsolate," AAHH 421
Other—"Tree of Life," CG 136, Marty Haugen
"Shepherd, Do You Tramp the Hills," HFTG 68

ANTHEMS

"O Taste and See," Ralph Vaughan Williams, OXU,
    SATB and soprano solo
"O Lord God," Paul Tschesnokov, BOM 7723
    (1500), SSAATTBB

MUSIC FOR THE SMALL CHURCH

"Come, Thou Fount of Every Blessing," Roland
    Martin (two-part mixed/organ), in *The Sewanee
    Composer's Project,* vol. 8, 1

OTHER VOCAL MUSIC

"What Wondrous Love Is This?" Linda Wells, FBM

ORGAN

Prelude on the chorale LIEBSTER JESU ("Blessed Jesus
    at Your Word")
    J. S. Bach, complete works (E-M)
    Marcel Dupe, *Seventy-Nine Chorales,* HWG (E)
    Sigfrid Karg-Elert, *Chorale Improvisations,* EM (M)
    Paul Manz, *Chorale Improvisations,* vol. 8, C (M)
    Flor Peeters, *Hymn Preludes for the Liturgical Year,*
        vol. 9, CFP (M)
    Johann Walter, complete works (E)
Postlude on the hymn tune WONDROUS LOVE ("What
    Wondrous Love Is This?")
    Samuel Barber, *Wondrous Love; Variations on a
        Shape-Note Hymn,* GS (D)
    Don Hustad, *Sacred Harp for the Organ,* HP (E)
    David Johnson, WONDROUS LOVE, AF (E)
    Gordon Young, *Prelude on* WONDROUS LOVE,
        CF (M)

THE CONFESSION OF 1967

For today's selection, see p. 225.

March 28, 2004

LECTIONARY READINGS

Isaiah 43:16–21
Philippians 3:4b–14
John 12:1–8

Psalm 126

CALL TO WORSHIP

When the Lord restored the fortunes of Zion,
   we were like those who dream.
Then our mouth was filled with laughter,
   and our tongue with shouts of joy;
It was said among the nations,
   "The Lord has done great things for them."
The Lord has done great things for us,
   let us rejoice!

PRAYER OF CONFESSION

God who makes all things new,
you send us rivers in the desert,
and bounty amidst famine.
Yet we do not trust you with our whole heart;
we do not look to you with a single eye;
we do not follow you with all our strength.

In mercy, forgive us for turning away from you.
Give us a new heart,
that we would rest in your love,
and enjoy your goodness,
revealed in Jesus Christ, our Savior.
Empower us by your Spirit,
that in all things we would offer glad witness
to the good news of your reign.

HYMNS FOR THE DAY

GATHERING	HB	LBW	NCH	PH	RIL	TFF	WOV
Sing Praise to God, Who Reigns Above	—	—	—	483	146	—	—
THE WORD							
O—My Hope Is Built on Nothing Less	368	293–4	403	379	459–0	192	—
When God Delivered Israel	—	—	—	237	133	—	—
E—Fight the Good Fight	359	461	—	307	—	—	—
Forgive Our Sins as We Forgive	—	307	—	347	—	—	—
G—Jesus, Thy Boundless Love to Me	404	336	—	366	454	—	—
O What Shall I Render	—	—	—	557	—	—	—
THE EUCHARIST							
Bread of the World in Mercy Broken	445	—	346	502	551	—	—
Bread of Heaven, on Thee We Feed	—	—	—	501	—	—	—
SENDING							
Lord, Dismiss Us with Thy Blessing	—	—	—	538	—	—	—

Fifth Sunday in Lent

Color: Purple

PSALM SETTINGS

METRICAL
"When God Delivered Israel," PH 237, 7.6.7.7.6.6,
    Saward
RESPONSORIAL
"The Lord Has Done Great Things for Us," HP 1,
    p. 114, Daw/Hackett

MULTICULTURAL/CONTEMPORARY

O—"Lay It All Down," LUYH 92
"Out in the Wilderness," W&P 115, Jay Beech
"I Will Do a New Thing," AAHH 568
Psalm—"Give Thanks with a Grateful Heart," LUYH
    114/W&P 41/CLUW 247/SNC 216, Henry
    Smith
"He Has Done Great Things for Me," AAHH 507
E—"La cruz excelsa al contemplar," El Himn 145
"A Charge to Keep I Have," AAHH 467
"Change My Heart, Oh God," W&P 28, Eddie
    Espinoza
G—"At the Foot of the Cross," W&P 11, Derek
    Bond
"More About Jesus," AAHH 565
Other—"To Know You More," Mar 76, Joe Horness

ANTHEMS

"Jesus, the Very Thought of Thee," Kay Hawkes
    Goodyear, CHM C02, SATB
"Springs in the Desert," Arthur B. Jennings, HWG,
    GCMR 580, SATB and tenor solo

MUSIC FOR THE SMALL CHURCH

"My Eyes for Beauty Pine," Herbert Howells (unison
    [SATB]/organ), OXU A14

OTHER VOCAL MUSIC

"Sing Praise to God Who Reigns Above," Lloyd
    Larson in *Sing Praise to God*, BP VC 7

ORGAN

Prelude on Luther's chorale setting of Psalm 130, AUS
    TIEFER NOT
    J. S. Bach, several setting, various publishers
        (E-M-D)
    Marcel Dupré, *Seventy-Nine Chorales for Organ*,
        HWG (M-E)
    Flor Peeters, *Thirty Chorale Preludes for Organ, Set
        II*, CFP (M)
"Hymn of the Passion" (tune of QUEM PASTORES),
    sung by a child's voice alternating with the chant
    "Behold the Lamb of God," found in *Enemy of
    Apathy*, IC (E)
Postlude on the hymn "Out of the Depth" (AUS TIEFE
    NOT)
    J. S. Bach, *Organ Works* (M-D)
    Jean Langlais, *Neuf Pièces*, BE (M)
    Flor Peeters, *Thirty Chorale Preludes*, CFP (M)
    Max Reger, *Thirty Short Preludes*, CFP (E)
    Friedrich Zachau, *Chorale Preludes by Masters of the
        Seventeenth and Eighteenth Centuries*, C (M)

THE CONFESSION OF 1967

For today's selection, see p. 225.

April 4, 2004

PROCLAMATION OF THE ENTRANCE INTO JERUSALEM

Luke 19:28–40
Psalm 118:1–2, 19–29

LECTIONARY READINGS

Isaiah 50:4–9a
Philippians 2:5–11
Luke 22:14–23:56 or Luke 23:1–49

Psalm 31:9–16

CALL TO WORSHIP

Blessed is the one
   who comes in the name of the Lord!
Peace in heaven,
   and glory in the highest heaven.
Give thanks to the Lord, for God is good;
   God's steadfast love endures forever!
Let those who trust the Lord say,
   "God's steadfast love endures forever."

PRAYER OF CONFESSION

Strong Savior,
we join voices in praise to you,
gladly proclaiming you as our King.
Yet we have not followed your rule.
We seek more to fulfill our own desires
than to accomplish your will,
we strive more to extend our influence
than to seek your kingdom.

Forgive us for saying one thing,
while living another.
Help us by your Spirit
to walk in your way of the cross,
that we would love God with all our heart,
and our neighbors as ourselves.

HYMNS FOR THE DAY

	HB	LBW	NCH	PH	RIL	TFF	WOV
GATHERING							
Prepare the Way, O Zion	—	26	—	13	—	—	—
All Glory, Laud and Honor	187	108	216–7	88	279	—	—
THE WORD							
O—Lord Christ, When First You Came to Earth	—	421	—	7	608	—	—
When We Are Tempted to Deny Your Son	—	—	—	86	—	—	—
E—At the Name of Jesus	143	179	—	148	336	—	—
G—Were You There?	201	92	229	102	—	81	—
O Sacred Head, Now Wounded	194	116–7	226	98	300	—	—
THE EUCHARIST							
Beneath the Cross of Jesus	190	107	190	92	310–1	—	—
SENDING							
Ride on, Ride on in Majesty!	188	121	215	90–1	280–1	—	—

Palm/Passion Sunday

Color: Red/Purple

PSALM SETTINGS

METRICAL
"This Is the Day the Lord Hath Made," PH 230,
   CM, Watts
RESPONSORIAL
"Hosanna," PH 232, Bevenot/Murray

MULTICULTURAL/CONTEMPORARY

ENTRANCE OF THE PALMS
"Filled with Excitement," CLUW 178/El Himn
   132/SNC 133, Ruben Ruiz Avila
"Hosanna," AAHH 224
Psalm—"This Is the Day," AAHH 108
LITURGY OF THE PASSION
O—"Come, Share the Lord," LUYH 126, Jeffery Leeds
"We Remember You," LUYH 132/W&P 152, Rick
   Founds
"Lord, My Strength," W&P 93, Dean Krippaehne
Psalm—"Shine on Me," AAHH 527
E—"He Is Exalted," W&P 55/SNC 41/Renew 238,
   Twila Paris
"Jesus, Name Above All Names," TFF 268/W&P 77,
   Naida Hearn
"I Bowed on My Knees," AAHH 599
"I Come to the Cross," Mar 122, Bob Somma and
   Bill Batstone
"Presenciasste la muerta del Senor," El Himn 142
G—"The Hand of Heaven," CG 124, French Carol
   Melody
"When Jesus Wept," CG 144, William Billings
"Open Our Eyes Lord," Mar 59/W&P 113/TFF 98,
   Bob Cull
"Remember Me," AAHH 434
"He Chose to Die," GLS, SATB, Patti Drennan
"Lone He Prays Within the Garden," HFTG 139
"Son of God, by God Forsaken," HFTG 38

ANTHEMS

"Hosanna in the Highest," David W. Music, CPH, C,
   98-2797, SATB with children's choir and percussion
"Let This Mind Be in You," Austin Lovelace, JFB
   F.E.C.8458, SATB and alto solo

MUSIC FOR THE SMALL CHURCH

"One with God Before Creation," Randall Sensmeier
   (SATB, keyboard), GIA G-4897
"Palm Sunday Processional," Rory Cooney
   (cantor/congregation/SATB/keyboard/optional
   brass), GIA G-5012

OTHER VOCAL MUSIC

"Beneath the Cross of Jesus," Dale Wood in *Songs of
   Reflection*, SMP 30/1109S
"Were You There?" Moses Hogan in *The Deep River
   Collection,* vol. 1, HL
"Ride on, King Jesus!" Hall Johnson, CF V2223

ORGAN

The prelude for this Sunday should be the Entrance
   Rite/Liturgy of the Palms; see the *Book of Common
   Worship,* pp. 252–67.
   "Hossana to the Son of David," Thomas Welks, O,
   SATB (M)
   "Hossana to the Son of David," Tomas Luis
   deVictoria, *First Motet Book,* C (M)
   Procession "All Glory Laud and Honor" [For an
   interesting alternative to VALET WILL ICH DIR
   GEBEN, tune 155 in the *Hymnal* (1982) is set as a
   procession with bells, tambourine, finger cym-
   bals, and drum. It is arranged for the congrega-
   tion singing a response and a cantor or choir
   singing verses. It can be sung in alternation with
   the more traditional tune.]
Postlude
   J. S. Bach, "Toccata and Fugue in D minor"
On the hymn tune THE KING'S MAJESTY ("Ride on,
   Ride on, in Majesty")
   Jan Bender, *Preludes for the Hymns in Worship,
   Supplement,* C (M)
   Leo Sowerby, "Prelude on THE KING'S MAJESTY,"
   HWG (D)

THE CONFESSION OF 1967

For today's selection, see p. 225.

April 8, 2004

LECTIONARY READINGS

Exodus 12:1–4 (5–10) 11–14
1 Corinthians 11:23–26
John 13:1–17, 31b–35

Psalm 116:1–2, 12–19

CALL TO WORSHIP

From generation to generation
    we celebrate this day as a festival to you, O Lord.
We remember with thanksgiving
    all your goodness to us.
We will lift the cup of salvation
    and call on the name of the Lord.
We are your people, your grateful guests,
    as we celebrate this sacrifice of thanksgiving.

PRAYER OF CONFESSION *(BCW)*

Eternal God,
whose covenant with us is never broken,
we confess that we fail to fulfill your will.
Though you have bound yourself to us,
we will not bind ourselves to you.
In Jesus Christ you serve us freely,
but we refuse your love
and withhold ourselves from others.
We do not love you fully
or love one another as you command.

In your mercy, forgive and cleanse us.
Lead us once again to your table
and unite us to Christ,
who is the bread of life
and the vine from which we grow in grace.

HYMNS FOR THE DAY

	HB	LBW	NCH	PH	RIL	TFF	WOV
GATHERING							
We Come as Guests Invited	—	—	—	517	—	—	—
THE WORD							
O—O God of Bethel, by Whose Hand	342	—	—	269	45	—	—
E—Be Known to Us in Breaking Bread	446	—	342	505	—	—	—
G—Thee We Adore	—	199	339	519	—	—	—
THE EUCHARIST							
Let Us Break Bread Together	—	212	330	513	545	123	—
By Gracious Powers	—	—	413	342	55	—	—
SENDING							
An Upper Room Did Our Lord Prepare	—	—	—	94	568	—	—

Maundy Thursday

Color: Purple (until church is stripped bare)

PSALM SETTINGS

METRICAL
"O Thou, My Soul, Return in Peace," PH 228, CM,
    Murrayfield Psalms/ The Psalter (1912)
RESPONSORIAL
"How Can I Repay the Lord?" p. 116, Weber

MULTICULTURAL/CONTEMPORARY

O—"We Bring the Sacrifice of Praise," W&P 150,
    Kirk Dearman
Psalm—"I Love the Lord, Who Heard My Cry," PH
    362
"My Tribute," AAHH 111
"I Love You, Lord," TFF 288/W&P 67, Laurie Klein
E—"Among Us and Before Us," LUYH 122, Iona
    Community, tune: gatehouse
"Bread, Blessed and Broken," LUYH 123/CG 17,
    Michael B. Lynch
"We Remember You," W&P 152, Rick Founds
"One Bread, One Body," WOV 710, John Foley
"The Master's Love," AAHH 611
G—"Jesus, Jesus," PH 367/WOV 765/CLUW 179/El
    Himn 138
"Jesus, Jesus, Fill Us with Your Love," two-part, GIA,
    arr. by Cindy Favreau
"Un mandamiento nuevo," El Himn 135
"The Bond of Love," AAHH 521
"Here I Am," Mar 115, Bill Batstone
"Lord, Help Us Walk Your Servant Way," HFTG 150

ANTHEMS

"Take the Body of Christ," Nikolai Bachmetiev, E.C.
    Schirmer, ECS 588, SATB
"To Thy Heavenly Banquet," Alexis Lvov, WAM
    W2400, SATB

MUSIC FOR THE SMALL CHURCH

"Love Consecrates the Humblest Act," arr. by Bradley
    Ellingboe (SATB/oboe), AF 98-10600

OTHER VOCAL MUSIC

"Let Us Break Bread Together," Jay Althouse in
    Spirituals for Solo Singers, AP
"Let Us Break Bread Together," Moses Hogan in *The
    Deep River Collection,* vol. 1, HL

ORGAN

Liturgical Note: There are two highly recommended
    and very complete services for Maundy Thursday:
    Book of Common Worship (WJN)
    New Handbook of the Christian Year (AB)
Prelude on the hymn tune HOLY MANNA
    Sue Mitchell Wallace, *Hymn Prisms*, HP (M)
    Wilbur Held, *Preludes and Postludes*, AF (M)
Or on the hymn tune ADORO TE DEVOTE ("Thee
    We Adore")
    Jean Langlais, *Suite Medievale*, SE (ME)
    Healey Willan, *Organ Music for the Communion
    Service,* CM (E)
Postlude: No music played; all depart in silence

April 9, 2004

LECTIONARY READINGS

Isaiah 52:13–53:12
Hebrews 10:16–25 or Hebrews 4:14–16; 5:7–9
John 18:1–19:42

Psalm 22

CALL TO WORSHIP

My God, my God why have your forsaken me?
   Why are you so far from helping me?
O God, we cry to you by day but you do not
    answer;
  we cry to you at night but find no rest.
To you our ancestors cried and you answered them.
   They trusted in you and were not put to shame.
O Lord, do not be far away from us.
  Come quickly to our aid, for you alone can
    deliver us.

PRAYER OF CONFESSION

Savior of the world,
we stagger under the weight
of our guilt and shame.
We have condemned the innocent one,
attacked the defenseless one,
hurled insults at the silent one,
maligned the truthful one.

Jesus, Lamb of God,
have mercy on us.
Jesus, bearer of our sins,
have mercy on us.
Jesus, redeemer of the world,
grant us peace.

HYMNS FOR THE DAY

	HB	LBW	NCH	PH	RIL	TFF	WOV
GATHERING							
Go to Dark Gethsemane (stanzas 1–3)	193	109	219	97	—	—	—
THE WORD							
O—O Sacred Head, Now Wounded	194	116–7	226	98	300	—	—
Alas, and Did My Savior Bleed	199	98	199–0	78	—	71	—
E—Blessing and Honor and Glory and Power	137	525	—	147	602	—	—
G—Calvary	—	—	—	96	—	85	—
Ah, Holy Jesus	191	123	218	93	285	—	—
Deep Were His Wounds, and Red	—	100	—	103	—	—	—
Were You There?	201	92	229	102	—	81	—
THE EUCHARIST							
My Song Is Love Unknown	—	94	222	76	284	—	—
SENDING							
Throned Upon the Awful Tree	197	—	—	99	—	—	—

Good Friday

Color: Stripped of color/black

PSALM SETTINGS

METRICAL
"Lord, Why Have You Forsaken Me?" PH 168, LM, Webber
RESPONSORIAL:
"My God, My God, Why Have You Abandoned Me?" P 16, Brubaker
RESPONSORIAL
"My God, My God, Why Have You Forsaken Me?" HP 1, p. 95, Daw/Hackett

MULTICULTURAL/CONTEMPORARY

O—"Our God Reigns," LUYH 84, Lenny Smith
"Amazing Love," W&P 8, Graham Kendrick
"O Perfect Love," AAHH 520
E—"Only by Grace," W&P 122, Gerritt Gustafson
"I Gave My Life for Thee," AAHH 233
G—"We Worship at Your Feet," spiritual song, LUYH 47
"Jesus, Remember Me," W&P 78/SNC 143/CLUW364/PH 599, Jacuqes Berthier
"He Never Said a Mumbalin' Word," PH 95
"Mi dulce buen Jesus," El Himn 144
"'Tis Finished! The Messiah Dies," CLUW 182
"Lamb of God," Twila Paris, arr. by Tome Fettke Lillenas
"O Come and Mourn," two-part, AGP, arr. by Hal H. Hopson
"Why Has God Forsaken Me?" handbells/SATB, GIA, Jane Marshall
Other—"Only by Grace," W&P 112, Gerritt Gustafson
"There Is a Redeemer," W&P 140/SNC 145/Renew 232, Melody Green

ANTHEMS

"Were You There?" Raymond H. Haan, MS MSM-50-3502, SATB with cello, soprano or tenor solo
"When I Survey the Wondrous Cross," Gilbert Martin, TP 312-49785, SSAATTBB

MUSIC FOR THE SMALL CHURCH

"Ah, Holy Jesus," Johann Crueger/G. Matheny (SATB/keyboard), HP A 568
"Be Not Far," Michael Birkley (two-part/piano/guitar), GIA G-5107
"Saw Ye My Savior?" David N. Johnson (solos/SATB/organ/optional flute), AF 11-1531

OTHER VOCAL MUSIC

"Were You There?" Moses Hogan in *The Deep River Collection*, HL
"Were You There?" Craig Courtney in *Music for the Master*, BP
"He Never Said a Mumbalin' Word," *Your Favorite Spirituals*, SP
"'Tis Finished! The Messiah Dies," Mary Jackson in *Winchester New, Sweet Singer/Hymns of Charles Wesley*, Steve Kimbrough, CHM

ORGAN

Liturgical Note: Silence should be in abundance. It would be preferable not to use any musical instruments to accompany singing. There is no need to turn on the organ or unlock the piano for this liturgy.
Prelude: A quiet prelude sung by the choir, congregation and soloists
Jacques Berthier, *Songs and Prayers from Taizé by Your Cross*, GIA (E) [During the prelude a rough life-sized cross could be carried in procession.]
Postlude: It is appropriate that the church be in silence following the benediction. Encourage people to remain in quiet prayer, meditating on the cross.

April 10, 2004

LECTIONARY READINGS

Genesis 1:1–2:4a
Psalm 136:1–9, 23–26

Genesis 7:1–5, 11–18; 8:6–18, 9:8–13
Psalm 46

Genesis 22:1–18
Psalm 16

Exodus 14:10–31; 15:20–21
Exodus 15:1b–13, 17–18

Isaiah 55:1–11
Isaiah 12:2–6

Proverbs 8:1–8, 19–21; 9:4b–6
Psalm 19

Ezekiel 36:24–28
Psalm 42 and 43

Ezekiel 37:1–14
Psalm 143

Zephaniah 3:14–20
Psalm 98

Romans 6:3–11
Psalm 114

Luke 24:1–12

(Nine readings from the Old Testament are provided. At least three are to be read. The reading from Exodus 14 is always included.)

HYMNS FOR THE DAY

	HB	LBW	NCH	PH	RIL	TFF	WOV
GENESIS 1							
Creating God, Your Fingers Trace	—	—	462	134	—	—	—
Morning Has Broken	—	—	—	469	—	—	—
PSALM 136							
We Thank You, Lord, for You Are Good	—	—	—	243	—	—	—
GENESIS 7							
Let All Things Now Living	—	557	—	554	—	—	—
PSALM 46							
God Our Help and Constant Refuge	—	—	—	192	—	—	—
GENESIS 22							
I Want Jesus to Walk with Me	—	—	490	363	—	66	660
The God of Abraham Praise	89	544	24	488	595	—	—
PSALM 16							
When in the Night I Meditate	—	—	—	165	—	—	—
EXODUS 14							
Come, Ye Faithful, Raise the Strain	205	132	230	114–5	315–6	—	—
Out of Deep, Unordered Water	—	—	—	494	—	—	—

Easter Vigil

Color: White

HYMNS FOR THE DAY

	HB	LBW	NCH	PH	RIL	TFF	WOV
ISAIAH 55							
Have Mercy, Lord, on Me	—	—	—	395	—	—	—
We Walk by Faith and Not by Sight	—	—	—	399	—	—	—
PROVERBS 8							
God Marked a Line and Told the Sea	—	—	568	283	—	—	—
PSALM 19							
The Heavens Above Declare God's Praise	—	—	—	166	—	—	—
EZEKIEL 36							
Thy Mercy and Thy Truth, O Lord	—	—	—	186	—	—	—
PSALM 42							
As Deer Long for the Streams	—	452	481	189	—	—	—
EZEKIEL 37							
Breathe on Me, Breath of God	235	488	292	316	—	—	—
PSALM 143							
When Morning Lights the Eastern Skies	—	—	—	250	—	—	—
ZEPHANIAH 3							
Deep in the Shadows of the Past	—	—	—	330	—	—	—
PSALM 98							
To God Compose a Song of Joy	—	—	36	219	—	—	—
ROMANS 6							
We Know That Christ Is Raised	189	—	—	495	528	—	—
LUKE 24							
Celebrate with Joy and Singing	—	—	—	107	—	—	—
THE EUCHARIST							
I Come with Joy to Meet My Lord	—	349	507	534	—	—	—
Jesus, Thou Joy of Loving Hearts	215	356	329	511	273	—	—
SENDING							
Eternal God, Whose Power Upholds	485	—	—	412	481	—	—

April 10, 2004

PSALM SETTINGS

PSALM 136:1–9, 23–26
METRICAL
"O Give Thanks unto the Lord," PCW, 7.7.7.7.7.7,
  Morgan
"O Thank the Lord," *Psalm Praise*, GIA 138, 8.8.7,
  Dudley-Smith
RESPONSORIAL
"Great Is His Love," P 139, Gelineau

PSALM 46
METRICAL
"God, Our Constant Help and Refuge," PH 192,
  8.7.8.7.3.3.7, Anderson
RESPONSORIAL
PH 193, Proulx/Murray
"The Lord of Hosts Is with Us," HP 1, p. 104,
  Daw/Hackett

PSALM 16
METRICAL
"When in the Night I Meditate," PH 165, CM,
  The Psalter (1912)
RESPONSORIAL
"Protect Me, O God," P 10, Barrett/Hopson

PSALM 19
METRICAL
"The Heavens Above Declare God's Praise," PH 166,
  CM, Webber
RESPONSORIAL
"Heaven and Earth Tell Your Glory," P 19, Monks of
  Saint Meinrad/Weber
"The Statutes of the Lord Rejoice the Heart," HP 2,
  p. 56, Daw/Hackett

PSALMS 42 AND 43
METRICAL
"As Deer Long for the Streams," PH 189, LM,
  Webber

RESPONSORIAL
"My Soul Is Thirsting for the Lord," PH 190,
  Mews/Gelineau

PSALM 143
METRICAL
"Lord, Hear Me in Your Faithfulness," NMP 223,
  CM, Webber
"Lord, Hear My Prayer, My Supplication," PsH 143,
  9.9.8.9.8, Bosch/Slenk
RESPONSORIAL
"Revive Me, O Lord, for Your Name's Sake," HP 1,
  p. 112, Daw/Hackett

PSALM 98
METRICAL
"New Songs of Celebration Render," PH 218,
  9.8.9.8.D, Routley
"Sing to the Lord New Songs," NMP 160, CM, Webber
RESPONSORIAL
"Sing to the Lord a New Song," HP 1, p. 49,
  Daw/Hackett

PSALM 114
METRICAL
"When Israel Fled from Egypt Land," PsH 114, LM,
  Harmsel/Bradbury
RESPONSORIAL
"Tremble, O Earth, at the Presence of the Lord,"
  HP 2, p. 46, Daw/Hackett

MULTICULTURAL/CONTEMPORARY

Genesis 1:1–2:4A—"Song Over the Waters," W&P
127, Marty Haugen
Psalm 46—"Be Still and Know," LUYH 82, Sylvia
Washer
Isaiah 12:2—"Surely It Is God," LUYH 81/SNC 74,
Jack Noble White
"Be Still My Soul," AAHH 135
"The Sun Was Bright That Easter Dawn," HFTG 14

Easter Vigil

Color: White

ANTHEMS

"The Whole Bright World Rejoices Now," Peter Crisafulli, MS MSM-50-4016A, SATB and instruments

"Alleluia, O Praise the Lord Most Holy," J. S. Bach, C 98-2101, SATB and instruments

MUSIC FOR THE SMALL CHURCH

"The First Day of Creation," Carol Doran (unison), in *New Hymns for the Lectionary*, OXU 14

"Let Your Alleluias Rise," K. Lee Scott (SATB, solo), AF 11-2549

"We Have Met Christ Raised and Living," Sally Ann Morris (unison or SATB), in *Giving Thanks in Song and Prayer*, 18

OTHER VOCAL MUSIC

"Jesus, the Very Thought of Thee," Dale Wood

"I Sing a Gentle Song," Dale Wood, SMP, SM 20

"I Know That My Redeemer Liveth," G. F. Handel/Wilbur Held in *Vocal Solos for Funerals and Memorial Services*, AF 11-10226

ORGAN

The organ and all musical instruments should remain silent until the singing of "Glory to God in the Highest."

Postlude on the hymn tune GELOBT SEI GOTT ("The Strife Is O'er")

J. S. Bach, several settings, various editions (M-D)

John Leavitt, *Hymn Preludes for the Church Year*, AF (M-E)

David Uhl, *Easter Suite for Trumpet, Organ and Timpani* (M-E)

John Ferguson, *New Liturgical Year*, AF (M)

Or David Johnson, "Trumpet tune in D Major," AF (M)

April 11, 2004

LECTIONARY READINGS

Acts 10:34–43 or Isaiah 65:17–25
1 Corinthians 15:19–26 or Acts 10:34–43
John 20:1–18 or Luke 24:1–12

Psalm 118:1–2, 14–24

CALL TO WORSHIP

Let there be songs of victory to you, O God,
  let the whole assembly sing of your salvation.
You are our strength and our salvation, O Lord;
  we have cried to you, and you have answered.
You are our God, and we will give thanks to you.
  You are our God, who has given us life.
Give thanks to God for the Lord is good,
  God's steadfast love endures forever!

PRAYER OF CONFESSION *(BCW)*

Almighty God,
in raising Jesus from the grave,
you shattered the power of sin and death.
We confess that we remain captive to doubt
  and fear,
bound by the ways that lead to death.
We overlook the poor and the hungry,
and pass by those who mourn;
we are deaf to the cries of the oppressed,
and indifferent to calls for peace;
we despise the weak,
and abuse the earth you made.

Forgive us, God of mercy.
Help us to trust your power
to change our lives and make us new,
that we may know the joy of life abundant
given in Jesus Christ, the risen Lord.

HYMNS FOR THE DAY

GATHERING	HB	LBW	NCH	PH	RIL	TFF	WOV
Christ the Lord Is Risen Today!	—	128	233	113	325	—	—
Christ Is Risen! Shout Hosanna!	—	—	—	104	—	—	—
Christ Has Arisen, Alleluia	—	—	—	—	—	96	—
THE WORD							
O—Blessing and Honor and Glory and Power	137	525	—	147	602	—	—
Christ Is Risen, Christ Is Living	—	—	—	109	—	—	—
Jesus Christ Is Risen Today	204	151	240	123	312	—	—
A—There Is a Balm in Gilead	—	—	553	394	465	185	—
At the Font We Start Our Journey	—	—	308	—	—	—	—
G—Thine Is the Glory	209	145	253	122	327	—	—
Low in the Grave He Lay	—	—	—	—	—	94	—
THE EUCHARIST							
Come, Risen Lord, and Deign to Be Our Guest	—	209	—	503	550	—	—
Christ Is Alive	—	363	—	108	—	—	—
SENDING							
Lift High the Cross	—	377	198	371	415	—	—

Easter Sunday
Resurrection of the Lord

Color: White/Gold

PSALM SETTINGS

METRICAL
Psalm 118, "Give Thanks Unto Our Gracious God,"
    PCW, 8.7.8.7.8.8.8.7, Morgan
RESPONSORIAL
"Alleluia!" PH 231, Bevenot/Murray

MULTICULTURAL/CONTEMPORARY

Gathering—"Cristo Vive (Christ Is Risen),"
    PH 109/El Himn 165
O/A—"He Is Lord," AAHH 285
E—"Lord, I Lift Your Name On High," W&P 90,
    Rick Founds
"He Is Exalted," W&P 55, Twila Paris
G—"You Are Mighty," LUYH 149, Craig Musseau
"Comes Mary to the Grave," CG 27, David Ilif
"Haven't You Heard?" CG 46, Alison Robertson
"We Will Glorify," W&P 154/SNC 21/AAHH 286,
    Twila Paris
"On the Third Day," HP, SATB, Allen Pote
"The Sun Was Bright That Easter Dawn," HFTG 14

ANTHEMS

"Christ the Lord Is Risen Again," John Rutter, OXU
    42.362, SATB
"This Is the Day," Jacobus Gallus, C 98-1702, double
    chorus or chorus and brass

MUSIC FOR THE SMALL CHURCH

"Myrrh-Bearing Mary," David Hurd (unison/key-
    board), in *Two New Hymntunes*, GIA G-3737
"Now the Green Blade Riseth," arr. by Shirley W.
    McRae (two-part/keyboard/flute/handbells),
    CG CGA795

OTHER VOCAL MUSIC

"There Is a Balm in Gilead," Lloyd Larson in *Sing
    Praise to God*, BP VC 7
"Rise Up, My Heart, with Gladness," J. S. Bach in
    Solos for the Church Year, Lloyd Pfautsch, LG/GS

ORGAN

Richard Purvis, PARTITA ON CHRIST IST ERSTANDEN,
    HWG (D)
Or prelude on the hymn tune EASTER HYMN
    William H. Harris, *Festal Voluntaries*, NOV (M)
    Austin Lovelace, *Fourteen Hymn Preludes*, AF (E)
    Flor Peeters, *Choral Fantasy on "Christ the Lord Has
        Risen"* with brass (M)
    C. V. Stanford, *Six Occasional Preludes*, S&B (M)
    Healey Willan, *The Parish Organist*, vol. 8, C (M)
Postlude on the hymn tune O FILII ET FILIAE ("O Sons
    and Daughters")
    Raymond Haan, Variations on O FILII ET FILIAE
        with brass, C (M)
    Carl Schalk *Festival Hymn Settings for the Small
        Parish Easter* with two instruments, C (E)
    Alexandre Guilmant *Historical Organ Recitals*,
        O FILII ET FILIAE, GS (D)
    Jean-François Dandrieu, *Offertoirs sur O Filii et
        Filiae*, EWE (M)
    Hermann Schroeder, *Preludes for the Hymns in
        Worship Supplement*, O FILII ET FILIAE, C (M-E)

THE CONFESSION OF 1967

For today's selection, see p. 225.

April 11, 2004

LECTIONARY READINGS

Isaiah 25:6–9
1 Corinthians 5:6b–8
Luke 24:13–49

Psalm 114

CALL TO WORSHIP

On this mountain God will make for all people
    a feast of rich food, a feast of well-matured wines,
and God will destroy on this mountain
    the shroud that is cast over all people,
    the sheet that is spread over all nations;
God will swallow up death forever.
    The Lord will wipe away the tears from every face.
This is our God who has come to save us,
    let us rejoice and be glad in God's salvation!

PRAYER OF CONFESSION

O God, Creator and Renewer of life,
forgive us when we fail to recognize your presence
accompanying us on life's journeys.
By your Spirit, open our eyes, ears, and hearts
that as we hear your word and break bread together
we may experience the presence
of the resurrected Christ among us. Amen.

HYMNS FOR THE DAY

GATHERING	HB	LBW	NCH	PH	RIL	TFF	WOV
Christ the Lord Is Risen Again	—	136	—	112	323	—	—
Good Christians All, Rejoice and Sing!	—	—	—	111	326	—	—
THE WORD							
A—All Hail the Power of Jesus' Name!	132	328–9	304	142–3	593–4	267	—
I Love to Tell the Story	383	390	522	—	—	228	—
E—Jesus Comes with Clouds Descending	234	27	—	6	605	—	—
The Head That Once Was Crowned with Thorns	211	173	—	149	335	—	—
G—O Sons and Daughters, Let Us Sing!	206	139	244	117	—	—	—
We Walk by Faith and Not by Sight	—	—	—	399	—	—	—
Show Me Your Hands, Your Feet, Your Side	—	—	—	—	—	—	109
THE EUCHARIST							
Lord, We Have Come at Your Own Invitation	—	—	516	—	—	—	—
SENDING							
Love Divine, All Loves Excelling	399	315	43	376	464	—	—

Easter Evening

PSALM SETTINGS

METRICAL
"When Israel Fled from Egypt Land," PH 114, LM,
    Harmsel/Bradbury
RESPONSORIAL
"Alleluia!" P 114 (Presbyterian 1)

MULTICULTURAL/CONTEMPORARY

Gathering—"Come and Rejoice," Renew 20
"Hoy Celebramos/Come, Celebrate," El Himn 165
G—"Haven't You Heard?" CG 46
"On Emmaus' Journey," HFTG 44
"Come to Us, Beloved Stranger," SNC 153

April 18, 2004

LECTIONARY READINGS

Acts 5:27–32
Revelation 1:4–8
John 20:19–31

Psalm 118:14–29 or Psalm 150

CALL TO WORSHIP

Look! God is coming with the clouds;
  every eye will see.
Even those who pierced him;
  and on his account all the tribes of the earth
    shall wail.
So it is to be
  I am the Alpha and Omega,
who is, who was and who is to come,
  the Almighty!

PRAYER OF CONFESSION

Almighty God,
we acknowledge that we belong to you,
and that you hold the keys of death and life.
Yet we have sought to preserve old ways of living,
rather than embracing the new life you have
    given us.
We have disbelieved your good news,
even when its signs are all around us.

Forgive our refusal to trust you.
Set us free by your Spirit
from the fear that binds us in unbelief.
Fill us with new life in Christ,
our risen Lord and Savior.

HYMNS FOR THE DAY

GATHERING	HB	LBW	NCH	PH	RIL	TFF	WOV
Christ the Lord Is Risen Again	—	136	—	112	323	—	—
Good Christians All, Rejoice and Sing!	—	—	—	111	326	—	—
THE WORD							
A—All Hail the Power of Jesus' Name!	132	328–9	304	142–3	593–4	267	—
I Love to Tell the Story	383	390	522	—	—	228	—
E—Jesus Comes with Clouds Descending	234	27	—	6	605	—	—
The Head That Once Was Crowned with Thorns	211	173	—	149	335	—	—
G—O Sons and Daughters, Let Us Sing!	206	139	244	117	—	—	—
We Walk by Faith and Not by Sight	—	—	—	399	—	—	—
THE EUCHARIST							
Lord, We Have Come at Your Own Invitation	—	—	—	516	—	—	—
SENDING							
Love Divine, All Loves Excelling	399	315	43	376	464	—	—

Second Sunday of Easter

Color: White/Gold

PSALM SETTINGS

METRICAL
Psalm 150, "Let Ev'ry Heart Lift Up God's Name in
  Praise," PCW, 8.8.8.4, Morgan
RESPONSORIAL
"Alleluia! Praise the Lord!" P 157, Hopson

MULTICULTURAL/CONTEMPORARY

A—"He Is Exalted," W&P 55/SNC 41, Twila Paris
Psalm 118—"This Is the Day," BH, arr. by Gerald
  Smith
"Great and Mighty," LUYH 29, Marlene Bigley
"Cantad al Senor, O Sing to the Lord," PH
  472/WOV 75/El Himn 1
"This Is the Day," AAHH 631
Psalm 150—"Praise Ye the Lord," PH 250/SNC 32,
  J. Jefferson Cleveland
"We'll Praise the Lord," AAHH 123
"Let All the World Sing Praises," Mar 216, Chris
  Falson
"Halle, Halle, Halle," HP, SATB, arr. by Hal H. Hopson
E—"Soon and Very Soon," W&P 128/WOV 744,
  Andraé Crouch
"Soon and Very Soon," HP, SATB, arr. by Jack
  Schrader
G—"Go in Peace and Serve the Lord," W&P 46,
  Handt Hanson
"There's Something About That Name," AAHH 301
"Show Me Your Hands, Your Feet, Your Side,"
  HFTG 109

ANTHEMS

"Peace I Leave with You," Walter L. Pelz, AF 11-1364,
  SATB
"The Head That Once Was Crowned with Thorns,"
  John Ferguson, GIA G-3750, SATB and brass
  quartet

MUSIC FOR THE SMALL CHURCH

"Gather Gladness from the Skies," Charles Callahan
  (unison/two-part/keyboard), MS MSM-50-4500

OTHER VOCAL MUSIC

"Lo, He Comes with Clouds Descending," Mary
  Jackson, BRYN CALFARIA in *Sweet Singer/Hymns
  of Charles Wesley*, Steven Kimbrough, CHM

ORGAN

Prelude on the hymn tune O FILII ET FILIAE
  Alex Wyton, *A Little Christian Year*, CF (M)
  Flor Peeters, *Hymn Preludes for the Liturgical Year*,
  CFP (M). [See also suggestions from last week.
  One could easily work up a short liturgical
  drama using the hymn "O Sons and Daughters"
  following the prelude based on the same tune.]
Postlude on the chant tune VICTIMAE PASCHALI LAUDES
  Charles Tournemire, *Cinq Improvisations*, DUR (D)
Or on the EASTER HYMN
  Wilbur Held, *Six Preludes on Easter Hymns*, C (E)
  Paul Manz, *Ten Chorale Improvisations*, vol. 6,
  C (M)

THE CONFESSION OF 1967

For today's selection, see p. 226.

April 25, 2004

LECTIONARY READINGS

Acts 9:1–6 (7–20)
Revelation 5:11–14
John 21:1–19

Psalm 30

CALL TO WORSHIP

Sing praises to the Lord,
   O you, God's faithful ones.
For God's anger is but for a moment,
   God's favor is for a lifetime.
O God, you have turned our mourning into dancing;
   you have clothed us with joy!
So that we may praise you and not be silent,
   O Lord our God, we will give thanks to you
      forever.

PRAYER OF CONFESSION

God of life,
you turn mourning into dancing,
the dark night of weeping
into the bright morning of gladness.
Your light has shined upon us,
claiming us as witnesses to your saving power.
Yet we keep silent, and hide your light.

Forgive our meager witness to the glad news
of your light breaking into our world,
in the life, death, and resurrection of Jesus;
empower us by your Spirit
to proclaim this Gospel to all.

HYMNS FOR THE DAY

GATHERING	HB	LBW	NCH	PH	RIL	TFF	WOV
Come, Ye Faithful, Raise the Strain	205	132	230	114–5	315–6	—	—
THE WORD							
A—Make Me a Captive, Lord	308	—	—	378	442	—	—
When I Had Not Yet Learned of Jesus	—	—	—	410	—	—	—
E—This Is the Feast of Victory	—	60	—	594	—	—	—
Blessing and Honor and Glory and Power	137	525	—	147	602	—	—
Let All That Is Within Me Cry, "Holy!"	—	—	—	—	—	282	—
G—Down to Earth, as a Dove	—	—	—	300	—	—	—
THE EUCHARIST							
What Wondrous Love Is This	—	385	223	85	—	—	—
SENDING							
Let Us Talents and Tongues Employ	—	—	347	514	—	232	754
At the Lamb's High Feast We Sing	—	210	—	—	—	—	—

Third Sunday of Easter

Color: White/Gold

PSALM SETTINGS

METRICAL
"Come, Sing to God," PH 181, CMD, Anderson
RESPONSORIAL
"Sing Praise to the Lord," P 27, Hopson/Byrd

MULTICULTURAL/CONTEMPORARY

Gathering—"Christ Is Alive," CLUW 190
A—"Let the Heaven Light Shine on Me," AAHH 630
"Amazing Love," W&P 8, Graham Kendrick
"The Power of Your Love," HP, SATB, Jane Holstein
Psalm—"How Can I Keep from Singing?" LUYH 34,
   Robert Lowry
"Praise His Holy Name," ES, SATB, arr. by Keith
   Hampton
"He Lifted Me," AAHH 232
E—"Alabare," two-part mixed, OCP, arr. by Ronald
   A. Nelson
"Glorify Thy Name," W&P 42, Donna Adkins
"Thou Art Worthy," AAHH 119
"Alleluia," SNC 149, tune from Honduras, arr. by
   John Bell
G—"More Love to Thee," GIA, SATB, arr. by Joseph
   Joubert
"Step by Step," W&P 132, arr. by Nylea Butler-
   Moore
"Haven't You Heard?" CG 46, Alison Robertson
"My Jesus I Love Thee," AAHH 574
"O Risen Christ, You Search Our Hearts,"
   HFTG 129

ANTHEMS

"Honor and Glory," J. S. Bach, PM, SSATB
"Worthy Is the Lamb," Handel's *Messiah*, any edition,
   SATB

MUSIC FOR THE SMALL CHURCH

"Feed My Lambs," Natalie Sleeth
   (unison/keyboard/flutes), CF CM7777

OTHER VOCAL MUSIC

"O for a Heart to Praise My God," Edwin T. Childs
   in *A Wesley Trilogy*, KM

ORGAN

Prelude based on the hymn tune O QUANTA QUALIA
   ("Blessing and Honor")
   Clarence Dickinson, Prelude on O QUANTA QUALIA,
   HWG (M) [Have the choir sing the text to the
   first stanza of "Blessing and Honor" to the final
   variation of this piece. A flourish of high-pitched
   handbells during the final variation would
   heighten the moment.]
   Philip Cranmer, *For Manuals Only*, OXU (E)
   Emma Lou Diemer, *Folk Hymn Sketches*, SMP (D)
   Richard Hillert: O QUANTA QUALIA, *The Concordia
   Hymn Prelude Series*, C (E)
Postlude: Chorale prelude on ERSTANDEN IST DER
   HEIL'GE CHRIST ("The Blessed Christ Is Ris'n
   Today"), J. S. Bach, various editions (M)
Chorale prelude on CHRISTUS, DER IST MEIN LEBEN
   ("Christ, You Are My Life")
   J. S. Bach, various editions (M)
   Pachelbel, various editions (E-M)
   Alexander Schreiner, *Organ Voluntaries*, JFB (E)

THE CONFESSION OF 1967

For today's selection, see p. 226.

May 2, 2004

LECTIONARY READINGS

Acts 9:36–43
Revelation 7:9–17
John 10:22–30

Psalm 23

CALL TO WORSHIP

From every nation and tribe they will cry out
  "Salvation belongs to our God,
who is seated on the throne,
  and to the Lamb!"
Amen! Blessing and glory and wisdom
  and thanksgiving and honor and power and might,
Be our God forever and ever!
  Amen!
We will worship God day and night in the temple,
  and the one who is seated on the throne will
    shelter us.

PRAYER OF CONFESSION

God of hope and safety,
like sheep who go astray,
we have wandered from your paths of life and light.
We have heard the Shepherd's voice calling us
    by name,
but we have turned instead to our own way.

Show us your tender mercy;
restore us in the security of your fold.
Lead us back to still waters,
seat us again at your bounteous table.
Fill us with your Spirit,
that we might bear glad witness
to your saving mercy,
revealed to us in the Great Shepherd,
Jesus Christ, our Lord.

HYMNS FOR THE DAY

	HB	LBW	NCH	PH	RIL	TFF	WOV
GATHERING							
O That I Had a Thousand Voices	—	560	—	475	—	—	—
THE WORD							
A—O Christ, the Healer	—	360	175	380	—	—	—
E—Ye Servants of God, Your Master Proclaim	27	252	305	477	598	—	—
O When the Saints Go Marching In	—	—	—	—	—	180	—
G—Near to the Heart of God	—	—	—	527	—	—	—
The King of Love My Shepherd Is (Psalm 23)	106	456	248	171	266–7	—	—
THE EUCHARIST							
You Satisfy the Hungry Heart	—	—	—	521	—	—	711
SENDING							
God, Bless Your Church with Strength!	—	—	—	418	—	—	—

Fourth Sunday of Easter

Color: White/Gold

PSALM SETTINGS

METRICAL
Psalm 23, "As Faithful Shepherds Tend Their Flocks,"
  PSW, CMD, Morgan
METRICAL
"The King of Love My Shepherd Is," PH 171,
  8.7.8.7, Baker
RESPONSORIAL
"My Shepherd Is the Lord," PH 173, Moore/Gelineau
RESPONSORIAL
"The Lord Is My Shepherd," HP 1, p. 23,
  Daw/Hackett

MULTICULTURAL/CONTEMPORARY

Psalm—"My Shepherd Is the Lord," *Psalms of
  Patience, Protest and Praise,* GIA, John Bell
E—"He Is Exalted," W&P 55, Twila Paris
"Shall We Gather at the River," WOV 690/TFF 179,
  Robert Lowry
G—"Like a Shepherd," SATB, HIN, Carl Nygard Jr.
Other—"Now We Remain," W&P 106, David Haas
"You Hear the Lambs a-Cryin'," *The Courage to Say
  No,* GIA, arr. by John Bell
"You, Lord, Are Both Lamb and Shepherd,"
  HFTG 64

ANTHEMS

"The Lord Is My Shepherd," John Rutter, OXU,
  SATB and oboe
"My Shepherd Will Supply My Need," Mark Wilberg,
  HIN HMCM24, SATB with harp, flute, and oboe

MUSIC FOR THE SMALL CHURCH

"Loving Shepherd of Thy Sheep," Philip Ledger
  (SATB/organ), Dean-Lorenz, HRD 244

OTHER VOCAL MUSIC

"The Good Shepherd," Franz Schubert in *Sacred Duet
  Masterpieces,* Carl Fredrickson, CF RB59
"The Lord Is My Shepherd," Edwin T. Childs in *Art
  Songs of the Hymnal,* vol. 2, WMP AO5V203
"The Lord Is My Shepherd," Craig Courtney in *Psalm
  Settings of Craig Courtney,* VC9, BP
"The Lord Is My Shepherd," Samuel Liddle in *Sing
  Solo Sacred,* Neil Jenkins, OXU
"The King of Love My Shepherd Is," Beck/Courtney
  in *Hymn Settings of John Ness Beck,* BP VC4

ORGAN

Prelude on hymn tunes to which Psalm 23 is set:
BROTHER JAMES' AIR
  Searle Wright, "Prelude on BROTHER JAMES' AIR,"
  OXU (M)
CRIMOND
  Raymond Hann, *A Second Book of Contemplative
  Hymn Tune Preludes,* HF (M)
RESIGNATION
  Alice Jordan, *The Organist's Companion,* MCA (E)
Postlude on the hymn tune HANOVER
  Robert Powell, variations on HANOVER, *The
  Organist's Companion,* MCA (M-E)
  Kenneth Leighton, *Six Fantasies on Hymn Tunes,*
  BR (D)
  Flor Peeters, *Thirty Short Preludes,* CFP (E)

THE CONFESSION OF 1967

For today's selection, see p. 226.

May 9, 2004

LECTIONARY READINGS

Acts 11:1–18
Revelation 21:1–6
John 13:31–35

Psalm 148

CALL TO WORSHIP

Praise the Lord!
  Sing to God a new song.
May God's praise be heard
  in the assembly of the faithful.
Let the faithful exult in glory,
  let them sing for joy!
Let us praise God's name with dancing,
  making melody to God with tambourine
    and lyre.
  Praise the Lord!

PRAYER OF CONFESSION

God of love,
you call us to love one another,
just as Jesus loved us.
You ordain us to be one with each other,
even as the Father and the Son are one.
Yet we disown our sisters and brothers;
our divisions defame your good name.

Forgive us in your great mercy.
Baptize us anew with your Spirit of love,
with grace to accept those whom you accept,
to love those whom you love,
to forgive one another as you have forgiven us,
and to live and work in united witness;
through Jesus Christ, our risen Lord.

HYMNS FOR THE DAY

	HB	LBW	NCH	PH	RIL	TFF	WOV
GATHERING							
With Glad, Exuberant Carolings	—	—	—	490	—	—	—
THE WORD							
A—Spirit of the Living God	—	—	283	322	—	101	—
We Are Your People	—	—	309	436	419	—	—
E—Here, O Our Lord, We See You Face to Face	442	211	336	520	549	—	—
O Holy City, Seen of John	508	—	613	453	—	—	—
I Want to Be Ready	—	—	616	—	—	41	—
G—Jesu, Jesu, Fill Us with Your Love	—	—	498	367	—	83	765
THE EUCHARIST							
Living Word of God Eternal	—	—	—	512	—	—	—
SENDING							
Today We All Are Called to Be Disciples	—	—	—	434	—	—	—

Fifth Sunday of Easter

Color: White/Gold

PSALM SETTINGS

METRICAL
Psalm 148, "Praise God in the Highest Heaven,"
    PCW, 8.7.8.7.8.7, Morgan
RESPONSORIAL
"Alleluia!" P 155, Hopson

MULTICULTURAL/CONTEMPORARY

Psalm—"Rise, Children, Gonna Praise the Lord,"
    MS, Michael Burkhardt
"Shout to the Lord," IM, arr. by Daniel Smith
"Come, Let Us Sing with Joy to the Lord," WL,
    Paul Tate
"Lift Every Voice and Sing," AAHH 540
E—"One More Step," CG 100, Sydney Carter
"Soon and Very Soon," W&P 128/TFF 38/WOV
    744, Andraé Crouch
"The Uncloudy Day," AAHH 589
G—"Family Song," LUYH 5, Steve Hampton
"No Greater Love," Mar 54, Tommy Walker
"The Bond of Love," AAHH 521
"Lord, Help Us Walk Your Servant Way," HFTG 150

ANTHEMS

Gloria (from the *Heiligmesse*), F. J. Haydn, WAM
    W2031, SATB
"Let All the World in Every Corner Sing," Dominick
    Argento, BH 6041, SATB with two trumpets, two
    trombones, timpani, and organ

MUSIC FOR THE SMALL CHURCH

"Love One Another," John L. Bell (SAB),
    GIA G-5158
"And God Shall Wipe Away All Tears," Eleanor Daley
    (unison/keyboard), HIN HMC1284
"I Want to Be Ready," arr. by J. Jefferson Cleveland
    and Verolga Nix (SATB/solo), in *Songs of Zion*,
    151

OTHER VOCAL MUSIC

"I Want to Be Ready," *Your Favorite Spirituals*, SP,
    HE-13
"I Want to Be Ready," Phillip McIntyre in *Spirituals
    for Church and Concert*, HTF/FBM FO114

ORGAN

Prelude on the hymn tune MORNING SONG ("O Holy
    City, Seen of John")
    Theodore Beck, *The Concordia Hymn Prelude Series*,
        vol. 1, C (E)
    David N. Johnson, *Preludes and Postludes*, AF (E)
    Gardner Reed, *Eight Preludes on Old Southern
        Hymns*, HWG (M)
Postlude on the hymn "At the Lamb's High Feast"
    John Ferguson, "At the Lamb's High Feast,"
        MSM (M)
    Jan Bender, *Kleine Choralvorspiel*, BAR (M)
    Paul Manz, *Ten Chorale Improvisations*, C (E)

THE CONFESSION OF 1967

For today's selection, see p. 226.

May 16, 2004

LECTIONARY READINGS

Acts 16:9–15
Revelation 21:10, 21:22–25:5
John 14:23–29 or John 5:1–9

Psalm 67

CALL TO WORSHIP

Let the peoples praise you, O God,
  let all the peoples praise you.
Let the nations be glad and sing for joy,
  for you, O God, judge the people with equity,
  and guide the nations of the earth.
Let the peoples praise you, O God,
  let all the peoples praise you.
The earth has yielded its increase;
  God, our God, has blessed us.
  Let all the earth worship God's holy name!

PRAYER OF CONFESSION

God of grace and glory,
the wideness of your mercy
extends beyond all we could even imagine.
In kindness you have drawn us to yourself,
claiming us who were far from you
as your own beloved people.
Yet we refuse mercy to those who offend us,
to those who differ from us,
to those we deem unlovely or unworthy.

Forgive our rush to judgment;
by your Spirit, tenderize our hearts,
so that we would show mercy to others,
even as we have received mercy,
through Jesus Christ, our risen Lord.

HYMNS FOR THE DAY

	HB	LBW	NCH	PH	RIL	TFF	WOV
GATHERING							
Praise Ye the Lord, the Almighty	1	543	22	482	145	—	—
THE WORD							
A—My Hope Is Built on Nothing Less	368	293–4	403	379	459–0	192	—
Out of Deep, Unordered Water	—	—	—	494	—	—	—
E—Glorious Things of Thee Are Spoken	434	358	307	446	393	—	—
G—Come Down, O Love Divine	—	508	289	313	444	—	—
Blessed Jesus, at Your Word	—	248	74	454	530	—	—
I've Got Peace Like a River	—	—	478	—	—	258	—
THE EUCHARIST							
Now to Your Table Spread	—	—	—	515	—	—	—
SENDING							
O Master, Let Me Walk with Thee	304	492	503	357	428	—	—

Sixth Sunday of Easter

Color: White/Gold

PSALM SETTINGS

METRICAL
Psalm 67, "God of Mercy and Compassion," PCW,
    8.7.8.7.D, Morgan
RESPONSORIAL
"O God, Let All the Nations Praise You!" PH 202,
    Bevenot/Kremer

MULTICULTURAL/CONTEMPORARY

Gathering—"Alabare," WOV 791
E—"Just to Behold His Face," AAHH 584
Psalm—"God Be Merciful," MS, Paul Bouman
"God Has Smiled on Me," AAHH 152
G—"Make Me a Channel of Your Peace," LUYH 109,
    Sebastian Temple
"You Are Mine," W&P 158, David Haas
"I've Got Peace Like a River," AAHH 492
"May God's Love Be Fixed Above You," HFTG 130

ANTHEMS

"Peace I Leave with You," Walter Pelz, AF 11-1364,
    SATB
"Heavenly Light," A. Kopylow, CF CM497, SATB

MUSIC FOR THE SMALL CHURCH

"The Song of the Tree of Life," Ralph Vaughan
    Williams (unison or two-part, piano), OXU T37

OTHER VOCAL MUSIC

"O Master, Let Me Walk with Thee," Dale Wood in
    Songs of Reflection, SMP 30/1109S

ORGAN

Prelude and postlude on the hymn tune DOWN
    AMPNEY ("Come Down, O Love Divine")
    Ronald Arnatt, *The Parish Organist*, vol. 11, C (E)
    Jan Bender, *Four Variations for Organ on* DOWN
        AMPNEY, AF (M)
    John Gardner, *Five Hymn Tune Preludes*, OXU (M)
    Philip Gehring, *Six Hymn Tune Preludes*, C (M)
    Henry Ley, "Prelude on DOWN AMPNEY," OXU (M)

THE CONFESSION OF 1967

For today's selection, see p. 227.

May 20, 2004

LECTIONARY READINGS

Acts 1:1–11
Ephesians 1:15–23
Luke 24:44–53

Psalm 47 or 93

CALL TO WORSHIP

Clap your hands, all you peoples;
   shout to God with loud songs of joy!
For God, the Most High, is awesome,
   Lord over all the earth.
God has gone up with a shout,
   ascending with the sound of a trumpet.
Sing praises to God, sing praises,
   for God alone is to be worshiped! Amen.

PRAYER OF CONFESSION *(BCW)*

Almighty God,
you have raised Jesus from death to life,
and crowned him Lord of all.
We confess that we have not bowed before him,
or acknowledged his rule in our lives.
We have gone along with the ways of the world,
and failed to give him glory.

Forgive us,
and raise us from sin,
that we may be your faithful people,
obeying the commands of our Lord Jesus Christ,
who rules the world
and is head of the church, his body.

HYMNS FOR THE DAY

	HB	LBW	NCH	PH	RIL	TFF	WOV
GATHERING							
Come, Christians, Join to Sing	131	—	—	150	357	—	—
THE WORD							
A—Lord, You Give the Great Commission	—	—	—	429	—	—	756
E—At the Name of Jesus Every Knee Shall Bow	143	179	—	148	336	—	—
He Is Lord	—	—	—	—	—	95	—
G—A Hymn of Glory Let Us Sing	—	157	259	141	332	—	—
THE EUCHARIST							
Fairest Lord Jesus	135	518	44	306	370	—	—
SENDING							
Rejoice, Ye Pure in Heart!	407	553	55/71	145–6	—	—	—

Ascension of the Lord

Color: White/Gold

PSALM SETTINGS

PSALM 47
METRICAL
"Clap Your Hands, O Faithful People," PCW,
8.7.8.7.8.7.7, Morgan
RESPONSORIAL
"Sing Out Your Praise to God" P 42, Hopson

PSALM 93
METRICAL
"God, Our Lord, a King Remaining," PH 213,
8.7.8.7.4444.7.7, Keble
RESPONSORIAL
"The Lord Is King," P 87, Phillips

MULTICULTURAL/CONTEMPORARY

Gathering—"He Is King of Kings," PH 153
A— "Go Now in Peace and Serve the Lord," W&P
46, Handt Hanson
"With Thy Spirit Fill Me," AAHH 322
Psalm—"Shout to the Lord," W&P 124, Darlene
Zachech
"Sing a New Song to God," SNC 33, Keven Bylsma
E—"Looking Forward in Faith," CG 73, Andrea
Steele
"Open Our Eyes, Lord," Mar 59/W&P 113, Bob Cull
"Lift Him Up," AAHH 547
G—"Haven't You Heard?" CG 46, Alison Robertson
"We Will Glorify," AAHH 286
"Lift Up Your Hearts, Believers," HFTG 69

ANTHEMS

"At the Name of Jesus," R. Vaughan Williams, OXU
40P100, SATB
"All Hail the Power of Jesus' Name," arr. by John F.
Wilson, HP 5990, SATB with optional brass and
timpani

MUSIC FOR THE SMALL CHURCH

"Christ, the Glory," J. F. Lallouette, arr. by Richard
Proulx (two-part mixed voices/organ),
GUA G-2288

OTHER VOCAL MUSIC

"O Clap Your Hands," Don McAfee in *The Solo
Psalmist*, PP 98, SMP
"This Son So Young," Louie White in *A Solo Cantata
for High Voice*, harp and organ, HWG

ORGAN

Chorale prelude on HEUT' TRIUMPHIRET GOTTES SOHN
("Today God's Son Triumphs")
J. S. Bach, *Orgel büchlein*, various editions (M) [Have
the choir sing the chorale prior to the organ
prelude.]
Or Olivier Messaien, movements from *The Ascension
Suite*, DUR (E-D)
Postlude
Olivier Messaien, "Outburst of Joy," *The Ascension
Suite*, DUR (D)
On the hymn tune SALVA FESTA DIES ("Hail Thee,
Festival Day")
S. Drummond Wolff, *Processional for Easter,
Ascension and Pentecost*, organ and brass, C (E)
Ralph Vaughan Williams, *The Concordia Hymn
Prelude Series,* vol. 11, C (E)
On the hymn tune DIADEMATA ("Crown Him with
Many Crowns")
Wilbur Held, *Hymn Preludes for the Pentecost
Season*, C (M)
Alec Wyton, *A Little Christian Year*, CF (E)

May 23, 2004

LECTIONARY READINGS

Acts 16:16–34
Revelation 22:12–34, 16–17, 20–21
John 17:20–26

Psalm 97

CALL TO WORSHIP

God rules over all creation,
   let the earth rejoice; let the many coastlands be glad!
The heavens proclaim God's righteousness;
   and all the people behold God's glory.
For you, O God, are most high over all the earth;
   You are exalted far above all gods.
Let us rejoice in the Lord
   and give thanks to God's holy name!

PRAYER OF CONFESSION

Holy Creator and Judge of all,
you made us to enjoy open fellowship,
both with yourself and with one another.
As the Son and the Father are One,
so we are created to live together in perfect unity.
Yet we have rebelled against your authority,
and have turned against one another.

In mercy, forgive us, and spare us our due
   judgment.
Fill us anew with your Spirit,
that we would richly manifest your rule
of righteousness, peace, and joy;
so enable us to walk rightly before you,
in loving unity with one another,
fulfilling your good and holy purpose for us.

HYMNS FOR THE DAY

GATHERING	HB	LBW	NCH	PH	RIL	TFF	WOV
Father, We Praise Thee	43	267	90	459	515	—	—
THE WORD							
A—Take My Life and Let It Be	310	406	448	391	475	—	—
If Thou but Trust in God to Guide Thee	344	453	410	282	151	—	—
E—Glorious Things of Thee Are Spoken	434	358	307	446	393	—	—
He Is Lord	—	—	—	—	—	95	—
G—O Savior, in This Quiet Place	—	—	555	390	—	—	—
THE EUCHARIST							
Sheaves of Summer	—	338	518	—	—	—	—
SENDING							
Alleluia! Sing to Jesus!	—	158	257	144	346	—	—

Seventh Sunday of Easter

Color: White/Gold

PSALM SETTINGS

METRICAL
Psalm 97, "God Reigns! Let Earth Rejoice!" PCW,
    SMD, Morgan
RESPONSORIAL
Psalm 97, "Rejoice, Rejoice, Let All the Earth
    Rejoice," P 93, Hopson

MULTICULTURAL/CONTEMPORARY

A—"How Can I Keep from Singing," CG 51, Robert
    Lowry
"For God So Loved the World," AAHH 153
Psalm—"The Lord Will Hear the Just/Proclaim God's
    Marvelous Deeds," SATB, GIA, Kenneth W. Louis
E—"Soon and Very Soon," LUYH 42/CLUW
    385/W&P 128/SNC 106/AAHH 193, Andraé
    Crouch
"While We Are Waiting, Come," AAHH 190
G—"One Bread, One Body," LUYH 130/CLUW
    237/W&P 111, John Foley
"As the Grains of Wheat," W&P 10, David Haas
"O How I Love Jesus," AAHH 291
Other—"Bind Us Together," WOV 748/W&P 18,
    Bob Gilman
"For All the World," HFTG 34

ANTHEMS

"E'en So, Lord Jesus, Quickly Come," Paul Manz,
    C 98-1054, SATB
"Draw Us in the Spirit's Tether," Harold Friedell,
    HWG CMR. 2472, SATB

MUSIC FOR THE SMALL CHURCH

"Most Glorious Lord of Life," William H. Harris
    (unison/two-part/organ), OXU E12
"Behold, I Am Coming Soon," Thomas Gieschen
    (unison or SATB), AF 11-2441

OTHER VOCAL MUSIC

"Take My Life," Craig Courtney in *Master for the
    Music*, VC1, BP

ORGAN

Prelude on the hymn tune WESTMINSTER ABBEY
    ("Christ Is Made the Sure Foundation")
    David Johnson, *Wedding Music*, A (M)
    Christopher Steel, *Six from the Sixties*, OXU (D)
    Robert Wetzler, *Processional on* WESTMINSTER ABBEY,
    C (E)
Postlude on the hymn tune HYFRYDOL ("Alleluia, Sing
    to Jesus")
    Wilbur Held, *Preludes and Postludes*, AF (E)
    Paul Manz, *Ten Chorale Improvisations*, vol. 1,
    C (M)
    Frederick Swann, *Hymns of Praise and Power*,
    FBM (M)
    Ralph Vaughan Williams, *Three Preludes Founded
    on Welsh Tunes*, S&B (M)

THE CONFESSION OF 1967

For today's selection, see p. 227.

May 30, 2004

LECTIONARY READINGS

Acts 2:1–21 or Genesis 11:1–9
Romans 8:14–17 or Acts 2:1–21
John 14:8–17 (25–27)

Psalm 104:24–34, 35b

CALL TO WORSHIP

In the last days it shall come to pass
   God's Spirit is poured out on all flesh,
sons and daughters shall prophesy,
   young men shall see visions,
   and old men shall dream dreams,
On the captives, both men and women
   God's Spirit will be poured out
   and they shall prophesy
Let us call upon the name of the Lord,
   who alone has given us salvation.

PRAYER OF CONFESSION *(BCW)*

Almighty God,
you poured your Spirit upon gathered disciples
creating bold tongues, open ears,
and a new community of faith.
We confess that we hold back the force of your
   Spirit among us.
We do not listen for your word of grace,
speak the good news of your love,
or live as a people made one in Christ.

Have mercy on us, O God.
Transform our timid lives by the power of your
   Spirit,
and fill us with a flaming desire to be your faithful
   people,
doing your will for the sake of Jesus Christ our
   Lord.

HYMNS FOR THE DAY

	HB	LBW	NCH	PH	RIL	TFF	WOV
GATHERING							
Come Sing, O Church, in Joy!	—	—	—	430	—	—	—
THE WORD							
A—Come, Holy Spirit, Our Souls Inspire	237	472–3	268	125	385	—	—
O Day Full of Grace	—	161	—	—	—	—	—
E—Come, O Spirit, with Your Sound	—	—	265	127	—	—	—
Holy Spirit, Light Divine	—	—	—	—	—	104	—
G—Come, Holy Spirit, Heavenly Dove	239	475	281	126	—	—	—
Like the Murmur of the Dove's Song	—	—	270	314	—	—	685
THE EUCHARIST							
Draw Us in the Spirit's Tether	—	—	337	504	—	—	703
There's a Sweet, Sweet Spirit in This Place	—	—	293	—	—	102	—
SENDING							
Wind Who Makes All Winds That Blow	—	—	271	131	—	—	—

Day of Pentecost

Color: Red

PSALM SETTINGS

METRICAL
"Your Spirit, O Lord, Makes Life to Abound," PH
    104, 10.10.11.11, *The Psalter* (1912)
RESPONSORIAL
"Lord, Send Out Your Spirit," P 105, Proulx

MULTICULTURAL/CONTEMPORARY

Gathering—"Wa, Wa, Wa Emimino (Come, O Holy
    Spirit Come)," WOV 681
A—"Come, Holy Spirit," LUYH 133, Iona Community
"Wind of the Spirit," W&P 157, Handt Hanson
"One Day," AAHH 235
Psalm— "Like the Murmur," spiritual song, CG 71,
    Peter Cutts
"Renew Thy Church, Her Ministries Restore,"
    AAHH 343
E—"Lord, Listen to Your Children," SATB, HP, Ken
    Medema, arr. by Jack Schrader
"Loving Spirit," CG 81, David Dell
"How Can You Recognize a Child of God?" AAHH 266
G—"Walk in the Spirit," LLB, SATB
"Every Time I Feel the Spirit," PH 315
"You Are Mine," W&P 158, David Haas
"Holy Spirit, with Light Divine," AAHH 315
"God Is Unique and One," HFTG 111

ANTHEMS

"I Will Sing with the Spirit," John Rutter, HIN
    HMC-1386, SATB
"Walking in the Spirit," Mark Hayes, HIN
    HMC-1036, SATB

MUSIC FOR THE SMALL CHURCH

"Wa Wa Wa Emimimo (Come, O Holy Spirit,
    Come)," Yoruba song (two-part choir or congrega-
    tion, leader), in C. Michael Hawn, *Halle Halle: We
    Sing the World Round*, CG CGC42, 38

"The Lone, Wild Bird," Dan Locklair (unison/organ),
    GIA G-2392
"Pentecost," arr. by Mark Schweizer (two-part, hand-
    bells, keyboard, optional percussion), in *The
    Sewanee Composer's Project*, vol. 7, SJM, 108

OTHER VOCAL MUSIC

"Spirit of Faith Come Down," Mary Jackson,
    BEALOTH, *Sweet Singer/Hymns of Charles Wesley*,
    Steven Kimbrough, CHM

ORGAN

Prelude on the plainsong VENI CREATOR SPIRITUS
    ("Come Holy Spirit")
    Maurice Duruflé, *Choral Variè Veni Creator*, DUR
        (M-D) [Choir can sing stanzas of the hymn
        between variations.]
    Nicolas de Gringy, VENI CREATOR SPIRITUS, various
        editions (M-D) [Choir can sing stanzas of the
        hymn between variations.]
    Wilbur Held, *Hymn Preludes for the Pentecost
        Season*, C (M)
    J. S. Bach, "Choral Prelude on KOMM, GOTT
        SCHÖPHER," various editions (M) [Choir can sing
        the chorale KOMM, GOTT SCHÖPHER as introit.]
Postlude
    Maurice Duruflé (final variation from VENI CREATOR)
    J. S. Bach (as in prelude)
    Flor Peeters, *Ten Chorale Preludes on Gregorian
        Hymns*, BSS (M-D)
    Paul Manz, *Ten Chorale Improvisations*, vol. 1, C (E)
    Olivier Messaien, "The Holy Trinity," movement
        based on the Spirit, DUR (M-D)

THE CONFESSION OF 1967

For today's selection, see p. 227.

June 6, 2004

LECTIONARY READINGS

Proverbs 8:1–4, 22–31
Romans 5:1–5
John 16:12–15

Psalm 8

CALL TO WORSHIP

Holy, holy, holy,
  Lord God Almighty!
How majestic is Your name,
  in all the earth!
Praise be to the Father, Son, and Holy Spirit,
  one God who calls us to be one people!
O Lord, our God, how majestic is your name
  in all the earth!

PRAYER OF CONFESSION *(BCW)*

God of grace, love, and communion,
we confess that we have failed to love you
with all our heart, soul, and mind;
and to love our neighbor as ourselves.
We ignore your commandments,
stray from your way, and follow other gods.

Have mercy on us.
Forgive our sin and raise us to new life
that we may serve you faithfully
and give honor to your holy name.

HYMNS FOR THE DAY

GATHERING	HB	LBW	NCH	PH	RIL	TFF	WOV
Holy God, We Praise Your Name	—	535	276	460	619	—	—
Holy, Holy, Holy! Lord God Almighty!	11	165	277	138	611	—	—
Come, All You People	—	—	—	—	—	138	717
THE WORD							
O—Immortal, Invisible, God Only Wise	85	526	1	263	7	—	—
E—Hope of the World	—	493	46	360	414	—	—
G—Sovereign Lord of All Creation	—	—	—	136	—	—	—
We All Believe in One True God	—	374	—	137	609	—	—
THE EUCHARIST							
Holy, Holy	—	—	—	140	—	289	—
SENDING							
Creating God, Your Fingers Trace	—	—	462	134	—	—	—

Trinity Sunday

Color: White

PSALM SETTINGS

METRICAL
"O Lord, Our God, How Excellent," PH 162, CM,
Anderson
METRICAL
"Lord, Our Lord, Thy Glorious Name," PH 163,
7.7.7.7, *The Psalter* (1912)
RESPONSORIAL
"O Lord, Our Governor," HP 1, p. 87, Daw/Hackett

MULTICULTURAL/CONTEMPORARY

Gathering— "Come, All You People," SNC 4, arr. by
John Bell
Psalm—"O Lord, Our Lord," Scottish traditional
from *Psalms of Patience, Protest and Praise,* GIA
"O Lord, How Excellent," AAHH 290
E—"When Our Confidence Is Shaken," CG 145,
David Lambert
"Blessings in the Love," AAHH 620
"When the Storms of Life Are Raging," SNC 200,
Albert Tindley
G—"Come, Spirit Come," LUYH 151, Walt Harrah
"Holy Ghost, with Light Divine," AAHH 315
"Let Your Spirit Teach Me, Lord," HFTG 13

ANTHEMS

"How Excellent Is Thy Name," Eugene Butler, BOU
837, SSAATB
"Come, Gracious Spirit," Dale Wood, AF 11-1571,
SATB

MUSIC FOR THE SMALL CHURCH

"Mighty God, Who Called Creation," Sally Ann
Morris (unison), in *Giving Thanks in Song and
Prayer,* 32

OTHER VOCAL MUSIC

"Trinity Sunday," Carl Smith in *Four George Herbert
Songs,* MS MSM, 40-905
"Lord, to Thee Do I Lift My Soul," Antonio Vivaldi
in *Solos for the Church Year,* Lloyd Pfautsch,
LG/GS

ORGAN

Based on the hymn tune GROSSER GOTT ("Holy God
We Praise Your Name")
See prelude suggestions for the Fifth Sunday in
Ordinary Time.
Or Jean Langlais, *Meditations on the Holy Trinity,*
DUR (M-D)
Olivier Messaien, quieter movements from the Holy
Trinity, DUR (M-D)
Postlude on the hymn tune NICEA ("Holy, Holy, Holy
Lord God Almighty")
Healey Willan, *Thirty-Six Short Preludes and
Postludes on Well-Known Hymn Tunes,* P (M)
Calvin Hampton, *The Church Organist's Library,*
MCA (M)
S. Drummond Wolff, Processional for Trinity on
"Holy, Holy" with brass, C (E)
Vachlav Nelhybel, NICEA, organ and brass,
AGP (M-E)
Or J. S. Bach, "Fugue in E-Flat," various editions (D)

THE CONFESSION OF 1967

For today's selection, see p. 227.

June 13, 2004

LECTIONARY READINGS

1 Kings 21:1–10 (11–14) 15–21a
Galatians 2:15–21
Luke 7:36–8:3

Psalm 5:1–8

CALL TO WORSHIP

Give ear to my words, O Lord,
  give heed to my sighing.
Listen to the sound of our cry,
  for to you alone do we pray.
O Lord, in the morning you hear my voice,
  in the morning I plead my case to you and watch.
Lead us, O God, in your righteousness.
  Make your way straight before us.
Let all who take refuge in you rejoice,
  let them ever sing for joy.
For you bless the righteous, O God,
  You cover them with favor.
  Let the whole assembly worship the Lord!

PRAYER OF CONFESSION

Gracious God,
even though you have given us all we need,
we resent the blessings you have given to others.
Our ingratitude deserves your righteous judgment;
yet we call upon you to forgive us in tender mercy.

Holy Christ, live in us by your Spirit.
Give us faith to trust in your goodness,
whatever our circumstance;
to walk with you in paths of service,
wherever you lead;
and to love you and our neighbors,
regardless of the cost;
to the glory of God.

HYMNS FOR THE DAY

GATHERING	HB	LBW	NCH	PH	RIL	TFF	WOV
O for a Thousand Tongues to Sing	141	559	42	466	362–3	—	—
THE WORD							
O—Wild and Lone the Prophet's Voice	—	—	—	409	—	—	—
E—Alas, and Did My Savior Bleed	199	98	199–0	78	—	71	—
Just as I Am, Without One Plea	272	296	207	370	467–8	—	—
G—Hear the Good News of Salvation	—	—	—	355	—	—	—
I Heard the Voice of Jesus Say	280	497	489	—	—	62	—
Said Judas to Mary	—	—	210	—	—	—	—
THE EUCHARIST							
My Faith Looks Up to Thee	378	479	—	383	446	—	—
SENDING							
I Come with Joy to Meet My Lord	—	—	349	507	534	—	—

Eleventh Sunday in Ordinary Time

Color: Green

PSALM SETTINGS

METRICAL
"As Morning Dawns," PH 161, LM, Anderson
RESPONSORIAL
Psalm 5, "Give Ear to All My Words," P 4, Hopson

MULTICULTURAL/CONTEMPORARY

Psalm—"Lord, My Strength," W&P 93, Dean
    Krippaehne
"Psalm 5," Mar 143, Bill Sprouse
"Precious Lord, Take My Hand," AAHH 471
E—"Grace," SATB, arr. by Mark Hayes, BP
"For by Grace," W&P 38, Thomas Ian Nicholas
"Only by Grace," W&P 112, Gerritt Gustafson
"Since Jesus Came into My Heart," AAHH 499
"Jesus, I Believe," Mar 130, Bill Batstone
G—"Will You Come and Follow Me," SATB, GIA,
    arr. by John Bell,
"Completely Yes," AAHH 551
"You, Lord," W&P 162, Handt Hanson

ANTHEMS

"The Best of Rooms," Randall Thompson, ECSP
    2672, SATB
"Hear Me, O Lord," Franz Schubert/Klein, Neil Kjos
    5480, SATB

MUSIC FOR THE SMALL CHURCH

"Drop, Drop, Slow Tears," Richard Shephard (two-
    part/organ), in *Canons & Crotchets: The York
    Minister Two-Part Anthem Book*, SJM, 31

OTHER VOCAL MUSIC

"O For a Thousand Tongues to Sing," Mary Jackson,
    AZMON in *Sweet Singer/Hymns by Charles Wesley*,
    Steven Kimbrough, CHM

ORGAN

Prelude on the chorale HERR JESU CHRIST ("Lord Jesus
    Christ Be Present Now")
    J. S. Bach, several settings, various editions (E-M)
    Jan Bender, *Kleine Choralvospiele*, BAR (E)
    Paul Manz, *Ten Chorale Improvisations*, vol. 3 and
        2, C (M)
    Max Reger, *Thirty Short Chorale Preludes*, CFP (E)
    Introit: Using the first stanza of the chorale:
        Lord Jesus Christ be present now, and let Your
            Holy Spirit bow
        all hearts in love and awe today to hear the truth
            and keep your way.
Postlude on the hymn tune BRESLAU ("Take Up Your
    Cross")
    David Willcoks, *Variations on Breslau*, OXU (D)
    Johann Walther, *The Parish Organist*, vol. 1, C (E)
    Max Reger, *Choralvorspiele*, BB (M)
J. S. Bach, one of the "Prelude and Fugues in
    G Major" (various editions) (E-M-D)

THE CONFESSION OF 1967

For today's selection, see p. 228.

June 20, 2004

LECTIONARY READINGS

1 Kings 19:1–4 (5–7) 8–15a
Galatians 3:23–29
Luke 8:26–39

Psalms 42 and 43

CALL TO WORSHIP

As a deer longs for flowing streams,
  so my soul longs for you, O God.
My soul thirsts for God,
  for the living God.
When shall I come and behold the face of God?
  My tears have been my food day and night,
Hope in God,
  even in distress we turn to You, O Lord,
  our help and our God.

PRAYER OF CONFESSION

Redeeming God,
through Jesus you have come
to set us free from sin and death.
Still, we cling to old ways of bondage,
rather than embracing your freedom.

Forgive us, merciful Savior;
for though we long for you,
we reject the liberation you offer us.
Open our eyes to the gift of your freedom;
and give us strength to stand firm in it.
Open our hearts to the depth of your love,
and stir us to love as we have been loved.
Unite us in the love and freedom of the Spirit,
that we may display your Good News to all.

HYMNS FOR THE DAY

	HB	LBW	NCH	PH	RIL	TFF	WOV
GATHERING							
O That I Had a Thousand Voices	—	560	—	475	—	—	—
THE WORD							
O—O God, Thou Faithful God	—	—	—	277	69	—	—
Lord, Why Have You Forsaken Me	—	—	—	168	—	—	—
E—Baptized in Water	—	—	—	492	—	—	693
In Christ There Is No East or West	479	359	394–5	439–0	410	214	—
The Church of Christ in Every Age	—	433	306	421	—	—	—
G—O Christ, the Healer	—	360	175	380	—	—	—
Live into Hope	—	—	—	332	—	—	—
THE EUCHARIST							
For the Bread Which You Have Broken	—	200	—	508–9	547	—	—
SENDING							
God of Grace and God of Glory	358	415	436	420	416	—	—

Twelfth Sunday in Ordinary Time

Color: Green

PSALM SETTINGS

METRICAL
"As Deer Long for the Streams," PH 189, LM, Webber

RESPONSORIAL
"My Soul Is Thirsting for the Lord," PH 190, Mews/Gelineau

MULTICULTURAL/CONTEMPORARY

O—"You Are My Hiding Place," W&P 160/Mar 160, Michael Ledner

"Blessed Quietness," AAHH 374

Psalm—"As the Deer," W&P 9, Martin Nystrom

"Hush! Hush! My Soul," AAHH 450

"Just as a Lost and Thirsty Deer," *Psalms of Patience, Protest and Praise*, GIA, John Bell

E—"One Bread, One Body," WOV 710/CG 98, John Foley

"In Christ There Is No East or West," AAHH 398

G—"Take, O Take Me as I Am," SNC 215, John Bell

ANTHEMS

"Like as the Hart Desireth the Waterbrooks," Herbert Howells, OXU 42.066, SATB and soprano solo

"Thy Perfect Love," John Rutter, OXU E 137, SATB

MUSIC FOR THE SMALL CHURCH

"Silence, Frenzied, Unclean Spirit," Carol Doran (unison), in *New Hymns for the Lectionary to Glorify the Maker's Name,* OXU 25

"Healer of Our Every Ill," Marty Haugen (SATB/congregation/c instrument/keyboard), GIA G-3478

OTHER VOCAL MUSIC

"Out of the Depths," Eugene Butler in *The Solo Psalmist*, PP 98, SMP

ORGAN

Introduce the hymn tune BRIDEGROOM to the text "Like the Murmur of the Dove's Song" (various new hymnals, copyrighted by HP)

Sue Mitchell Wallace, *Hymn Prisms*, HP (E)

Choral Call to Worship: Have the choir sing the verses of "Like the Murmur" and the congregation sing the end of each stanza of "Come, Holy Spirit, Come."

Postlude on the chorale LIEBSTER JESU ("Blessed Jesus, at Your Word")

J. S. Bach, *Orgelbüchlein,* various editions (E)

Flor Peteers, *Hymn Preludes for the Liturgical Year,* CFP (M)

Johann Walther, collected works, various editions (E)

Or J. S. Bach, "Prelude and Fugue in A Major," various editions (M)

THE CONFESSION OF 1967

For today's selection, see p. 228.

June 27, 2004

LECTIONARY READINGS

2 Kings 2:1–2, 6–14
Galatians 5:1, 13–25
Luke 9:51–62

Psalm 77:1–2, 11–20

CALL TO WORSHIP

Let us call to mind the deeds of the Lord,
  we will remember Your wonders of old.
We will meditate on your work,
  and muse on your mighty deeds.
Your way, O God, is holy,
  what god is so great as our God?
You are the God who works wonders;
  You have displayed your might among the
      peoples,
  and we have come to worship You!

PRAYER OF CONFESSION

Mighty deliverer,
you open to us the highways of freedom,
yet we stay on familiar paths of bondage.
When Jesus calls us to follow,
we try to justify our desire our own way.
We are neither ready nor fit for your service.
Still, you claim us as your own.

In mercy, forgive us,
renew us, empower us—
that we may live by the Spirit,
bearing good fruit to your honor and glory.

HYMNS FOR THE DAY

	HB	LBW	NCH	PH	RIL	TFF	WOV
GATHERING							
I Sing the Mighty Power of God	84	—	12	288	10	—	—
THE WORD							
O—Many and Great, O God, Are Thy Things	—	—	3	271	—	—	—
E—Make Me a Captive, Lord	308	—	—	378	442	—	—
O Jesus, I Have Promised	307	503	493	388	—	—	—
G—When We Are Tempted to Deny Your Son	—	—	—	86	—	—	—
Take Up Your Cross, the Savior Said	293	398	204	393	—	—	—
I Can Hear My Savior Calling	—	—	—	—	—	146	—
THE EUCHARIST							
Spirit of God, Descend Upon My Heart	236	486	290	326	445	—	—
SENDING							
Eternal God, Whose Power Upholds	485	—	—	412	481	—	—

Thirteenth Sunday in Ordinary Time

Color: Green

PSALM SETTINGS

METRICAL

"I Cried Out to God to Help Me," PsH 77,
8.8.7.7.D, Otte/Goudimel

RESPONSORIAL

Psalm 77, "I Remember Your Deeds, O My God,"
P 66, Hughes

MULTICULTURAL/CONTEMPORARY

O—"Shine, Jesus Shine," WOV 651/W&P 123,
Graham Kendrick

"Draw Me into Your Presence," Mar 23, Teresa Muller

Psalm—"Rock of Ages," AAHH 559

E—"Spirit of the Living God," W&P 129/PH 322,
Daniel Iverson

"Spirit of God, Unseen as the Wind," CG 117,
Scottish folk melody

"Spirit Song," SNC 212, John Wimber

"Lead Me, Guide Me," TFF 70/AAHH 474

G—"The Summons," W&P 137, John Bell

"Guide My Feet, Lord," SATB, HP, arr. by John
Carter

"O Christ, Who Called the Twelve," HFTG 55

ANTHEMS

"I Want Jesus to Walk with Me," spiritual arr. by
Moses Hogan, HL 08740785, SATB and solo

"Lo, There Came a Fiery Chariot," from *Elijah* by
Mendelssohn, GS, SATB

MUSIC FOR THE SMALL CHURCH

"Freedom Is Coming," arr. by Henry H. Leck
(SATB), in *Two South African Freedom Songs*,
WAM W1248-1

"Come, Follow Me," John Leavitt (SAB/organ/oboe),
GIA G-3028

"The Summons (Will You Come and Follow Me?),"
John L. Bell, (unison), GIA

OTHER VOCAL MUSIC

"Spirit of God, Descend Upon My Heart," Ron
Harris in *Art Songs of the Hymnal*, vol. 3, WMP

ORGAN

Prelude based on Ralph Vaughan-Williams's "The
Call" from *Five Mystical Songs*
Organ: Charles Heaton, *The Concordia Hymn
Prelude Series*, vol. 39, C
Solo for baritone (or alto) from *Five Mystical Songs*
Organ: Alec Wyton, *The Bristol Collection*,
HF (E)

Postlude based on the hymn tune SONG 34 ("Forth in
Your Name, O Lord")
Walter Pelz, *The Concordia Hymn Prelude Series*,
vol. 38, C (E)
Charles V. Stanford, *Six Short Preludes and Postludes
for Organ*, GM (M)

Or J. S. Bach, "Prelude and Fugue in A Major," various editions (M)

THE CONFESSION OF 1967

For today's selection, see p. 228.

July 4, 2004

LECTIONARY READINGS

2 Kings 5:1–14
Galatians 6:(1–6) 7–16
Luke 10:1–11, 16–20

Psalm 30

CALL TO WORSHIP

Sing praises and give thanks to God
   You, God's faithful ones.
Let us give thanks to God
   and praise God's holy name.
For God has turned our mourning into dancing
   and has clothed us with joy.
O Lord, our God, we will give thanks to you
   forever and ever! Amen.

PRAYER OF CONFESSION

God of mercy and justice,
you turn mourning into dancing,
darkness into light,
sorrow into joy.
Yet we look to our own wisdom to guide us;
we rely on our own strength to protect us.

In mercy, forgive us.
Empower us by your Spirit
to entrust ourselves fully to your way,
that we may faithfully display and proclaim
the good news of your abundant goodness,
through Jesus Christ, our Lord.

HYMNS FOR THE DAY

	HB	LBW	NCH	PH	RIL	TFF	WOV
GATHERING							
Stand Up and Bless the Lord	—	—	—	491	499	—	
THE WORD							
O—O God, in a Mysterious Way	112	483	412	270	36	—	—
E—In the Cross of Christ I Glory	195	104	193–4	84	297–8	—	—
Lord, Make Us Servants of Your Peace	—	—	—	374	—	—	—
G—Lord, You Give the Great Commission	—	—	—	429	—	—	756
All Who Love and Serve Your City	—	436	—	413	485	—	—
THE EUCHARIST							
Jesus, Thou Joy of Loving Hearts	215	356	329	510	273	—	—
God the Sculptor of the Mountains	—	—	—	—	—	222	—
SENDING							
Lead On, O King Eternal	332	495	573	447	423	—	—

Fourteenth Sunday in Ordinary Time

Color: Green

PSALM SETTINGS

METRICAL
"Come Sing to God," PH 181, CMD, Anderson
RESPONSORIAL
"Sing Praise to the Lord," P 27, Hopson/Byrd

MULTICULTURAL/CONTEMPORARY

Psalm—"Mourning into Dancing," W&P 99,
Tommy Walker
"He Lifted Me," AAHH 232
E—"At the Foot of the Cross," W&P 11, Derek Bond
"At the Cross," AAHH 264
"I Come to the Cross," Mar 122, Bill Batstone
G—"Glory and Praise to Our God," W&P 43, Daniel
Schutte
"Here I Am," Mar 115, Bill Batstone
"As You Go, Tell the World," AAHH 633
"Not Alone, but Two by Two," HFTG 83

ANTHEMS

"Lift High the Cross," Nicholson/Larson, HF A-6735,
SATB with optional brass
"I Have Longed for Thy Saving Health," William
Byrd/Alfred Whitehead, HWG, CMR 1679,
SATB

MUSIC FOR THE SMALL CHURCH

"O Christ, Who Called the Twelve," Sally Ann Morris
(unison), in *Giving Thanks in Song and Prayer*,
GIA G-4930, 16

OTHER VOCAL MUSIC

"Great Peace Have They," Jean Baptiste Lully in
Sacred Duet Masterpieces, CF

ORGAN

Prelude based on the hymn tune ROCKINGHAM
("When I Survey the Wondrous Cross")
Robert Powel, *Eleven Chorale Preludes on Hymn
Tunes*, HF (M)
Healey Willan, *Thirty-Six Short Preludes and
Postludes on Well-Known Hymn Tunes* (E)
Postlude on ABBOT'S LEIGH, ("Lord, You Give the
Great Commission")
Austin Lovelace, ABBOT'S LEIGH, HPC (M)
Kimberly Patterson, *The Concordia Hymn Prelude
Series*, 19, C (E)b

THE CONFESSION OF 1967

For today's selection, see p. 228.

July 11, 2004

LECTIONARY READINGS

Amos 7:7–17
Colossians 1:1–14
Luke 10:25–37

Psalm 82

CALL TO WORSHIP

Let us give thanks to God,
Who has enabled us to share in the inheritance
  Of the saints in light.
O God, we praise you,
  For you have delivered us out of darkness
And transformed us
  into the kingdom of your beloved Son,
For all things, in heaven and on earth
  Are reconciled through Christ
  who made peace through the blood of his cross.
Who lives and reigns with you and the Holy Spirit,
  One God forever and ever. Amen.

PRAYER OF CONFESSION

God of all compassion,
you call us to show your kindness
to neighbors and strangers alike,
even as you have shown us your tender mercy,
in Jesus Christ, who rescued us from darkness.
Yet we pass by the needy you call us to serve,
leaving your ministry of mercy to others.

Have mercy on us, O Lord.
Stir up in us your Spirit of mercy,
that we may gladly aid those in distress,
even as you have been merciful to us.
Make us beacons of your hope, comfort,
  and justice,
that the poor and needy may know
the good news of your reign.

HYMNS FOR THE DAY

GATHERING	HB	LBW	NCH	PH	RIL	TFF	WOV
To God Be the Glory	—	—	—	485	355	264	—
THE WORD							
O—What Does the Lord Require	—	—	—	405	176	—	—
E—Called as Partners in Christ's Service	—	—	495	343	—	—	—
Celebrate with Joy and Singing	—	—	—	107	—	—	—
G—Jesu, Jesu, Fill Us with Your Love	—	—	498	367	—	83	765
We Meet You, O Christ	—	—	—	311	—	—	—
THE EUCHARIST							
Fill My Cup	—	—	—	350	—	—	—
SENDING							
Lord, Whose Love through Humble Service	—	423	—	427	—	—	—

Fifteenth Sunday in Ordinary Time

Color: Green

PSALM SETTINGS

METRICAL
"God Stands in Heaven's Council Hall," NMP,
    p. 130, LMD, Webber
RESPONSORIAL
"Arise, O God, and Rule the Earth," HP 2, p. 84,
    Daw/Hackett

MULTICULTURAL/CONTEMPORARY

Psalm—"God Leads Us Along," AAHH 136
E—"God Has Smiled on Me," LUYV 69/SNC 191,
    Isaiah Jones Jr.
"Look Forward in Faith," CG 73, Andrea Steele
"Through the Blood," AAHH 259
G—"Send Me, Jesus," WOV 773/Renew 308, South
    African
"The Living Church," AAHH 523
"Stop by, Lord," Doris Wesley Bettis, GIA Pub, SATB
Other—"Help Me, Jesus," Bonnemere TFF 224
"We Sing Your Praise, O Christ," HFTG 93

ANTHEMS

"Draw Us in the Spirit's Tether," HF, HWG
    CM4-2472, SATB
"Blessed Is the Man," Jane Marshall, HIN HMC-627,
    SATB

MUSIC FOR THE SMALL CHURCH

"Listen to the Cloud That Brightens," Carol Doran
    (unison) in *New Hymns for the Lectionary to
    Glorify the Maker's Name*, OXU, 42

OTHER VOCAL MUSIC

"Acquaint Now Thyself with Him," Michael Head,
    BH

ORGAN

J. S. Bach, Partita on O GOD THOU FAITHFUL GOD,
    various editions (ME-MD)
Or prelude on the hymn tune AZMON ("O for a
    Thousand Tongues")
    Alec Wyton, *Preludes and Fanfares*, SMP (M)
    Paul Manz, *Ten Chorale Improvisations*, vol. 9,
        C (M) [Suggestion: As an introit on the tune
        have the choir or soloist sing stanzas interspersed
        with variant harmonizations by John Ferguson,
        Hymn Harmonizations, Ludwid Music (M)]
Postlude
    J. S. Bach, final partite, O GOD THOU FAITHFUL
        GOD (MD)
Or on the gregorian melody UBI CARITAS ("Where
    Charity and Love Prevail")
    Dom Paul Benoit, *Pièces d'Orgue*, JFB (M) [A
        soloist could sing several stanzas of the hymn text
        "Where Charity and Love Prevail" unaccompa-
        nied to the gregorian tune.]

THE CONFESSION OF 1967

For today's selection, see p. 228.

July 18, 2004

LECTIONARY READINGS

Amos 8:1–12
Colossians 1:15–28
Luke 10:38–42

Psalm 52

CALL TO WORSHIP

Christ is the image of the invisible God,
   the firstborn of all creation,
for in Christ all things in heaven and on earth were
   created,
   things visible and invisible,
Christ is before all things,
   and in him all things hold together,
for all things, in heaven and on earth
   are reconciled to God through Christ.
   Alleluia! Amen!

PRAYER OF CONFESSION

God of our salvation,
in Jesus Christ you show us your fullness
of grace, beauty, and truth.
Yet we are distracted by many things,
while we neglect the one thing needful—
to know him, love him, and serve him.

Forgive us for turning away from the One
through whom you seek and save the lost.
Pour out your Spirit upon us,
that we may know Christ more fully,
and be made ambassadors of the good news,
that in Christ you give the world
a sure hope of glory.

HYMNS FOR THE DAY

GATHERING	HB	LBW	NCH	PH	RIL	TFF	WOV
I Greet Thee, Who My Sure Redeemer Art	144	—	251	457	366	—	—
THE WORD							
O—O God of Earth and Altar	511	428	582	291	80	—	—
My Lord! What a Morning	—	—	—	449	—	40	627
E—Christ, You Are the Fullness	—	—	—	346	—	—	—
G—Blessed Jesus, at Your Word	—	248	74	454	530	—	—
They Crucified my Savior	—	—	—	—	90	—	—
THE EUCHARIST							
Jesus, the Very Thought of Thee	401	316	507	310	—	—	—
SENDING							
Guide Me, O Thou Great Jehovah	339	343	18–9	281	50	—	—

Sixteenth Sunday in Ordinary Time

Color: Green

PSALM SETTINGS

METRICAL
"Mighty Mortal, Boasting Evil," PsH 52, 8.7.8.7.D,
   Otte/Butler
RESPONSORIAL
"Lord, You Are My Strength," P 50, Presbyterian 8

MULTICULTURAL/CONTEMPORARY

Psalm—"How Can I Keep from Singing?" LUYH 34,
   Robert Lowry
"Just When I Need Him," AAHH 379
G—"We Have Come into His House," AAHH
   174/TFF 136, Bruce Ballinger
"Lord, Grant Us Grace to Know the Time,"
   HFTG 142

ANTHEMS

"The Best of Rooms," Randall Thompson,
   E. C. Schirmer, ECS No. 2672, SATB
"God Is Our Refuge and Strength," Kenneth Pool,
   BRM 564, SSAATTBB

MUSIC FOR THE SMALL CHURCH

"The Best of Rooms," Charles Wood (two-part,
   piano), in *The Sewanee Composer's Project*,
   vol. 2, 39

OTHER VOCAL MUSIC

"My Lord, What a Morning," in *Your Favorite
   Spirituals*, SP
"My Lord, What a Morning," Mark Hayes in *Ten
   Spirituals for Solo Voice*, AP

ORGAN

Prelude on the hymn tune SLANE ("Be Thou My
   Vision")
   Paul Manz, *Ten Chorale Improvisations*, vol. 9, C (E)
   Jan Bender, *Variations on SLANE Organ and Violin*,
   AF (D)
   Alice Jordan, *The Organist's Companion*, BM (M)
Postlude on the chorale LIEBSTER JESU ("Blessed Jesus,
   at Your Word")
   J. S. Bach, several settings, various editions (E-M)
   Jan Bender, *Kleine Choralvorspiele*, Barenreitter (E)
   Egil Hovland, *Orgelkoraler*, L (M)
   Johann Walther, *Chorale Preludes of the Old Masters*,
   CFP (E)

THE CONFESSION OF 1967

For today's selection, see p. 229.

July 25, 2004

LECTIONARY READINGS

Hosea 1:2–10
Colossians 2:6–15
Luke 11:1–13

Psalm 85

CALL TO WORSHIP

Steadfast love and faithfulness will meet;
  righteousness and peace will kiss each other.
Faithfulness will spring up from the ground,
  and righteousness will look down from the sky.
God will give what is good,
  and the land will yield its increase.
Righteousness will go before the Lord,
and will make a path for our God's steps.

PRAYER OF CONFESSION

God of steadfast love,
you call us to serve and love you alone;
yet we bow to interests of wealth and power,
and long after that which does not last.
Still you claim us as your own,
ever calling us back to yourself.

In mercy, heal our crooked ways.
Restore us to live as you intend,
in steadfast love and faithfulness,
in righteousness and peace;
that we may display to the world around us
the glory of your coming kingdom,
where your will is done,
on earth as it is in heaven.

HYMNS FOR THE DAY

GATHERING	HB	LBW	NCH	PH	RIL	TFF	WOV
O Day of Radiant Gladness	70	251	66	470	511	—	—
We Have Come into His House	—	—	—	—	—	136	—
THE WORD							
O—Have Mercy on Us, Living Lord	—	—	—	195	—	—	—
O God of Every Nation	—	416	—	289	—	—	—
E—We Know That Christ Is Raised and Dies No More	189	—	495	528	—	—	—
Hail Thee, Festival Day!	—	142	262	120	—	—	—
Jesus, We Are Gathered	—	—	—	—	—	140	—
G—Let All Who Pray the Prayer Christ Taught	—	—	—	349	—	—	—
Forgive Our Sins as We Forgive	—	307	—	347	—	—	—
THE EUCHARIST							
Let Us Break Bread Together	447	212	330	513	545	—	—
SENDING							
O Christ, the Great Foundation	—	—	387	443	—	—	—

Seventeenth Sunday in Ordinary Time

Color: Green

PSALM SETTINGS

METRICAL
Psalm 85, "The Lord Has Long with Favor Looked,"
  PCW, CMD, Morgan
RESPONSORIAL
"Lord, Show Us Your Love," P 76, Hopson

MULTICULTURAL/CONTEMPORARY

O—"Hosea, Come Back to Me," Renew 126,
  Gregory Norbet
"Father, I Adore You," W&P 37/AAHH 330, Terry
  Coehlo
Psalm—"Psalm 85," GS 20, arr. by Ray Makeever
"God Is So Good," Mar 186/AAHH 156, traditional
E—"Spirit Song," LUYH 13/W&P 130/SNC
  212/AAHH 321, John Wimber
"Water Life," W&P 145, Handt Hanson
G—"Seek Ye First," W&P 122/TFF 149/WOV
  783/PH 333, Karen Lafferty
"Sweet Hour of Prayer," AAHH 442
"Lord, Teach Us How to Pray," HFTG 22

ANTHEMS

"The Lord's Prayer," Albert Hay Malotte/Carl Deis,
  GS 7943, SATB
"Christ Is Made the Sure Foundation," Milburn Price,
  CF CM7926, SATB with brass

MUSIC FOR THE SMALL CHURCH

"Seek, and You Shall Find," Douglas E. Wagner
  (unison/two-part, piano), BM BSC00175
"Increase Our Faith," David Hass (cantor/choir/
  congregation/keyboard), GIA G-4736

OTHER VOCAL MUSIC

"O Lord, Whose Mercies Numberless," G. F. Handel,
  LG/GS

ORGAN

Prelude on the chorale VATER UNSER ("The Lord's
  Prayer")
  J. S. Bach, several preludes in various editions
  (M-D)
  Georg Böhm, *Organ Masters of the Seventeenth &
  Eighteenth Centuries*, CFP (E)
  Flor Peeters, *Thirty Chorale Preludes*, CFP (M)
  Friedrich Zachau, *Short Chorale Preludes*, OXU (M)
Postlude on the chorale VATER UNSER
  Paul Bunjes, *The Hymns of Martin Luther*, organ
  and solo instruments, AF (E)
  Felix Mendelssohn, "Organ Sonata," several edi-
  tions (D)
  Johann Pachelbel, collected works, various
  editions (M)

THE CONFESSION OF 1967

For today's selection, see p. 229.

August 1, 2004

LECTIONARY READINGS

Hosea 11:1–11
Colossians 3:1–11
Luke 12:13–21

Psalm 107:1–9, 43

CALL TO WORSHIP

Our ancestors cried to the Lord in their trouble,
and God delivered them from their distress.
O give thanks to the Lord, for God is good,
God's steadfast love endures forever.
For God's steadfast love we give thanks to the Lord,
for God's wonderful works to humankind.
For God satisfies the thirsty,
and the hungry he fills with good things.

PRAYER OF CONFESSION

Source of all good things,
we have stored up treasure that does not last,
and filled ourselves with bread that does
not sustain.
We have looked to other providers,
when only you can truly satisfy
our deepest hunger and thirst.

Forgive us for seeking elsewhere
what you have already given us
so richly in Jesus, our Lord.
Stir our hearts by your Spirit,
to set our affections on things above,
on treasures that last forever.
Clothe us with the new self,
that Christ may be our all in all.

HYMNS FOR THE DAY

	HB	LBW	NCH	PH	RIL	TFF	WOV
GATHERING							
Glorious Things of Thee Are Spoken	434	358	307	446	393	—	—
THE WORD							
O—Loving Spirit	—	—	—	323	—	—	683
E—O God, Our Faithful God	—	504	—	277	69	—	—
G—Be Thou My Vision	303	—	451	339	67	—	776
I'd Rather Have Jesus	—	—	—	—	—	233	—
THE EUCHARIST							
Come, Risen Lord, and Deign to Be Our Guest	—	209	—	503	550	—	—
SENDING							
Lord, Dismiss Us with Thy Blessing	79	259	77	538	—	—	—

Eighteenth Sunday
in Ordinary Time

Color: Green

PSALM SETTINGS

METRICAL
"Thanks Be to God Our Savior," PsH #107,
    7.6.7.6.6.7.6.7, Diephouse/Grotenhuis
RESPONSORIAL
"Give Thanks to the Lord," HP 2, p. 41,
    Daw/Hackett

MULTICULTURAL/CONTEMPORARY

O—"Be My Home," W&P 16, Handt Hanson
"Just a Closer Walk with Thee," AAHH 455
Psalm—"Certainly, Lord," AAHH 678
E—"Christ, You Are the Fullness," PH 346
"You Are My Hiding Place," W&P 160, Michael
    Ledner
"Christ Is All," AAHH 363
G—"Give Thanks with a Grateful Heart," LUYH
    114/W&P 41/CLUW 247/SNC 216, Henry
    Smith
"Lord, Whose Then Shall They Be," HFTG 11

ANTHEMS

"Be Thou My Vision," John Rutter, HIN
    HMC-1035, SATB
"Give Me Jesus," L. L. Fleming, AF 11-0540,
    SSATBB

MUSIC FOR THE SMALL CHURCH

"O, My People, Turn to Me," Robert Buckley Farlee
    (unison), in *Three Biblical Songs*, AF 11-10604
"If You Believe and I Believe," Hal H. Hopson
    (SATB/keyboard/optional flute), AF 11-11192

OTHER VOCAL MUSIC

"Be Thou My Vision," Richard Walters in *Hymn
    Classics*, HL
"Be Thou My Vision," Edwin T. Childs in *Art Songs
    of the Hymnal*, vol. 2, WMP

ORGAN

Prelude on the hymn tune ENGELBERG ("We Know
    That Christ Is Raised")
    Sue Mitchell Wallace, *Hymn Prisms*, HP (M)
    Dale Wood, *Preludes and Postludes*, AF (E)
Postlude on the hymn tune HANOVER
    Robert Powell, *The Organist's Companion*, BM (E)
    C. H. H. Parry, *Seven Chorale Preludes*, OXU (D)
    Flor Peeters, *Hymn Preludes for the Church Year*,
    CFP (M)

THE CONFESSION OF 1967

For today's selection, see p. 229.

August 8, 2004

LECTIONARY READINGS

Isaiah 1:1, 10–20
Hebrews 11:1–3, 8–16
Luke 12:32–40

Psalm 50:1–8, 22–23

CALL TO WORSHIP

The Mighty One, God our creator,
  speaks and summons the earth,
**From the rising of the sun to its setting
  out of Zion, God shines forth.**
God calls to the heavens above and to the earth,
  that God may judge the people:
**The heavens declare God's righteousness,
  for God alone is judge.**
Let all who made a covenant with God,
  gather together before God's presence.
**Let us bring to God our offering,
  thanksgiving as a sacrifice, honoring our God.**

PRAYER OF CONFESSION

**Faithful God,
you call us to paths unknown,
inviting us to trust your Spirit's leading,
even when we cannot see the destination.
Countless generations have borne witness
that you keep your covenant promises;
yet we shrink back from your call,
trusting more in our own limited wisdom,
than in your boundless faithfulness.**

**Forgive our unbelief in your promises.
Give us a willing heart
to follow your call wherever it leads;
grant that we be counted among the faithful,
ever testifying of your rich goodness
to all who trust in you.**

HYMNS FOR THE DAY

GATHERING	HB	LBW	NCH	PH	RIL	TFF	WOV
Holy God, We Praise Your Name	—	535	276	460	619	—	—
THE WORD							
O—Lord, Who May Dwell Within Your House	—	—	—	164	—	—	—
What Does the Lord Require?	—	—	—	405	176	—	—
E—How Firm a Foundation	369	507	407	361	172	—	—
How Clear Is Our Vocation, Lord	—	—	—	419	433	—	—
If Thou but Trust in God to Guide Thee	344	453	410	282	151	—	—
We've Come This Far by Faith	—	—	—	—	—	197	—
G—"Sleepers, Wake!" A Voice Astounds Us	—	31	112	17	606	—	—
Rejoice! Rejoice, Believers	231	25	—	15	—	—	—
God, Whose Giving Knows No Ending	—	408	565	422	—	—	—
THE EUCHARIST							
Jesus, Priceless Treasure	414	457–8	480	365	448	—	—
SENDING							
Great Is Thy faithfulness	—	—	423	276	155	283	771

Nineteenth Sunday
in Ordinary Time

Color: Green

PSALM SETTINGS

METRICAL
Psalm 50, "The Mighty One, the Lord of Hosts,"
 PCW, CMD, Morgan
RESPONSORIAL
"Out of Zion, Perfect in Its Beauty," HP 1, p. 56,
 Daw/Hackett
RESPONSORIAL
"Exalt the Lord Our God," P 46, Hopson

MULTICULTURAL/CONTEMPORARY

O—"The First Song of Isaiah," Renew 122, Jack
 Nobler
"Close to Thee," AAHH 553
Psalm—"Sing to the World," CG 113, Ernest Sands
"What a Mighty God We Serve," AAHH 478
"Let the Giving of Thanks," from *Psalms of Patience,
 Protest and Praise*, GIA, John Bell
E—"Be My Home," W&P 16, Handt Hanson/Paul
 Murakami
"Faith of Our Fathers," AAHH 409
G—"Here I Stand," LUYH 89, Iona Community
"Now in This Banquet," W&P 104, Marty Haugen
"Ain't-a That Good News," AAHH 592

ANTHEMS

"Keep Your Lamps," arr. by Andre Thomas, HIN
 HMC-577, SATB with conga drums
"Write Your Blessed Name," K. Lee Scott, HP A632,
 SATB

MUSIC FOR THE SMALL CHURCH

"Have No Fear, Little Flock," Carolyn Johnson
 (SATB/keyboard), AF 0-8006-7454-5
"Give Me Oil in My Lamp," Max V. Exner
 (two/three-part/piano), CG CGA659

OTHER VOCAL MUSIC

"How Firm a Foundation," Richard Walters in *Hymn
 Classics*, HL

ORGAN

Prelude and postlude on the chorale WACHET AUF
 ("Sleepers Wake")
 Paul Manz, *Ten Chorale Improvisations*, vols. 4 and
 10, C (M)
 Max Reger, *Choralfantasien*, CFP (D)
 Harold Rohlig, *Wake, Awake, for Night Is Flying*,
 organ and trumpet, C (M)
 Johann Walther, complete works, or *The Concordia
 Hymn Prelude Series*, C (E)

THE CONFESSION OF 1967

For today's selection, see p. 229.

August 15, 2004

LECTIONARY READINGS

Isaiah 5:1–7
Hebrews 11:29–12:2
Luke 12:49–56

Psalm 80:1–2, 8–19

CALL TO WORSHIP

O God, you call your people your beloved vineyard,
   Your pleasant planting;
You, O God, expected justice, but saw bloodshed;
   righteousness but heard a cry!
Restore us, O God of hosts;
   let your face shine, that we might be saved.
You, O God, expected the vineyard to yield grapes,
   but it has yielded wild grapes.
Turn again, O God of hosts;
   look down from heaven, and see;
   have regard for this vine.
Restore us, O God of hosts;
   let your face shine, that we might be saved.

PRAYER OF CONFESSION

God of peace and judgment,
you sent Jesus to be our pioneer,
to blaze for us the path that leads to life
      and blessing.
But we are afraid to follow his way of the cross;
we are more eager to avoid suffering
than to embrace the joy of his rewards.

Forgive us for heeding our fears,
rather than Christ's call.
Enable us by your Spirit to set aside
the weights that hold us back;
strengthen us to persevere in following Jesus,
trusting our destiny into your good hands,
whether in life or in death.

HYMNS FOR THE DAY

GATHERING	HB	LBW	NCH	PH	RIL	TFF	WOV
God, Who Stretched the Spangled Heavens	—	463	556	268	29	—	—
Come, We That Love the Lord	—	—	379–2	—	575–6	135	742
THE WORD							
O—The One Is Blest	—	—	—	158	—	—	—
E—Fight the Good Fight	359	461	—	307	—	—	—
Take Up Your Cross, the Savior Said	293	398	204	393	268	—	—
When We Are Tempted to Deny Your Son	—	—	—	86	—	—	—
G—Lead On, O King Eternal	332	495	573	447	423	—	—
How Great Thou Art	—	532	—	467	—	—	—
THE EUCHARIST							
We Come as Guests Invited	—	—	—	517	—	—	—
SENDING							
Guide My Feet	—	—	497	354	—	153	—

Twentieth Sunday in Ordinary Time

Color: Green

PSALM SETTINGS

METRICAL
"Hear Us, O Shepherd of Your Chosen Race," PsH
    80, 10.10.10.10.10.10, Polman/Wainwright
RESPONSORIAL
"Restore Us, O God of Hosts," HP 1, p. 59,
    Daw/Hackett

MULTICULTURAL/CONTEMPORARY

O—"We've Come to Praise You," Mar 80, Amy
    Grant/Beverly Darnall
Psalm—"Revive Us Again," AAHH 569
E—"May You Run and Not Be Weary," W&P 97,
    Handt Hanson
"Life's Railway to Heaven," AAHH 472
Other—"Be Bold, Be Strong," W&P 15, Morris
    Chapman
"Guide My Feet," TFF 153
"God, Whose Purpose Is to Kindle," HFTG 80

ANTHEMS

"If Thou but Suffer Good to Guide Thee," from
    Three Chorales, J. S. Bach, GS Octave no. 10053,
    SATB
"Where Cross the Crowded Ways of Life," David
    Stanley York, CF CM7952, SATB with optional
    brass and timpani

MUSIC FOR THE SMALL CHURCH

"Prayer for Today," Margaret Tucker (SATB/unison
    setting available), CG, CGA855/CGA358

OTHER VOCAL MUSIC

"Guide Me Ever, Great Redeemer," Dale Wood in
    Songs of Reflection, SMP30/1109S

ORGAN

Sinfonia for Organ and Trumpet, Carlo Pallavicino,
    GIA (M)
Liturgical Meditations Flute and Organ, Jacques
    Berthier, GIA (E)
Or on the chorale GROSSER GOTT
    Wilbur Held, *Hymn Preludes for the Pentecost
    Season*, C (M)
    Theodore Beck, *Fourteen Organ Chorale Preludes*,
    AF (E)
    Max Reger, *A Little Christian Year*, CF (E) [If your
    sending hymn this morning is "Guide My Feet"
    it might follow the Blessing and Sending. A
    dancer could lead the congregation in a proces-
    sion from the sanctuary. Or, following the hymn,
    the organist might improvise on the hymn tune.]

THE CONFESSION OF 1967

For today's selection, see p. 230.

August 22, 2004

LECTIONARY READINGS

Jeremiah 1:4–10
Hebrews 12:18–29
Luke 13:10–17

Psalm 71:1–6

CALL TO WORSHIP

In you, O Lord, I take refuge;
　　let me never be put to shame.
In your righteousness deliver me and rescue me;
　　incline your ear to me and save me.
Be to me a rock and a refuge.
　　A strong fortress to save me,
for you are our rock and a mighty fortress,
　　our God in whom we trust.

PRAYER OF CONFESSION

God of consuming fire,
all creation worships you,
acknowledging your boundless majesty,
trembling before your holy judgment.
Yet we indulgently seek to please ourselves,
and cravenly seek to please others,
rather than seeking only to please you.

In mercy, forgive us.
Burn away all in us that dishonors you;
ignite in us the fire of your Spirit,
that we may serve you only,
and worship you wholly,
for the sake of Jesus, our Lord.

HYMNS FOR THE DAY

	HB	LBW	NCH	PH	RIL	TFF	WOV
GATHERING							
Praise Ye the Lord, the Almighty	1	543	22	482	145	—	—
We Have Come into His House	—	—	—	—	—	136	—
THE WORD							
O—I'm Gonna Live So God Can Use Me	—	—	—	369	—	—	—
Lord, When I Came into This Life	—	—	—	522	—	—	—
E—Come, Thou Fount of Every Blessing	379	499	459	356	449	—	—
Come, All You Servants of the Lord	—	—	—	242	—	—	—
G—Christ Is Risen! Shout Hosanna!	—	—	—	104	—	—	—
Heal Me, O Lord	—	—	—	—	189	—	—
THE EUCHARIST							
God of the Sparrow	—	—	32	272	—	—	—
SENDING							
Lord, Whose Love Through Humble Service	—	423	—	427	—	—	—

Twenty-First Sunday in Ordinary Time

Color: Green

PSALM SETTINGS

METRICAL
Psalm 71, "In You, O Lord, I Put My Trust," PH 71,
  LM, Walhout/Wischmeier
RESPONSORIAL
"My Tongue Will Proclaim Your Righteousness,"
  HP 1, p. 63, Daw/Hackett
RESPONSORIAL
"My Tongue Will Proclaim Your Righteousness,"
  P 63, Barrett/Hopson

MULTICULTURAL/CONTEMPORARY

O—"Open Our Eyes, Lord," W&P 113/Mar 59,
  Bob Cull
Psalm—"Bless the Lord My Soul," LUYH 71/CLUW
  120/SNC 256, Jacques Berthier
"Praise You," AAHH 110
E—"I Come with Joy," CG 57, American folk melody
G—"We Won't Leave Here Like We Came,"
  AAHH 407
Other—"Canticle of the Turning," W&P 26, Kelly
  Willard

ANTHEMS

"Go Not Far from Me," Zingarelli, GS 4889, SATB
"Guide Me, O Thou Great Jehova," arr. by Bertieg
  and Lugo, APG 808026-00921-8, SATB

MUSIC FOR THE SMALL CHURCH

"Jesus, When You Walked This Earth," Sally Ann
  Morris (unison or SATB), in *Giving Thanks in
  Song and Prayer*, 36

OTHER VOCAL MUSIC

"Come, Thou Fount of Every Blessing," Richard
  Walters in *Hymn Classics*, HL

ORGAN

Prelude on the chorale SCHMÜCKE DICH ("Deck
  Thyself, My Soul")
  J. S. Bach, several settings, various editions (M-D)
  David N. Johnson, "Deck Thyself, My Soul,"
    AF (M)
  Johannes Brahms, *Eleven Chorale Preludes*, various
    editions (E)
Postlude
  S. Bach, "Prelude and Fugue in G (Eight Little),"
    various editions (M-E)
  Dietrich Buxtehude, "Toccata and Fugue in F,"
    various editions (M)
  Myron D. Casner, "Postlude on SCHMÜCKE DICH,"
    C (M)

THE CONFESSION OF 1967

For today's selection, see p. 230.

August 29, 2004

LECTIONARY READINGS

Jeremiah 2:4–13
Hebrews 13:1–8, 15–16
Luke 14:1, 7–14

Psalm 81:1, 10–16

CALL TO WORSHIP

Sing aloud to God our strength,
  shout for joy to the God of Jacob!
Raise a song, sound the tambourine,
  on lyre and harp make melody to God.
Let us offer to God our sacrifice of praise,
  for you alone are worthy.
For you, O God, declared never to forsake us.
  So we sing with joy and will not be afraid.

PRAYER OF CONFESSION

God of tender care,
like a mother, you have fed and defended us,
protecting us from that which would destroy,
blessing us with abundant fruitfulness.
Yet we live as though we were self-sufficient,
leaning on our own understanding,
rather than trusting you with all our heart.

Show us your mercy in Christ Jesus.
Forgive our stubborn ingratitude;
empower us to live by your Spirit
in confident assurance
that your designs for us are best,
your provisions most bountiful,
and your glory our greatest joy.

HYMNS FOR THE DAY

GATHERING	HB	LBW	NCH	PH	RIL	TFF	WOV
Sing Praise to God, Who Reigns Above	—	—	6	483	146	—	—
THE WORD							
O—Not Unto Us, O Lord of Heaven	—	—	—	227	—	—	—
E—Where Cross the Crowded Ways of Life	507	429	543	408	482	—	—
Lord Jesus, Think on Me	270	309	301	248	—	—	—
G—Here, O Our Lord, We See You Face to Face	442	211	336	520	549	—	—
O Praise the Gracious Power	—	—	54	471	—	—	750
I'm a-Goin'-a-Eat at the Welcome Table	—	—	—	—	—	263	—
THE EUCHARIST							
Draw Us in the Spirit's Tether	—	—	337	504	—	—	703
SENDING							
The Church of Christ in Every Age	—	433	306	421	—	—	—

Twenty-Second Sunday in Ordinary Time

Color: Green

PSALM SETTINGS

METRICAL
"Sing a Psalm of Joy," PH 81, 5.6.5.5.5.6,
   Post/Grotenhuis
RESPONSORIAL
"Let the People Praise You, O God," P 72,
   Presbyterian 2

MULTICULTURAL/CONTEMPORARY

Psalm—"God Is So Good," TFF 275/AAHH 156
E—"Come to the Table," W&P 33, Martin Nystrom
"We Are an Offering," W&P 146, Dwight Liles
G—"Now in This Banquet," W&P 104, Marty
   Haugen
"God Never Fails," AAHH 159
"Christ, the One Who Tells the Tale," HFTG 24

ANTHEMS

"Easter Canticle," John Ness Beck, BP BP1200, SATB
"Shout Glory Hallelujah," Hal H. Hopson, LAP
   10/1925LA, SATB

MUSIC FOR THE SMALL CHURCH

"The Love of God Comes Close," John L. Bell
   (unison/keyboard/flute), GIA G-5049
"Lord, Keep Us Steadfast," arr. by Donald Johns
   (two-part mixed/keyboard), AF 11-10424

OTHER VOCAL MUSIC

"O Master, Let Me Walk with Thee," Dale Wood in
   Songs of Reflection, SMP 30/1109S

ORGAN

Prelude on the hymn tune MILES LANE ("All Hail the
   Power of Jesus' Name")
   Alex Rowley, *Choral Preludes Based on Famous
      Hymn Tunes*, EA (M)
   David N. Johnson, *The Concordia Hymn Prelude
      Series*, vol. 32, C (E)
   Healey Willan, *Thirty-Six Short Preludes and Fugues*,
      CFP (M)
Postlude
   Jean Langalis, *Suite Mèdièval Acclamations*,
      SAL (M-D)
   Henry Purcell, "C-Bell" (trumpet tune), various
      editions (M)
   François Couperin, *Mass for the Parish Offertory*,
      various editions (M)
   Clerambault, *Dialogue sur les grandes jeux*, various
      editions (M-E)

THE CONFESSION OF 1967

For today's selection, see p. 230.

September 5, 2004

LECTIONARY READINGS

Jeremiah 18:1–11
Philemon 1–21
Luke 14:25–33

Psalm 139:1–6, 13–18

CALL TO WORSHIP

O Lord, you have searched me and known me.
    You know when I sit down and when I rise up.
You discern my thoughts from far away.
    You search my path and my lying down,
    and are acquainted with all my ways.
How weighty to me are your thoughts, O God!
    How vast is the sum of them!
I try to count them—they are more than the sand,
    I come to the end—I am still with you.

PRAYER OF CONFESSION

O Lord, you search us and know us.
You know the secrets of our heart,
even better than we do.
You know how we have run away from your call;
still you are ready to receive us again,
ready to use us again.

In mercy, forgive and heal
our inclination to wander.
Fashion us by your Spirit
into vessels fit for good use;
that we may bear faithfully
what you have entrusted to our care—
treasures of Christ's saving work
for a lost and broken world.

HYMNS FOR THE DAY

GATHERING	HB	LBW	NCH	PH	RIL	TFF	WOV
O Worship the King, All Glorious Above!	26	548	26	476	2	—	—
THE WORD							
O—Kind Maker of the World	—	—	—	79	—	—	—
Breathe on Me, Breath of God	235	488	292	316	—	—	—
Spirit of the Living God	—	—	283	322	—	101	—
E—Help Us Accept Each Other	—	—	388	358	—	—	—
G—Take Up Your Cross, the Savior Said	293	398	204	393	268	—	—
Take Thou Our Minds, Dear Lord	306	—	—	392	434	—	—
I Shall Not Be Moved	—	—	—	—	—	147	—
THE EUCHARIST							
Take My Life and Let It Be	310	406	448	391	475	—	—
Must Jesus Bear the Cross Alone	290	—	—	—	—	237	—
SENDING							
Lift High the Cross	—	377	198	371	415	—	—

Twenty-Third Sunday in Ordinary Time

Color: Green

PSALM SETTINGS

METRICAL
Psalm 139, "Thou, O Lord, Hast Searched and
   Known Me," PCW, 8.7.8.7.D, Morgan
RESPONSORIAL
"Lord, You Have Searched Me," P 143, Hopson

MULTICULTURAL/CONTEMPORARY

O—"Change My Heart, O God," W&P 28, Eddie
   Espinoza
Psalm—"I Was There to Hear Your Borning Cry,"
   W&P 69/WOV 770, John Ylvisaker
"I Know the Lord Has Laid His Hands on Me,"
   AAHH 360
G—"I Want Jesus to Walk with Me," traditional,
   TFF 66/WOV 660/AAHH 563
"For God Risk Everything!" HFTG 26

ANTHEMS

"Psalm 139," Allen Pote, CG CGA-610, SATB
"Who Is the One We Love the Most," Carl Schalk,
   C 98-3404, SATB

MUSIC FOR THE SMALL CHURCH

"Consecrated, Lord, to Thee," Wayne Wold (two-
   part/keyboard), AF 11-10330

OTHER VOCAL MUSIC

"Spirit of Faith, Come Down," Mary Jackson,
   BEALOTH, *Sweet Singer/Hymns of Charles Wesley*,
   Steven Kimbrough, CHM

ORGAN

Prelude on the hymn tune SURSUM CORDA
   Harald Rohlig, *Preludes for the Hymns in Worship*,
   C (E)
Or Jan Bender, "Partita on 'O God, Our Help in Ages
   Past,'" AF (M)
   David N. Johnson, *Music for Worship with East
   Pedals*, AF (E)
   C. H. H. Parry, chorale prelude on DUNDEE, from
   Seven Chorale Preludes, NOV (M)
Postlude: Chorale prelude on ST. DENIO ("How Firm a
   Foundation")
   Harold Rohlig, *The Parish Organist*, C (two
   versions) (E-M)
   Robert J. Powell, *Eleven Chorale Preludes on Hymn
   Tunes*, HF (E)
Or Johann Pachelbel, "Toccata in E Minor," various
   editions (M)
Chorale preludes on BREESLAU ("Take Up Your
   Cross")
   Paul Manz, *Ten Chorale Improvisations*, vol. 8,
   C (M)

THE CONFESSION OF 1967

For today's selection, see p. 231.

September 12, 2004

LECTIONARY READINGS

Jeremiah 4:11–12, 22–28
1 Timothy 1:12–17
Luke 15:1–10

Psalm 14

CALL TO WORSHIP

We rejoice, O God, that you call us to this place
   to sing your praise and offer our lives.
For you have searched for us and found us,
   You rejoice in our salvation.
You strengthen us and call us to serve,
   You have appointed us to service in Christ,
to the ruler of the ages, immortal, invisible,
   The only God,
   Be honor and glory forever and ever. Amen.

PRAYER OF CONFESSION

Holy Redeemer,
we confess that our sins are great;
they lead us astray from your ways of peace.
Yet you do not leave us alone;
in Christ you come to seek and save the lost.

We acknowledge that we need a Savior,
and rejoice in the sure hope of Christ's saving work.
As recipients of your tender mercy,
we offer ourselves to be bearers of your mercy.
Equip us by your Spirit as your ambassadors,
to show the world your healing love in Christ,
working faithfully for your kingdom and
     righteousness,
proclaiming the good news of your salvation.

HYMNS FOR THE DAY

GATHERING	HB	LBW	NCH	PH	RIL	TFF	WOV
Praise the Lord, God's Glories Show	—	—	—	481	142	—	—
THE WORD							
O—All Who Love and Serve Your City	—	436	—	413	485	—	—
Come, Ye Thankful People, Come	525	407	422	551	18	—	—
E—Immortal, Invisible, God Only Wise	85	526	1	263	7	—	—
Amazing Grace, How Sweet the Sound	275	448	547–8	280	456	—	—
G—Lord, Speak to Me That I May Speak	298	403	531	426	436	—	—
Savior, Like a Shepherd Lead Us	380	481	252	387	—	—	—
THE EUCHARIST							
You Satisfy the Hungry Heart	—	—	—	521	—	—	711
Give Me a Clean Heart	—	—	—	—	—	216	—
SENDING							
There's a Spirit in the Air	—	—	294	433	—	—	—

Twenty-Fourth Sunday in Ordinary Time

Color: Green

PSALM SETTINGS

METRICAL

"The Foolish in Their Hearts Deny," PsH 14, CMD,
Post/Van Oss

RESPONSORIAL

"O, That Salvation Would Come from Zion," P 8,
Ferguson

MULTICULTURAL/CONTEMPORARY

O—"Awesome God," W&P 13/AAHH 126, Rich
Mullins

"God, the Sculptor of the Mountains," TFF 222,
John Thornburg/Amanda Husberg

G—"Softly and Tenderly Jesus Is Calling," WOV
734/Renew 147, Will Thompson

"God Leads Us Along," AAHH 136

"Shepherd, Do You Tramp the Hills?" HFTG 68

ANTHEMS

"Come and Taste," arr. by Alice Parker, LG 51342,
SATB

"Immortal, Invisible," Eric H. Thiman, *Novello
Anthology* 1140, SATB

MUSIC FOR THE SMALL CHURCH

"Come and Taste," arr. by Alice Parker (SATB),
LG 51342

"Immortal, Invisible," Eric H. Thiman (SATB),
Novello Anthology 1140

OTHER VOCAL MUSIC

"Savior, Like a Shepherd Lead Us," William Bradbury,
Five American Gospel Songs, Luigi Zaninelli, HF

ORGAN

Prelude on LAUDA ANIMA ("Praise My Soul")

Kevin Norris, *Reflections on Six Hymn Tunes*,
AMSI (M)

Richard, Wienhorst, *The Concordia Hymn Prelude
Series,* C (E)

Or J. S. Bach, "Passacaglia in C Minor," various
editions (D)

Postlude

Johann Pachelbel, "Toccata in G," various
editions (M)

Healey Willan, chorale prelude based on DURHAM
("When All Thy Mercies, O My God"), *Thirty-
Six Short Preludes and Postludes on Well-Known
Hymn Tunes*, CFP (M)

THE CONFESSION OF 1967

For today's selection, see p. 231.

September 19, 2004

LECTIONARY READINGS

Jeremiah 8:18–9:1
1 Timothy 2:1–7
Luke 16:1–13

Psalm 79:1–9

CALL TO WORSHIP

Help us, O God of our salvation,
　for the glory of your name;
deliver us and forgive our sins,
　for your name's sake.
Do not remember against us our iniquities,
　let your compassion come speedily to meet us.
We are your people, the flock of your pasture,
　we give thanks to you forever.
　　From generation to generation we will recount
　　　your praise.

PRAYER OF CONFESSION

Lord of all,
you have entrusted us with much treasure,
and commissioned us to use it wisely and diligently,
that your kingdom of love and justice may increase.
Yet we have shown ourselves unfaithful,
even with small things you have entrusted to us.

Forgive our carelessness with your treasures.
Stir us up by your Spirit to dedicate back to you
all you have so richly bestowed upon us.
Keep us ever mindful
that all that we have, and all that we are,
comes from you and belongs to you,
through the redeeming work of Jesus our Lord.

HYMNS FOR THE DAY

	HB	LBW	NCH	PH	RIL	TFF	WOV
GATHERING							
Father, We Praise Thee	43	267	90	459	515	—	—
THE WORD							
O—There Is a Balm in Gilead	—	—	553	394	465	185	737
When Jesus Wept	—	—	192	312	—	—	—
E—When I Had Not Yet Learned of Jesus	—	—	—	410	—	—	—
All Hail the Power of Jesus' Name!	132	328–9	304	142–3	593–4	267	—
G—As Those of Old Their Firstfruits Brought	—	—	—	414	—	—	—
Let Justice Flow Like Streams	—	—	588	—	—	48	763
We Give Thee but Thine Own	312	410	—	428	427	—	—
THE EUCHARIST							
Now to Your Table Spread	—	—	—	515	—	—	—
SENDING							
God, Whose Giving Knows No Ending	—	408	565	422	—	—	—

Twenty-Fifth Sunday in Ordinary Time

Color: Green

PSALM SETTINGS

METRICAL
"In Your Heritage the Nations," PsH 79, 8.7.8.7.D,
The Psalter (1912)
RESPONSORIAL
"O God, Come to Our Help and Save Us," P 69,
Hughes/Gelineau

MULTICULTURAL/CONTEMPORARY

O—"There Is A Balm in Gilead," PH 394/AAHH
524
Psalm—"I Love the Lord, He Heard My Cry,"
AAHH 395
E—"Lord, for the Years," CG 74, Michael Baughen
G—"Until I Found the Lord," AAHH 454
Other—"From Where the Sun Rises," W&P 40,
Graham Kendrick
"Here Is Love," Mar 116, Robert Lowry

ANTHEMS

"There Is a Balm in Gilead," William Dawson, Neil
Kjos T104, SSATB
"First Fruits," Austin Lovelace, AGP HSA103, SATB
with flute, optional trumpet
"Great Day," spiritual, arr. by Brazeal Dennard,
SP A-1895, SATB and high solo voice
"Where Cross the Crowded Ways of Life," David
Stanley York, CF CM7952, SATB with optional
brass and timpani

MUSIC FOR THE SMALL CHURCH

"Balm in Gilead," Mark Shepperd (SATB), AF
11-10923

OTHER VOCAL MUSIC

"Children of the Heavenly Father," John Ferguson in
Three Swedish Folk Hymns for Medium Solo Voice,
AF 11-5360

ORGAN

Prelude on MIT FREUDEN ZART ("Sing Praise to God
Who Reigns Above")
Jan Bender, *Organ Fantasy on* MIT FREUDEN ZART,
CMP (D)
Hugo Distler, *Klein Orgelchoral-Bearbeitungen*,
BAR (M)
Alec Wyton, *A Little Christian Year*, CF (E)
Postlude on the chorale NUN DANKET ("Now Thank
We All Our God")
Jan Bender, *The Parish Organist*, C (E)
Wilbur Held, *Hymn Preludes for the Autumn
Festivals*, C (M)
Flor Peeters, *Hymn Preludes for the Liturgical Year*,
CFP (M)
Or J. S. Bach, "Prelude and Fugue in A Major," vari-
ous editions (M)

THE CONFESSION OF 1967

For today's selection, see p. 231.

September 26, 2004

LECTIONARY READING

Jeremiah 32:1–3a, 6–15
1 Timothy 6:6–19
Luke 16:19–31

Psalm 91:1–6, 14–16

CALL TO WORSHIP

You who live in the shelter of the Most High
   Who abide in the shadow of the Almighty will say
     to the Lord,
"My refuge and my fortress,
  my God in whom I trust."
Under God's wings we will find refuge,
   For God is our shield and our buckler.
To God alone be all glory and honor,
  Forever and ever. Amen.

PRAYER OF CONFESSION

Protector and Provider of all,
we have sought to increase treasure and bolster
  security,
more than we have cultivated justice, godliness,
  and love.
We love money and influence,
with little regard for the evil such love breeds.

In mercy, forgive our selfish greed.
Quicken our hearts by your Spirit,
that we may care more for that which lasts,
than for treasures that quickly fade.
Grant us courage to live in the way of the cross,
as faithful disciples of your Son,
our Lord and Savior, Jesus Christ.

HYMNS FOR THE DAY

	HB	LBW	NCH	PH	RIL	TFF	WOV
GATHERING							
God of Grace and God of Glory	358	415	436	420	416	—	—
THE WORD							
O—O God, What You Ordain Is Right	366	446	415	284	153	—	—
O God, in a Mysterious Way	112	483	412	270	36	—	—
E—Fight the Good Fight	359	461	—	307	—	—	—
He Is King of kings	—	—	—	153	—	—	—
G— Where Cross the Crowded Ways of Life	507	429	543	408	482	—	—
Lord, Whose Love through Humble Service	—	423	—	427	—	—	—
All to Jesus I Surrender	—	—	—	—	—	235	—
THE EUCHARIST							
Thee We Adore	—	199	339	519	—	—	—
SENDING							
Come, Labor on	287	—	532	415	75	—	—

Twenty-Sixth Sunday in Ordinary Time

Color: Green

PSALM SETTINGS

METRICAL
Psalm 91, "Deep in the Shelter of the Lord I Dwell,"
    PCW, 10.10.10.10, Morgan
RESPONSORIAL
"God Is Our Refuge," P 85 (Presbyterian 6)

MULTICULTURAL/CONTEMPORARY

Psalm—"On Eagle's Wings," W&P 110/WOV 779,
    Michael Joncas
"Whoever Lives Beside the Lord," in *Psalms of
    Patience, Protest and Praise*, John Bell, GIA
E—"Just When I Need Him," AAHH 379
"Only Trust Him," AAHH 369
G—"Oh the Life of the World," CG 97, Ian
    Galloway
"Come, You Sinners, Poor and Needy," AAHH 361
"God, Whose Purpose Is to Kindle," HFTG 80

ANTHEMS

"Great Day," arr. by Brazeal & Dennard, SP A-1895,
    SATB and high solo voice
"Where Cross the Crowded Ways of Life," David
    Stanley York, CF CM7952, SATB with optional
    brass and tympani

MUSIC FOR THE SMALL CHURCH

"Move Me," Richard Alan Henderson
    (SATB/solo/keyboard) in *Songs of Zion*, 185

OTHER VOCAL MUSIC

"He Is King of Kings," Hall Johnson

ORGAN

Prelude on DIX and/or ENGLANDS LANE ("For the
    Beauty of the Earth")
    William H. Harris, *Festival Voluntaries,* NOV (M)
    Dennis Janzer, *Variations on* DIX, *The Organist's
        Companion,* vol. 8, MCA (M)
    Flor Peters, *Hymn Preludes for the Liturgical Year,*
        C. F. Peters (M)
    Alec Wyton, *Preludes for Christian Praise,* SMP (E)
ENGLANDS LANE
    Myron Casner, *The Parish Organist,* C (E)
    Flor Peeters, *Little Chorale Suite for Organ,* JBC (M)
        [Construct a "Concertato" using the two tunes,
        and several of the organ settings for each. Have
        one or more of your choirs introduce each organ
        setting, alternating the tunes. Invite the congre-
        gation to join the final stanza as the call to
        worship.]
Postlude
    Nicolas Clarembault, "Trumpet in Dialogue,"
        Treasury of Early Organ Music, MP (E)
    Deiterich Buxtehude, "Fuge in C Major," *Treasury
        of Early Organ Music,* MP (M)

THE CONFESSION OF 1967

For today's selection, see p. 232.

October 3, 2004

LECTIONARY READINGS

Lamentations 1:1–6
2 Timothy 1:1–14
Luke 17:5–10

Lamentations 3:1–26 or Psalm 137

CALL TO WORSHIP

The steadfast love of the Lord never ceases,
  God's mercies never come to an end.
They are new every morning:
  Great is your faithfulness.
"The Lord is my portion," says my soul.
  Therefore all my hope is in God.
Praise the Lord!
  For God's steadfast love endures forever.

PRAYER OF CONFESSION

Faithful God,
You have given us a rich and godly heritage,
through the sure testimony and holy example
of our mothers and fathers in the faith.
But we let the light of our faith grow dim;
we stray from the paths they commend to us.

Forgive us, and renew us by your Holy Spirit.
Fan in us a new and brighter flame of faith,
that, like those who have gone before us,
our words and deeds would mightily declare
the good news of your salvation,
given to all in Jesus Christ, our Lord.

HYMNS FOR THE DAY

	HB	LBW	NCH	PH	RIL	TFF	WOV
GATHERING							
For the Fruit of All Creation	—	563	425	553	21	—	760
THE WORD							
O—Great Is Thy Faithfulness	—	—	423	276	155	283	771
O Hear Our Cry, O Lord	—	—	—	206	—	—	—
All Who Love and Serve Your City	—	436	—	413	485	—	—
Give to the Winds Thy Fears	—	—	404	286	149	—	—
Why Are Nations Raging?	—	—	—	159	—	—	—
E—Holy Spirit, Truth Divine	240	257	63	321	—	—	—
Holy Spirit, Light Divine	—	—	—	—	—	104	—
Now Thank We All Our God	9	533–4	419	555	61	—	—
Take the Name of Jesus with You	411	—	—	—	—	159	—
G—The Church of Christ in Every Age	—	433	306	421	—	—	—
THE EUCHARIST							
O Master, Let Me Walk with Thee	304	492	503	357	428	—	—
Lord, Whose Love Through Humble Service	—	423	—	427	—	—	—
SENDING							
God Be with You Till We Meet Again	78	—	81	540	—	—	—

Twenty-Seventh Sunday in Ordinary Time

Color: Green

PSALM SETTINGS

METRICAL
Psalm 137, "By the Streams of Babylon," PCW,
    7.7.7.7.D, Morgan
METRICAL
"By the Babylonian Rivers," PH 246, 8.7.8.7, Bash
RESPONSORIAL
"By the Waters of Babylon We Cried for Our Home,"
    P 140, Hopson

MULTICULTURAL/CONTEMPORARY

Gathering—"Here, O Lord, Your Servants Gather,"
    PH 465
"Uyai Mose," SNC 4, Alexander Gondo
Lamentations 3—"Great Is Thy Faithfulness,"
    CG 43/WOV 771/Renew 149/AAHH 158,
    William Runyan
Psalm 137—"By the Babylonian Rivers," PH
    246/WOV 656
E—"I Know Who Holds Tomorrow," AAHH 415
G—"Good Soil," W&P 52/WOV 713, Handt
    Hanson
Communion—"We Are One in Christ Jesus,"
    SNC 179, Alice Parker
Other—"A Song of Unity," W&P 1, David Jahn
"I Will Trust in the Lord," AAHH 391
"When Our Confidence Is Shaken," HFTG 4

ANTHEMS

"Great Lord God, Thy Kingdom Shall Endure,"
    G. F. Handel, TP 312-41125, SATB
"Let Nothing Ever Grieve Thee," Johannes Brahms,
    CFP 6093, SATB

MUSIC FOR THE SMALL CHURCH

"By the Babylonian Rivers," Richard Erickson (SATB,
    two flutes), AF 11-10814
"How Can It Be, the Life of Jesus," Sally Ann Morris
    (unison/SATB/keyboard), in *Giving Thanks in
    Song and Prayer*, 66

OTHER VOCAL MUSIC

"He's Got the Whole World in His Hands," Edward
    Boatner in *The Story of the Spirituals*, MCA

ORGAN

Prelude on the chant UBI CARITAS ("Where Charity
    and Love Prevail")
    Ten Communion Pieces for Organ, WLSM (E)
    Dom Paul Benoit, *Pieces d'Orgue*, JFB (M)
    Jean Langlais, from *Suite Médiéval*, SAL (M)
Postlude
    Dieterich Buxtehude, "Prelude in C Major (Jig),"
        various editions (M)
    David Hurd, *Three Fugues*, SEL (M-D)
    Robert Lind, variations on KEDRON, PAR (M)

THE CONFESSION OF 1967

For today's selection, see p. 232.

October 10, 2004

LECTIONARY READINGS

Jeremiah 29:1, 4–7
2 Timothy 2:8–15
Luke 17:11–19

Psalm 66:1–12

CALL TO WORSHIP

Make a joyful noise to God,
  all the earth;
we will sing the glory of God's name;
  and give to God glorious praise!
Bless our God, O peoples,
  let the sound of God's praise be heard.
Let all the earth worship you,
  and sing praises to your holy name.

PRAYER OF CONFESSION

God of healing grace,
we were lost and broken—
you sent us a Savior, Jesus the Christ,
who mended our brokenness,
and renewed our strength.
Yet we have taken for granted your boundless
    goodness,
freely given us when we were in desperate need.
We have defrauded you of your due gratitude.

In tender mercy, forgive us;
by your Spirit, lead us,
that we would demonstrate genuine thanksgiving,
through gracious words and glad service;
loving as we have been loved,
and giving as we have received.

HYMNS FOR THE DAY

	HB	LBW	NCH	PH	RIL	TFF	WOV
GATHERING							
Earth and All Stars	—	558	—	458	33	—	—
When Morning Gilds the Skies	41	545–6	86	487	365	—	—
THE WORD							
O—The Lord's My Shepherd, I'll Not Want	104	451	—	170–4	89–0	—	—
Fret Not for Those Who Do Wrong Things	—	—	—	188	—	—	—
E—Christ Is Made the Sure Foundation	433	367	400	416–7	392	—	—
O God, Our Faithful God	—	504	—	277	69	—	—
G—Praise Ye the Lord, the Almighty	1	543	22	482	145	—	—
Live into Hope	—	—	—	332	—	—	—
Thank You, Lord	—	—	—	—	—	293	—
When I Think of the Goodness of Jesus	—	—	—	—	—	269	—
THE EUCHARIST							
Jesus, Thy Boundless Love to Me	404	336	—	366	454	—	—
SENDING							
Savior, Again to Thy Dear Name We Raise	77	262	80	539	517	—	—

Twenty-Eighth Sunday in Ordinary Time

Color: Green

PSALM SETTINGS

METRICAL
"Come, Everyone, and Join with Us," PsH 66, CMD, Post/Grotenhuis

RESPONSORIAL
"Be Joyful in God All You Lands," HP 1, p. 24, Daw/Hackett

MULTICULTURAL/CONTEMPORARY

Psalm—"Awesome God," W&P 13, Rich Mullins
"Let All the World Sing Praises," Mar 216, Chris Falson
"Come, Let Us Sing," AAHH 502
E—"Broken in Love," W&P 24, Handt Hanson
"Always Remember," AAHH 640
G—"Glory and Praise to Our God," W&P 43, Daniel Schutte
"I Thank You, Jesus," AHH 532
"Banned and Banished by Their Neighbors," HFTG 7

ANTHEMS

"Christ Is Made the Sure Foundation," Milburn Price, CF CM7926, SATB with brass
"Praise Ye the Lord," W. A. Mozart/Lynn, TP 312-40059, SATB with soprano solo

MUSIC FOR THE SMALL CHURCH

"Banned and Banished," Stephen P. Folkemer (two-part), GIA G-4907

OTHER VOCAL MUSIC

"Praise to the Lord, the Almighty," Richard Walters in *Hymn Classics*, HL

ORGAN

Prelude on the hymn tune EARTH AND ALL STARS ("Earth and All Stars")
David Cherwin, *Interpretations Based on Hymn Tunes*, AMSI (M)
Sue Mitchell Wallace, *Hymn Prisms*, HP (M)
Alec Wyton, *Variants on* EARTH AND ALL STARS, AF (D)
Postlude
J. S. Bach, "Prelude and Fugue in G Major," various editions (D)
William Rowan, *Ferland's March and Recessional*, MS (M)
William H. Bates, "Partita on ENGELBERG," C (M)

THE CONFESSION OF 1967

For today's selection, see p. 232.

October 17, 2004

LECTIONARY READINGS

Jeremiah 31:27–34
2 Timothy 3:14–4:5
Luke 18:1–8

Psalm 119:97–104

CALL TO WORSHIP

O children of Zion, be glad
   And rejoice in the Lord your God;
The threshing-floor shall be full of grain,
   The vats shall overflow with wine and oil.
You shall eat in plenty and be satisfied,
   And praise the name of the Lord your God,
For the Lord alone is our God, and there is
   no other,
   Let us praise the name of the Lord!

PRAYER OF CONFESSION

God of the Covenant,
you promise to write your law in our hearts,
that we would be your faithful people,
even as you are our faithful God.
You have confirmed your promise to us
in your free gift of grace through Jesus Christ.
Still, we stray from your ways,
even though they are written upon our hearts.
We have violated your holy calling.

Forgive us; by your Spirit, renew us
in our knowledge of you and our love for you.
Grant us strength and courage to live with integrity,
according to the deepest longings of our heart,
to your honor and glory forever.

HYMNS FOR THE DAY

	HB	LBW	NCH	PH	RIL	TFF	WOV
GATHERING							
God Is Here!	—	—	70	461	—	—	719
THE WORD							
O—Song of Zechariah	592	2	733	601–2	564–7	—	725
The God of Abraham Praise	89	544	24	488	595	—	—
E—Lord, Speak to Me That I May Speak	298	403	531	426	436	—	—
With Grateful Hearts Our Faith Professing	—	—	—	497	—	—	—
G—What a Friend We Have in Jesus	385	439	506	403	507	—	—
Precious Lord, Take My Hand	—	—	472	404	—	193	731
Eternal Spirit of the Living Christ	—	441	520	—	—	—	—
When the Storms of Life Are Raging	—	—	—	—	—	198	—
Stand by Me	—	—	—	—	—	198	—
THE EUCHARIST							
There Is a Balm in Gilead	—	—	553	394	465	185	737
SENDING							
Lord, Dismiss Us with Thy Blessing	79	259	77	538	—	—	—

Twenty-Ninth Sunday in Ordinary Time

Color: Green

PSALM SETTINGS

METRICAL

"My Mind Is on Your Law All Day," NMP, p. 202, LM, Webber

RESPONSORIAL

"O Lord, My Delight Is in Your Law," P 123 (Presbyterian 5)

MULTICULTURAL/CONTEMPORARY

Psalm—"Lead Me, Guide Me," TFF 70/AAHH 474

"Wonderful Words of Life," AAHH 332

E—"Thy Word," TFF 132/W&P 144, Amy Grant

"I'll Tell It Wherever I Go," AAHH 514

G—"Lord, Listen to Your Children," W&P 91, Handt Hanson

ANTHEMS

"Here, O My Lord, I See Thee Face to Face," Perry W. Whitlock, OXU A42, SSATBB

"Precious Lord, Take My Hand," Roy Ringweld, SP A-981, SATB with soprano solo

MUSIC FOR THE SMALL CHURCH

"O Lord, Hear My Prayer," Jacques Berthier (congregation), in *Songs & Prayers from Taizé*, 20, GIA G-3719

OTHER VOCAL MUSIC

"Pass Me Not, O Gentle Savior," Dale Wood in *Songs of Reflection*, Dale Wood, SMP

ORGAN

Prelude and postlude on the hymn tune LEONI ("The God of Abraham Praise")

Richard Hillert, *The Concordia Hymn Prelude Series*, vol. 42 (E)

Hal H. Hopson, *Five Preludes on Familiar Hymns*, HF (M)

Seth Bingham, "Toccata on LEONI," HWG (D)

Flor Peeters, *Hymn Preludes for the Liturgical Year*, vol. 6, CFP (M)

Richard Proulx, "Prelude on LEONI," AF (M)

Gordon Young, *Nine Hymn Preludes for Organ*, HP (M)

THE CONFESSION OF 1967

For today's selection, see p. 233.

October 24, 2004

LECTIONARY READINGS

Joel 2:23–32
2 Timothy 4:6–8, 16–18
Luke 18:9–14

Psalm 65

CALL TO WORSHIP

Praise is due to you, O God,
    For you answer our prayers.
By awesome deeds you answer us with deliverance
    O God of our salvation.
You are the hope of the ends of the earth
    And of the farthest seas.
The whole world is clothed in your glory.
    Let us shout and sing together for joy!

PRAYER OF CONFESSION

God of compassion,
you show yourself merciful to the needy,
exalting the humble, and humbling the exalted.
When we were low, you lifted us up,
and fed us with the bounty of your goodness.
But we have set aside the tender ways of humility;
we have become rich in our own eyes,
vainly proud of our strength and accomplishments.

Merciful God, forgive our arrogance,
our complacent sense of self-sufficiency.
Renew in us a meek spirit;
teach us to clothe ourselves in humility,
that we will seek always to give you all glory,
for all your wondrous works on our behalf.

HYMNS FOR THE DAY

GATHERING	HB	LBW	NCH	PH	RIL	TFF	WOV
Let All Things Now Living	—	557	—	554	—	—	—
THE WORD							
O—Come, Ye Thankful People, Come	525	407	422	551	18	—	—
All Hail to God's Anointed	146	87	104	205	232	—	—
E—Fight the Good Fight	359	461	—	307	—	—	—
As Morning Dawns, Lord, Hear Our Cry	—	—	—	161	—	—	—
Guide My Feet	—	—	—	354	—	153	—
G— O Savior, in This Quiet Place	—	—	555	390	—	—	—
Song of Mary	596	6	119	600	—	—	730
In a Lowly Manger Born	—	417	162	—	—	—	—
THE EUCHARIST							
Jesus, Remember Me	—	—	—	599	—	—	740
SENDING							
When in Our Music God Is Glorified	—	555	561	264	508	—	802

Thirtieth Sunday in Ordinary Time

Color: Green

PSALM SETTINGS

METRICAL
"Praise Is Your Right, O God, in Zion," PH 201,
  9.6.9.6.D, Wiersma
RESPONSORIAL
"In You Our Praise Is Due in Zion, O God," P 55,
  Hopson

MULTICULTURAL/CONTEMPORARY

Gathering—"Gather Us In," SNC 8, Marty Haugen
Psalm—"Psalm 65," SNC 222, Darlene Zschech
E—"Guide My Feet Lord," arr. by John Carter, HP,
  SATB
"Let It Be Said of Us," Mar 217, Steve Fry
"He'll Understand and Say 'Well Done,'" AAHH 413
G—"O Lord, Listen to Your Children," Ken
  Medema, arr. by Jack Schrader, HP
"Thy Way, O Lord," AAHH 444

ANTHEMS

"Canticle for Pentecost" from *Two for Pentecost*, Erik
  Routley, HIN HMC-267, SATB
"Fight the Good Fight with All Thy Might" from *Five
  Hymns in Popular Style*, John Gardner, OXU
  42.874, SATB with orchestra or two pianos

MUSIC FOR THE SMALL CHURCH

"I Have Fought the Good Fight," Thomas Gieschen
  (unison or SATB), AF 11-2448

OTHER VOCAL MUSIC

"Acquaint Now Thyself with Him," Michael Head,
  BH

ORGAN

Prelude on the tune AZMON ("O For a Thousand
  Tongues to Sing")
  Austin Lovelace, *Eight Hymn Preludes*, AF (M)
  Paul Manz, *Ten Chorale Improvisations*, vol. 9
    C (M)
  Alec Wyton, *Preludes and Fanfares*, JFB (M)
Or J. S. Bach, "Prelude and Fugue in A Major" (vari-
  ous editions) (MD)
Postlude on WER NUR DEN LIEBEN GOTT ("If Thou But
  Suffer God to Guide You")
  J. S. Bach, several settings, various editions (E-M)
  William Albright, *Chorale Partita in an Old Style*,
    EV (D)
  Ernst Pepping, *Fünfundzwanzig Orgelchoräle*
    BSS (E)

THE CONFESSION OF 1967

For today's selection, see p. 233.

October 31, 2004

LECTIONARY READING

Habakkuk 1:1–4, 2:1–4
2 Thessalonians 1:1–4, 11–14
Luke 19:1–10

Psalm 119:137–144

CALL TO WORSHIP

You are righteous, O Lord,
    And your judgments are right.
You have appointed your decrees in righteousness
    And in all faithfulness.
Your righteousness is an everlasting righteousness
    And your law is truth.
Your decrees are righteous forever;
    Give us understanding that we may live.

PRAYER OF CONFESSION

God of the future,
you grant visions and dreams
to those who look to your Spirit for guidance,
who incline their ears to hear your Word anew.
You sustain with your power
all who purpose to follow you.
Grateful for our strong and wide heritage,
staked out by men and women of courage and faith,
we have been afraid to step out like they did,
when your Spirit urges your people further forward.

Forgive our fear of where you may lead,
and of what you may require of us.
Open our hearts and eyes to a fresh vision of Jesus,
who ever leads us forward into your coming
        kingdom.

HYMNS FOR THE DAY

GATHERING	HB	LBW	NCH	PH	RIL	TFF	WOV
Awake My Soul, and with the Sun	50	269	—	456	71	—	—
O God, Our Help in Ages Past	111	320	25	210	1	—	—
THE WORD							
O—Why Are Nations Raging	—	—	—	159	—	—	—
O God of Earth and Altar	511	428	582	291	80	—	—
E—I Sing a Song of the Saints of God	—	—	295	364	401	—	—
I Love Thy Kingdom, Lord	435	368	312	441	409	—	—
Wonderful Grace of Jesus	—	—	—	—	—	184	—
G— Help Us Accept Each Other	—	—	388	358	—	—	—
Hear the Good News of Salvation	—	—	—	355	—	—	—
THE EUCHARIST							
Sheaves of Summer	—	—	338	518	—	—	—
SENDING							
God, Bless Your Church with Strength	—	—	—	418	—	—	—

Reformation Day

Thirty-First Sunday in Ordinary Time

Color: Green

PSALM SETTINGS

METRICAL

Psalm 119e: "Lord, Thou Art Righteous Always,"
PCW, 7.6.7.6.D, Morgan

RESPONSORIAL

"O Lord, My Delight Is in Your Law," P 124
(Presbyterian 5)

MULTICULTURAL/CONTEMPORARY

Psalm—"Step by Step," W&P 132, arr. by Nylea
Butler-Moore

E—"Christ in Us Be Glorified," Mar 176, Morris
Chapman

G—"I'm Forever Grateful," Mar 44, Mark Atrogge

"Your Grace and Mercy," AAHH 270

"When Jesus Passed through Jericho," HFTG 52

ANTHEMS

"Glory to God," by J. S. Bach/Christiansen, Schmitt
Music 1436, SSATB

"How Long Wilt Thou Forget Me?" Austin Lovelace,
JFB F.E.C.8783, SATB

MUSIC FOR THE SMALL CHURCH

"When Jesus Passed through Jericho," Sally Ann
Morris (unison or SATB) in *Giving Thanks in
Song and Prayer*, 99

OTHER VOCAL MUSIC

"The Goodness of God," C. P. E. Bach in *Solos for the
Church Year*, Lloyd Pfautsch, LG/G. Schirmer, Inc.

ORGAN

Prelude on the chorale EIN FESTE BURG ("A Mighty
Fortress")

J. S. Bach, several versions, various editions (M-D)

Calvin Hampton, *The Church Organist's Library*,
vol. 2, BM (E)

Wilbur Held, *Hymn Preludes for the Autumn
Festivals*, C (M)

Alexander Schreiner, *Organ Voluntaries*, CF (E)

Johann Walther, *Chorale Preludes by Masters of the
Seventeenth and Eighteenth Centuries*, CFP

Russell Schultz Widmar, *The Organist's Companion*,
BM (E)

Louis Vierne "Andante" from the *First Symphony*,
various editions (D)

THE CONFESSION OF 1967

For today's selection, see p. 234.

November 1, 2004

LECTIONARY READINGS

Daniel 7:1–3, 15–18
Ephesians 1:11–23
Luke 6:20–31

Psalm 149

CALL TO WORSHIP

Praise the Lord!
   Sing to God a new song.
As long as we live we will sing aloud
   God's praises in the assembly of the faithful.
Let God's children be glad,
   let all God's children rejoice!
With our whole being we will sing and dance
   giving praise to the God of our salvation.

PRAYER OF CONFESSION (BCW)

Eternal God,
in every age you have raised up men and women
to live and die in faith.
We confess that we are indifferent to your will.
You call us to proclaim your name,
but we are silent.
You call us to do what is just,
but we remain idle.
You call us to live faithfully,
but we are afraid.

In your mercy, forgive us.
Give us courage to follow in your way,
that joined with those from ages past,
who have served you with faith, hope, and love,
we may inherit the kingdom you promised
     in Jesus Christ.

HYMNS FOR THE DAY

GATHERING	HB	LBW	NCH	PH	RIL	TFF	WOV
For All the Saints	425	174	299	526	—	—	—
Come, We That Love the Lord	—	—	379	—	575–6	135	—
THE WORD							
O—Love Divine, All Loves Excelling	399	315	43	376	—	—	—
Ye Watchers and Ye Holy Ones	34	175	—	451	—	—	—
E—Lord, Enthroned in Heavenly Splendor	—	172	258	154	537	—	—
At the Name of Jesus	143	179	—	148	336	—	—
G—Blest Are the Uncorrupt in Heart	—	—	—	233	—	—	—
Jesus, the Very Thought of Thee	401	316	507	310	—	—	—
Wade in the Water	—	—	—	—	—	114	—
THE EUCHARIST							
O Holy City, Seen of John	508	—	613	453	—	—	—
Near to the Heart of God	—	—	—	527	—	—	—
SENDING							
Lord of the Living	—	—	—	529	—	—	—
Great Day	—	—	—	445	—	164	—

All Saints' Day

PSALM SETTINGS

METRICAL
"Sing Praise to the Lord," PsH 149, 10.10.11.11,
The Psalter (1912)
RESPONSORIAL
"Sing to the Lord a New Song" HP 2, p. 28,
Daw/Hackett

MULTICULTURAL/CONTEMPORARY

Gathering—"Christ the Victorious," CLUW 380
O—"Bring Forth Thy Kingdom," W&P 22, Marty
Haugen
Psalm—"Blessed Be the Name," AAHH 299
E—"Open Our Eyes, Lord," W&P 113, Bob Cull
"Looking Forward in Faith," CG 73, Andrea Steele
G—"The Gift of Love," AAHH 522

ANTHEMS

"Sine Nomine," R. Vaughan Williams, CF CM6637,
SATB
"Blessed Are They," from *Requiem*, Johannes Brahms,
GS, SATB

MUSIC FOR THE SMALL CHURCH

"Listen to the Cloud That Brightens," Carol Doran
(unison, keyboard), in *New Hymns for the
Lectionary*, OXU 42
"Jerusalem, Jerusalem," arr. by Russell Schulz-Widmer
(two-part mixed), AF 11-10646

OTHER VOCAL MUSIC

"Come, Thou Fount of Every Blessing," Richard
Walters in *Hymn Classics*, HL
"Come, Peace of God," Eugene Bulter in *Sacred Songs*,
Dale Wood, SMP

"Come, Come Ye Saints," Sacred Harp, Ovid Young
in *Twenty-One Classic Duets*, BLP
"Children of the Heavenly Father," John Ferguson in
Three Swedish Folk Hymns, AF 11-5360

ORGAN

Liturgical note: The Russian Orthodox responsorial
setting of "The Beatitudes," as found in the
Hymnal 1982 or the Canadian Anglican hymnal
Common Praise, is an excellent reflective introduc-
tion to worship involving choirs, congregation,
and soloists. This is a good beginning for either All
Saints or the Reign of Christ.
Prelude and postlude on the hymn tune SINE NOMINE
("For All the Saints")
   Jan Bender, "Fantasy on SINE NOMINE," AF (D)
   Hugo Gehrke, *The Parish Organist*, C (E)
   Wilbur Held, *Organ Music for Funerals and
     Memorial Services*, AF (E)
   Robert Lind, "Fantasia on SINE NOMINE," PAR (M-
     D)
   Flor Peeters, *Hymn Preludes for the Liturgical Year*,
     CFP (M)
   Richard Proulx, "Variations of SINE NOMINE,"
     MS (M)
Or Michael Burkhardt, DEO GRACIAS (four-movement
suite); use I and III for offertory and IV for
postlude (M/M-D)
J. S. Bach, "Prelude in D Major," various editions
(M-D)

November 7, 2004

LECTIONARY READING

Haggai 1:15b–2:9
2 Thessalonians 2:1–5, 13–17
Luke 20:27–38

Psalm 145:1–5, 17–21 or Psalm 98

CALL TO WORSHIP

The Lord is gracious and merciful,
  slow to anger and abounding in steadfast love.
The Lord is good to all,
  and God's compassion is over all creation.
All your works shall give thanks to you, O Lord,
  and all your faithful shall bless you.
Our mouths shall speak the praise of the Lord,
  and all flesh will bless God's holy name forever
    and ever.

PRAYER OF CONFESSION

God of steadfast promise,
we have yearned for earlier days,
when all seemed well, and our cause seemed strong.
We have abandoned hope in your good promise,
that you will complete the good work you started
    in us.
Our eyes have been upon ourselves,
rather than upon you.

Forgive us for giving up faith in you,
for discounting your enduring promises to us.
Fill us anew with your Spirit,
that we may press forward in joy and confidence,
doing your good work, trusting in your purposes,
witnessing to the good news of Jesus Christ—
good news that will never be silenced.

HYMNS FOR THE DAY

GATHERING	HB	LBW	NCH	PH	RIL	TFF	WOV
To God Be the Glory	—	—	—	485	355	264	—
O Sing a New Song to the Lord	—	—	—	216	—	—	—
THE WORD							
O—O Come, O Come, Emmanuel	147	34	116	9	184	—	—
God Is My Strong Salvation	347	—	—	179	95	—	—
E—Give Thanks, O Christian People	—	—	—	552	—	—	—
I Want Jesus to Walk with Me	—	—	490	363	—	66	660
If Thou but Trust in God to Guide Thee	344	453	410	282	151	—	—
G—O Sons and Daughters, Let Us Sing!	206	139	244	117	—	—	—
Thine Is the Glory	209	145	253	122	327	—	—
THE EUCHARIST							
For the Bread Which You Have Broken	—	200	—	508–9	547	—	—
Let Us with a Gladsome Mind	28	521	16	244	136	—	—
SENDING							
Eternal God, Whose Power Upholds	485	—	—	412	481	—	—

Thirty-Second Sunday in Ordinary Time

Color: Green

PSALM SETTINGS

PSALM 145:1–5, 17–21
Metrical: Psalm 145, "I Will Ever Sing Thy Praises,"
    PCW, 8.7.8.7.D, Morgan
METRICAL
"O Lord, You Are My God and King," PH 252,
    LMD, *The Psalter* (1912)
RESPONSORIAL
"The Lord Is Gracious and Full of Compassion,"
    HP 2, p. 22, Daw/Hackett

PSALM 98
METRICAL
"To God Compose a Song of Joy," PH 219, CM,
    Duck
RESPONSORIAL
"Sing to the Lord a New Song," HP 1, p. 49,
    Daw/Hackett
RESPONSORIAL
"All the Ends of the Earth Have Seen the Salvation of
    Our God," P 95, Hallock

MULTICULTURAL/CONTEMPORARY

Gathering—"Praise Our God Above," PH 480
O—"If You Believe and I Believe," Zimbabwean,
    from *Sent by the Lord*, John Bell, GIA
Psalm—"Psalm 145," SNC 27, Casiodoro Cardenas
"I Will Bless Thee, O Lord," AAHH 530
"Awesome God," LUYH 23, Rich Mullins
"Praise, I Will Praise You, Lord," LUYH 48, Claude
    Fraysse
E—"Stand in the Congregation," W&P 131, Bill
    Batstone
"Spirit Song," AAHH 321

ANTHEMS

"The Eyes of All Wait Upon Thee," Jean Berger,
    AF 11-1264, SATB
"I Want Jesus to Walk with Me," spiritual, arr. by
    Moses Hogan, HL 08740785, SATB and solo

MUSIC FOR THE SMALL CHURCH

"Now, Let Us All in Hymns of Praise," Sally Ann
    Morris (unison), in *Giving Thanks in Song and
    Prayer*, 40 (also available as a separate anthem for
    SATB/organ/trumpet, GIA)

OTHER VOCAL MUSIC

"I Want Jesus to Walk with Me," Edward Boatner,
    GM

ORGAN

Prelude on the hymn tune MIT FREUDEN ZART ("Sing
    Praise to God Who Reigns Above")
    Hugo Distler, *Kleinne Orgelchoral*, BAR (M)
    Ernnst Pepping, *Grosses Orgelbuch*, BSS (M)
    Alec Wyton, *A Little Christian Year*, CF (E)
Postlude
    Charles Callahan, "Aria," MS (M)
    J. S. Bach, "Prelude in E Flat," various editions (D)
    Alfred V. Fedak, "Fantasia on ST. ANNE," SEL
        (M-D)
    Wilbur Held, ST. DENIO ("Those Wonderful
        Welsh"), Set 2, MS (M)
    Harald Rohlig, ST. DENIO, *The Parish Organist*,
        vol. 12, C (M-E)

THE CONFESSION OF 1967

For today's selection, see p. 234.

November 14, 2004

LECTIONARY READINGS

Isaiah 65:17–25
2 Thessalonians 3:6–13
Luke 21:5–19

Isaiah 12

CALL TO WORSHIP

Give thanks to the Lord,
   call on God's name;
Make known God's deeds among the nations;
   proclaim the greatness of God's name.
Sing praises to the Lord,
   shout aloud and sing for joy!
Let it be known in all the earth,
   great in our midst is the Holy One of Israel.

PRAYER OF CONFESSION

Sovereign Creator,
just as your creating Word brought forth
the natural order, and all that is in it,
so you promise to create new heavens and
   a new earth,
free from injustice, oppression, and brokenness.
Yet we live in fear and despair,
as though sin and war and death were final words.

In mercy, forgive us for doubting the Gospel.
Transform us by your Spirit,
that we would witness ceaselessly
to the certain triumph of your grace,
inaugurated in the life, death, and resurrection,
of Jesus Christ, the Lord and Savior of all.

HYMNS FOR THE DAY

GATHERING	HB	LBW	NCH	PH	RIL	TFF	WOV
When the Morning Stars Together	—	—	453	486	510	—	—
Praise, My Soul, the King of Heaven	31	549	—	478–9	144	—	—
THE WORD							
O—O Day of Peace	—	—	—	450	—	—	762
Isaiah the Prophet Has Written of Old	—	—	108	337	—	—	—
E—Jesus, Our Divine Companion	—	—	—	305	—	—	—
G—Jesus Walked This Lonesome Valley	—	—	—	80	—	—	—
By Gracious Powers	—	—	413	342	55	—	—
Here from All Nations	—	—	—	—	582	—	—
In Bethlehem a Newborn Boy	—	—	—	35	—	—	—
THE EUCHARIST							
Let Us Talents and Tongues Employ	—	—	347	514	—	232	754
SENDING							
Lead On, O King Eternal	332	495	573	447	423	—	—

Thirty-Third Sunday in Ordinary Time

Color: Green

PSALM SETTINGS

METRICAL
"Surely It Is God Who Saves Me," PsH 193, CRC
RESPONSORIAL
"Canticle of Thanksgiving," P 175

MULTICULTURAL/CONTEMPORARY

O—"Surely It Is God," LUYH 81/SNC 74, Jack Noble White
"Lord, My Strength," W&P 93, Dean Krippaehne
E—"Beauty for Brokenness," W&P 17, Graham Kendrick
"Don't Tell Me of a Faith That Fears," in *Love and Anger*, GIA, John Bell
"We Must Work," AAHH 557

ANTHEMS

"I Will Give Thanks," Allen Pote, FP 3-75001, SATB with optional trumpets
"Thanks Be to Thee, O Lord," ECS 1732, SATB with alto solo

MUSIC FOR THE SMALL CHURCH

"I Want a Principle Within," Lloyd Pfautsch (two-part mixed), AB APM-399

OTHER VOCAL MUSIC

"A Simple Song," from Mass, Leonard Bernstein, BH

ORGAN

Prelude on the chorale HERR JESU CHRIST ("Lord Jesus Christ, Be Present Now")
  J. S. Bach, HERR JESU CHRIST, several settings, various publishers (E-M)
  Paul Manz, *Improvisations on Herr Jesu Christ*, MS (M)
  Georg Telemann, HERR JESU CHRIST, *Twelve Easy Preludes*, KAL (E)
Postlude
  Cesar Franck, "Chorale in A," DUR (M-D)
  Sr. T. Hytrek, *Suite Gloriosa*, organ (optional congregation), Descant (M-D)
  David N. Johnson, *Earth and All Stars*, AF (M)
  Gerald Near, *Passacaglia for Organ*, AF (M)
  Johann Pachelbel, "Toccata in C Major," various editions (M)
  Ernst Pepping, MIT FREUDEN ZART, *Kleines Orgelbuch*, BSS (M)

THE CONFESSION OF 1967

For today's selection, see p. 234.

November 21, 2004

LECTIONARY READINGS

Jeremiah 23:1–6
Colossians 1:11–20
Luke 23:33–43

Luke 1:68–79

CALL TO WORSHIP

Blessed be the Lord God of Israel,
   Who has come to the people and set them free.
God has raised up for us a mighty savior,
   Born of the house of his servant David.
God has shown the mercy promised to our ancestors,
   And has remembered God's holy covenant.
To give light to those who sit in darkness,
   And the shadow of death,
   And to guide our feet into the way of peace!

PRAYER OF CONFESSION *(BCW)*

Righteous God,
you have crowned Jesus Christ as Lord of all.
We confess that we have not bowed before him,
and are slow to acknowledge his rule.
We give allegiance to the powers of this world,
and fail to be governed by justice and love.

In your mercy, forgive us.
Raise us to acclaim him as ruler of all,
that we may be loyal ambassadors,
obeying the commands of our Lord Jesus Christ.

HYMNS FOR THE DAY

GATHERING	HB	LBW	NCH	PH	RIL	TFF	WOV
Alleluia! Sing to Jesus!	—	158	257	144	346	—	—
Lift High the Cross	—	377	198	371	415	—	—
God, Our Lord, a King Remaining	90	—	—	213	117	—	—
THE WORD							
O—My Shepherd Will Supply My Need	—	—	247	172	—	—	—
Lord, Enthroned in Heavenly Splendor	—	172	258	154	537	—	—
Crown Him with Many Crowns	213	170	301	151	600	—	—
E—Christ, You Are the Fullness	—	—	—	346	—	—	—
Immortal, Invisible, God Only Wise	85	526	1	263	7	—	—
All Hail the Power of Jesus' Name!	132	328–9	304	142–3	593–4	267	—
G—Come, Christians, Join to Sing	131	—	—	150	357	—	—
The Head That Once Was Crowned with Thorns	211	173	—	149	335	—	—
Alleluia! Sing to Jesus!	—	158	257	144	346	—	—
THE EUCHARIST							
Jesus, Remember Me	—	—	—	599	—	—	740
A Hymn of Glory Let Us Sing	—	157	259	141	332	—	—
SENDING							
Rejoice, Ye Pure in Heart!	407	553	55	71	145–6	—	—

Reign of Christ
or Christ the King

Color: White

PSALM SETTINGS

METRICAL
"Blessed Be the God of Israel," PH 601
RESPONSORIAL
"Canticle of Zechariah," P 159, Weaver setting

MULTICULTURAL/CONTEMPORARY

Gathering—"Jesus Es Mi Rey Soberano (Our King and Our Sovereign, Lord Jesus)," PH 157
"Cameroon Processional," ES
"The King of Glory," W&P 136, Israeli traditional
Psalm—"Blest Be the Lord," CG 15a, Bernadette Farrell
"Guide My Feet," AAHH 131
E—"Looking Forward in Faith," CG 73, Andrea Steele
"At the Cross," Mar 91, Ralph Hudson
"These Things Are True of You," Mar 248, Tommy Walker
G—"Jesus, Remember Me," WOV 740/W&P 78, Jacques Berthier
"Calvary," AAHH 239
"We Will Glorify," SNC 21/AAHH 286, Twila Paris
"King Jesus Is His Name," HP, SATB, arr. by Jack Schrader
"Son of God, by God Forsaken," HFTG 38

ANTHEMS

"The Head That Once Was Crowned with Thorns," John Ferguson, GIA G-3750, SATB and brass quartet
"Rejoice Ye Pure in Heart," Richard Dirkson, HF A5677, SATB with brass

MUSIC FOR THE SMALL CHURCH

"Lord Christ, When First You Came to Earth," Sally Ann Morris (unison or SATB), in *Giving Thanks in Song and Prayer*, 88
"Name of All Majesty," K. Lee Scott (SATB/ keyboard/optional brass), MS MSM-50-7020

OTHER VOCAL MUSIC

"Ye Servants of God," Timothy and Steven Kimbrough, HANOVER in *Sweet Sing/Hymns of Charles Wesley*, CHM

ORGAN

Prelude on the hymn tune DARWALL'S 14 ("Rejoice, the Lord Is King")
　　Charles Callahan, "Partita on DARWALL'S 148TH," seven movements, MS (E-M)
　　Healey Willan, DARWALL'S 148, *Thirty-Six Short Preludes*, CFP (M)
　　Percy Whitlock, DARWALL'S 148TH, *Six Hymn Preludes*, OXU (M)
Postlude on the hymn tune CONDITOR ALME SIDERUM ("Creator of the Stars")
　　Joseph Ahrens, *Das Heilige Jahr*, WM (M)
　　J. S. Bach, various editions, several settings (E-M)
J. S. Bach, "Toccata in D Minor (Dorian)," various editions (M-D)
J. S. Bach, "Prelude in D Minor (Eight Little)," various editions (E)
Alex Rowley, *Festal Voluntaries*, OXU (E)

THE CONFESSION OF 1967

For today's selection, see p. 234.

November 25, 2004

October 11, 2004 *(Canada)*

LECTIONARY READINGS

Deuteronomy 26:1–11
Philippians 4:4–9
John 6:25–35

Psalm 100

CALL TO WORSHIP

Make a joyful noise to the Lord, all the earth.
  Worship the Lord with gladness;
  Come in to God's presence with singing.
Know that the Lord is God,
  It is God that made us,
  We are God's people, the sheep of his pasture.
Enter God's gates with thanksgiving,
  enter the courts with praise.
  Give thanks to God!
For the Lord is good,
  God's steadfast love endure to all generations!

PRAYER OF CONFESSION

Gracious God,
You give us an abundance of good things,
richly to enjoy and use for your glory.
Yet we have been anxious to hoard your gifts,
and to acquire still more for ourselves.
We have not trusted your promises,
and have not sought your kingdom first.

Forgive our ingratitude for all you have given,
our fear that your provision will not be enough,
and our failure to be generous with others,
even as you have lavished generosity upon us.
Bring to fullness in us the good fruit of your Spirit,
that we would live in joyous faith, hope, and love;
for the sake of Jesus Christ, our Lord.

HYMNS FOR THE DAY

GATHERING	HB	LBW	NCH	PH	RIL	TFF	WOV
Come, Ye Thankful People, Come	525	407	422	551	18	—	—
THE WORD							
O—Hoy celebramos con gozo al Dios	—	—	246	—	—	—	—
E—As Those of Old Their Firstfruits Brought	—	—	—	414	—	—	—
G—Rejoice, Ye Pure in Heart!	402	553	55/71	145–6	—	—	—
Bread of Heaven, on Thee We Feed	—	—	—	501	—	—	—
THE EUCHARIST							
For the Bread Which You Have Broken	449	200	—	508	542	—	—
SENDING							
Let All Things Now Living	—	557	—	554	—	—	—
Thank You, God, for Water, Soil, Air	—	—	559	266	22	—	—

Thanksgiving Day

Color: Green

MULTICULTURAL/CONTEMPORARY

Gathering—"Every Hill Seems to Be Aflame," CLUW 243

Psalm—"Let There Be Praise," W&P 87, Melodie Tunney/Dick Tunney

"He Has Made Me Glad," TFF 291, Leona von Brethorst

"Come, Praise God! Sing Hallelujah," SNC 38, Subranto Atmodjo

"We Have Come into This House," AAHH 174

E—"Con Que Pagremos (What Shall I Render)," PH 557

"Give Thanks with a Grateful Heart," LUYH 114/W&P 41/CLUW 247/SNC 216, Henry Smith

"I Must Tell Jesus," AAHH 375

G—"Here Is Bread," W&P 58, Graham Kendrick

"Eat This Bread," CG 31, Jacques Berthier

Other—"I Thank You, Jesus," AAHH 532

ORGAN

Prelude and postlude on the chorale NUN DANKET ("Now Thank We All Our God")

J. S. Bach, complete works, various editions (M-D)

Wilbur Held, *Hymn Preludes for the Autumn Festivals*, C (M)

Don Hustad, *The Collected Works of Don Hustad*, HOP (M)

V. Nelhybel, *Now Thank We All Our God*, organ, brass, timpani, AGP (M)

Alice Parker, *Now Thank We All Our God*, choir, organ, congregation, brass, and percussion (M-D)

Flor Peeters, *Hymn Preludes for the Liturgical Year*, vol. 23, CFP (M)

Inclusive Language Text of the Confession of 1967*

PREFACE

9.01 The church confesses its faith when it bears a present witness to God's grace in Jesus Christ.

9.02 In every age, the church has expressed its witness in words and deeds as the need of the time required. The earliest examples of confession are found within the Scriptures. Confessional statements have taken such varied forms as hymns, liturgical formulas, doctrinal definitions, catechisms, theological systems in summary, and declarations of purpose against threatening evil.

9.03 Confessions and declarations are subordinate standards in the church, subject to the authority of Jesus Christ, the Word of God, as the Scriptures bear witness to him. No one type of confession is exclusively valid, no one statement is irreformable. Obedience to Jesus Christ alone identifies the one universal church and supplies the continuity of its tradition. This obedience is the ground of the church's duty and freedom to reform itself in life and doctrine as new occasions, in God's providence, may demand.

9.04 The United Presbyterian Church in the United States of America acknowledges itself aided in understanding the gospel by the testimony of the church from earlier ages and from many lands. More especially it is

---

*This inclusive language text of the Confession of 1967 was prepared informally by the Rev. Cynthia A. Jarvis (associate pastor, Nassau Presbyterian Church, Princeton, N.J.) and Professor Freda A. Gardner for use at the October 21–22, 1982, Symposium on "The Confession of 1967: Contemporary Implication." Subsequently the text was reviewed with professors Daniel Migliore and Edward Dowey, and later by a group of scholars solicited by the Rev. Dr. Christian Iosso. After receiving a referral from the 214th General Assembly (2002), the text was revised once more by the Office of Theology and Worship. Additional copies of the confession (with a helpful introduction by Joseph Small) are available for $2.00 each ($1.00 in quantities of ten or more) from Presbyterian Distribution Service by calling (800) 524–2612.

guided by the Nicene and Apostles' Creeds from the time of the early church; the Scots Confession, the Heidelberg Catechism, and the Second Helvetic Confession from the era of the Reformation; the Westminster Confession and Shorter Catechism from the seventeenth century; and the Theological Declaration of Barmen from the twentieth century.

9.05 The purpose of the Confession of 1967 is to call the church to that unity in confession and mission which is required of disciples today. This Confession is not a "system of doctrine," nor does it include all the traditional topics of theology. For example, the Trinity and the Person of Christ are not redefined, but are recognized and reaffirmed as forming the basis and determining the structure of the Christian faith.

9.06 God's reconciling work in Jesus Christ and the mission of reconciliation to which he has called his church are the heart of the gospel in any age. Our generation stands in peculiar need of reconciliation in Christ. Accordingly, this Confession of 1967 is built upon that theme.

THE CONFESSION

NOVEMBER 30, 2003   FIRST SUNDAY OF ADVENT

9.07 In Jesus Christ, God was reconciling the world to himself. Jesus Christ is God with humankind. He is the eternal Son of the Father, who became human and lived among us to fulfill the work of reconciliation. He is present in the church by the power of the Holy Spirit to continue and complete his mission. This work of God, the Father, Son, and Holy Spirit is the foundation of all confessional statements about God, humanity, and the world. Therefore, the church calls all people to be reconciled to God and to one another.

I: GOD'S WORK OF RECONCILIATION

SECTION A: THE GRACE OF OUR LORD JESUS CHRIST

1. Jesus Christ

DECEMBER 7, 2003   SECOND SUNDAY OF ADVENT

9.08 In Jesus of Nazareth, true humanity was realized once for all. Jesus, a Palestinian Jew, lived among his own people and shared their needs, temptations, joys, and sorrows. He expressed the love of God in word and deed and became a brother to all kinds of sinful men and women. But his complete obedience led him into conflict with his people. His life and teaching judged their goodness, religious aspirations, and national hopes. Many rejected him and demanded his death. In giving himself freely for them, he took upon himself the judgment under which everyone stands convicted. God raised him from the dead, vindicating him as Messiah and Lord. The victim of sin became victor, and won the victory over sin and death for all.

DECEMBER 14, 2003   THIRD SUNDAY IN ADVENT

9.09   God's reconciling act in Jesus Christ is a mystery which the Scriptures describe in various ways. It is called the sacrifice of a lamb, a shepherd's life given for his sheep, atonement by a priest; again it is ransom of a slave, payment of debt, vicarious satisfaction of a legal penalty, and victory over the powers of evil. These are expressions of a truth which remains beyond the reach of all theory in the depths of God's love for humankind. They reveal the gravity, cost, and sure achievement of God's reconciling work.

DECEMBER 21, 2003   FOURTH SUNDAY IN ADVENT

9.10   The risen Christ is the savior of all people. Those joined to him by faith are set right with God and commissioned to serve as God's reconciling community. Christ is head of this community, the church, which began with the apostles and continues through all generations.

DECEMBER 28, 2003   FIRST SUNDAY AFTER CHRISTMAS

9.11   The same Jesus Christ is the judge of all people. His judgment discloses the ultimate seriousness of life and gives promise of God's final victory over the power of sin and death. To receive life from the risen Lord is to have life eternal; to refuse life from him is to choose the death which is separation from God. All who put their trust in Christ face divine judgment without fear, for the judge is their redeemer.

2. Human Sin

JANUARY 4, 2004   SECOND SUNDAY AFTER CHRISTMAS

9.12   The reconciling act of God in Jesus Christ exposes the evil in people as sin in the sight of God. In sin, people claim mastery of their own lives, turn against God and each other, and become exploiters and despoilers of the world. They lose their humanity in futile striving and are left in rebellion, despair, and isolation.

9.13   Wise and virtuous men and women through the ages have sought the highest good in devotion to freedom, justice, peace, truth, and beauty. Yet all human virtue, when seen in the light of God's love in Jesus Christ, is found to be infected by self-interest and hostility. All people, good and bad alike, are in the wrong before God and helpless without God's forgiveness. Thus everyone falls under God's judgment. No one is more subject to that judgment than those who assume that they are guiltless before God or morally superior to others.

JANUARY 18, 2004   SECOND SUNDAY IN ORDINARY TIME

9.14   God's love never changes. Against all who oppose the divine will, God expresses love in wrath. In the same love, God bore judgment and shameful death in Jesus Christ, to bring all people to repentance and new life.

SECTION B: THE LOVE OF GOD

JANUARY 25, 2004   THIRD SUNDAY IN ORDINARY TIME

9.15   God's sovereign love is a mystery beyond the reach of the human mind. Human thought ascribes to God superlatives of power, wisdom, and goodness. But God reveals divine love in Jesus Christ by showing power in the form of a servant, wisdom in the folly of the cross, and goodness in receiving sinful men and women. The power of God's love in Christ to transform the world discloses that the Redeemer is the Lord and Creator who made all things to serve the purpose of God's love.

FEBRUARY 1, 2004   FOURTH SUNDAY IN ORDINARY TIME

9.16   God has created the world of space and time to be the sphere of God's dealings with humankind. In its beauty and vastness, sublimity and awfulness, order and disorder, the world reflects to the eye of faith the majesty and mystery of its Creator.

FEBRUARY 8, 2004   FIFTH SUNDAY IN ORDINARY TIME

9.17   God has created human beings for a personal relation with himself that they may respond to the love of the Creator. God has created male and female and given them a life which proceeds from birth to death in a succession of generations and in a wide complex of social relations. God has endowed humans with capacities to make the world serve their needs and to enjoy its good things. Life is a gift to be received with gratitude and a task to be pursued with courage. People are free to seek life within the purpose of God: to develop and protect the resources of nature for the common welfare, to work for justice and peace in society, and in other ways to use their creative powers for the fulfillment of human life.

FEBRUARY 15, 2004   SIXTH SUNDAY IN ORDINARY TIME

9.18   God expressed love for all humankind through Israel, whom God chose to be a covenant people to serve him in love and faithfulness. When Israel was unfaithful, God disciplined the nation with judgment and maintained the covenant through prophets, priests, teachers, and true believers. These witnesses called all Israelites to a destiny in which they would serve God faithfully and become a light to the nations. The same witnesses proclaimed the coming of a new age, and a true servant of God in whom God's purpose of Israel and for humanity would be realized.

FEBRUARY 22, 2004   TRANSFIGURATION OF THE LORD

9.19   Out of Israel, God in due time raised up Jesus. His faith and obedience were the response of the perfect child of God. He was the fulfillment of God's promise to Israel, the beginning of the new creation, and the pioneer of the new humanity. He gave history its meaning and direction and called the church to be his servant for the reconciliation of the world.

SECTION C: THE COMMUNION OF THE HOLY SPIRIT

FEBRUARY 29, 2004   FIRST SUNDAY IN LENT

9.20   God the Holy Spirit fulfills the work of reconciliation in human life. The Holy Spirit creates and renews the church as the community in which people are reconciled to God and to one another. The Spirit enables people to receive forgiveness as they forgive one another and to enjoy the peace of God as they make peace among themselves. In spite of their sin, the Spirit gives people power to become representatives of Jesus Christ and his gospel of reconciliation to all.

1. The New Life

MARCH 7, 2004   SECOND SUNDAY IN LENT

9.21   The reconciling work of Jesus was the supreme crisis in the life of humankind. His cross and resurrection become personal crisis and present hope for women and men when the gospel is proclaimed and believed. In this experience, the Spirit brings God's forgiveness to all, moves people to respond in faith, repentance, and obedience, and initiates the new life in Christ.

MARCH 14, 2004   THIRD SUNDAY IN LENT

9.22 The new life takes shape in a community in which people know that God loves and accepts them in spite of what they are. They therefore accept themselves and love others, knowing that no one has any ground on which to stand, except God's grace.

MARCH 21, 2004   FOURTH SUNDAY IN LENT

9.23 The new life does not release people from conflict with unbelief, pride, lust, and fear. They still have to struggle with disheartening difficulties and problems. Nevertheless, as they mature in love and faithfulness in their life with Christ, they live in freedom and good cheer, bearing witness on good days and evil days, confident that the new life is pleasing to God and helpful to others.

MARCH 28, 2004   FIFTH SUNDAY IN LENT

9.24 The new life finds its direction in the life of Jesus, his deeds and words, his struggles against temptation, his compassion, his anger, and his willingness to suffer death. The teaching of apostles and prophets guides men and women in living this life, and the Christian community nurtures and equips them for their ministries.

APRIL 4, 2004   PALM/PASSION SUNDAY

9.25 The members of the church are emissaries of peace and seek the good of all in cooperation with powers and authorities in politics, culture, and economics. But they have to fight against pretensions and injustices when these same powers endanger human welfare. Their strength is in their confidence that God's purpose rather than human schemes will finally prevail.

APRIL 11, 2004   EASTER

9.26 Life in Christ is life eternal. The resurrection of Jesus is the sign that God will consummate the work of creation and reconciliation beyond death and bring to fulfillment the new life begun in Christ.

2. The Bible

9.27 The one sufficient revelation of God is Jesus Christ, the Word of God incarnate, to whom the Holy Spirit bears unique and authoritative witness through the Holy Scriptures, which are received and obeyed as the word of God written. The Scriptures are not a witness among others, but the witness without parallel. The church has received the books of the Old and New Testaments as prophetic and apostolic testimony in which it hears the word of God and by which its faith and obedience are nourished and regulated.

9.28 The New Testament is the recorded testimony of apostles to the coming of the Messiah, Jesus of Nazareth, and the sending of the Holy Spirit to the Church. The Old Testament bears witness to God's faithfulness in his covenant with Israel and points the way to the fulfillment of God's purpose in Christ. The Old Testament is indispensable to understanding the New, and is not itself fully understood without the New.

9.29 The Bible is to be interpreted in the light of its witness to God's work of reconciliation in Christ. The Scriptures, given under the guidance of the Holy Spirit, are nevertheless words of human beings, conditioned by the language, thought forms, and literary fashions of the places and times at which they were written. They reflect views of life, history, and the cosmos which were then current. The church, therefore, has an obligation to approach the Scriptures with literary and historical understanding. As God has spoken the divine word in diverse cultural situations, the church is confident that God will continue to speak through the Scriptures in a changing world and in every form of human culture.

9.30 God's word is spoken to the church today where the Scriptures are faithfully preached and attentively read in dependence on the illumination of the Holy Spirit and with readiness to receive their truth and direction.

II: THE MINISTRY OF RECONCILIATION

Section A: The Mission of the Church

1. Direction

MAY 16, 2004   SIXTH SUNDAY OF EASTER

9.31   To be reconciled to God is to be sent into the world as God's reconciling community. This community, the church universal, is entrusted with God's message of reconciliation and shares God's labor of healing the enmities which separate people from God and from each other. Christ has called the church to this mission and given it the gift of the Holy Spirit. The church maintains continuity with the apostles and with Israel by faithful obedience to his call.

MAY 23, 2004   SEVENTH SUNDAY OF EASTER

9.32   The life, death, resurrection, and promised coming of Jesus Christ has set the pattern for the church's mission. His human life involves the church in the common life of all people. His service to men and women commits the church to work for every form of human well-being. His suffering makes the church sensitive to all human suffering so that it sees the face of Christ in the faces of persons in every kind of need. His crucifixion discloses to the church God's judgment on the inhumanity that marks human relations, and the awful consequences of the church's own complicity in injustice. In the power of the risen Christ and the hope of his coming, the church sees the promise of God's renewal of human life in society and of God's victory over all wrong.

MAY 30, 2004   DAY OF PENTECOST

9.33   The church follows this pattern in the form of its life and in the method of its action. So to live and serve is to confess Christ as Lord.

2. Forms and Order

JUNE 6, 2004   TRINITY SUNDAY

9.34   The institutions of the people of God change and vary as their mission requires in different times and places. The unity of the church is compatible with a wide variety of forms, but it is hidden and distorted when variant forms are allowed to harden into sectarian divisions, exclusive denominations, and rival factions.

JUNE 13, 2004   ELEVENTH SUNDAY IN ORDINARY TIME

9.35   Wherever the church exists, its members are both gathered in corporate life and dispersed in society for the sake of mission in the world.

JUNE 20, 2004   TWELFTH SUNDAY IN ORDINARY TIME

9.36   The church gathers to praise God, to hear God's word for humankind, to baptize and to join in the Lord's Supper, to pray for and present the world to God in worship, to enjoy fellowship, to receive instruction, strength, and comfort, to order and organize its own corporate life, to be tested, renewed, and reformed, and to speak and act in the world's affairs as may be appropriate to the needs of the time.

JUNE 27, 2004   THIRTEENTH SUNDAY IN ORDINARY TIME

9.37   The church disperses to serve God wherever its members are, at work or play, in private or in the life of society. Their prayer and Bible study are part of the church's worship and theological reflection. Their witness is the church's evangelism. Their daily action in the world is the church in mission to the world. The quality of their relation with other persons is the measure of the church's fidelity.

JULY 4, 2004   FOURTEENTH SUNDAY IN ORDINARY TIME

9.38   Each member is the church in the world, endowed by the Spirit with some gift of ministry and is responsible for the integrity of his or her witness in each particular situation. Each member is entitled to the guidance and support of the Christian community and is subject to its advice and correction. In turn, each member, in her or his own competence, helps to guide the church.

JULY 11, 2004   FIFTEENTH SUNDAY IN ORDINARY TIME

9.39   In recognition of special gifts of the Spirit and for the ordering of its life as a community, the church calls, trains, and authorizes certain members for leadership and oversight. The persons qualified for these duties in accordance with the polity of the church are set apart by ordination or other appropriate act and thus made responsible for their special ministries.

9.40 The church thus orders its life as an institution with a constitution, government, officers, finances, and administrative rules. These are instruments of mission, not ends in themselves. Different orders have served the gospel, and none can claim exclusive validity. A Presbyterian polity recognizes the responsibility of all members for ministry and maintains the organic relation of all congregations in the church. It seeks to protect the church from exploitation by ecclesiastical or secular power and ambition. Every church order must be open to such reformation as may be required to make it a more effective instrument of the mission of reconciliation.

3. Revelation and Religion

9.41 The church in its mission encounters other religions and in that encounter becomes conscious of its own human character as a religion. God's revelation to Israel, expressed within Semitic culture, gave rise to the religion of the Hebrew people. God's revelation in Jesus Christ called forth the response of Jews and Greeks and came to expression within Judaism and Hellenism as the Christian religion. The Christian religion, as distinct from God's self-revelation, has been shaped throughout its history by the cultural forms of its environment.

9.42 Christians find parallels between other religions and their own and must approach all religions with openness and respect. Repeatedly God has used the insight of non-Christians to challenge the church to renewal. But the reconciling word of the gospel is God's judgment upon all forms of religion, including the Christian. The gift of God in Christ is for all. The church, therefore, is commissioned to carry the gospel to all whatever their religion may be and even when they profess none.

4. Reconciliation in Society

9.43 In each time and place, there are particular problems and crises through which God calls the church to act. The church, guided by the Spirit, humbled by its own complicity and instructed by all attainable knowledge, seeks to discern the will of God and learn how to obey in these concrete situations.

<table>
<tr><td>AUGUST 15, 2004</td><td style="text-align:right">TWENTIETH SUNDAY
IN ORDINARY TIME</td></tr>
</table>

AUGUST 15, 2004   **TWENTIETH SUNDAY IN ORDINARY TIME**

9.44 a. God has created the peoples of the earth to be one universal family. In his reconciling love, God overcomes the barriers between sisters and brothers and breaks down every form of discrimination based on racial or ethnic difference, real or imaginary. The church is called to bring all people to receive and uphold one another as persons in all relationships of life: in employment, housing, education, leisure, marriage, family, church, and the exercise of political rights. Therefore, the church labors for the abolition of all racial discrimination and ministers to those injured by it. Congregations, individuals, or groups of Christians who exclude, dominate, or patronize others, however subtly, resist the Spirit of God and bring contempt on the faith which they profess.

AUGUST 22, 2004   **TWENTY-FIRST SUNDAY IN ORDINARY TIME**

9.45 b. God's reconciliation in Jesus Christ is the ground of the peace, justice, and freedom among nations which all powers of government are called to serve and defend. The church, in its own life, is called to practice the forgiveness of enemies and to commend to the nations as practical politics the search for cooperation and peace. This search requires that the nations pursue fresh and responsible relations across every line of conflict, even at risk to national security, to reduce areas of strife and to broaden international understanding. Reconciliation among nations becomes peculiarly urgent as countries develop nuclear, chemical, and biological weapons, diverting human power and resources from constructive uses and risking the annihilation of humankind. Although nations may serve God's purposes in history, the church which identifies the sovereignty of any one nation or any one way of life with the cause of God denies the Lordship of Christ and betrays its calling.

AUGUST 29, 2004   **TWENTY-SECOND SUNDAY IN ORDINARY TIME**

9.46 c. The reconciliation of humankind through Jesus Christ makes it plain that enslaving poverty in a world of abundance is an intolerable violation of God's good creation. Because Jesus identified himself with the needy and exploited, the cause of the world's poor is the cause of his disciples. The church cannot condone poverty, whether it is the product of unjust social structures, exploitation of the defenseless, lack of national resources, absence of technological understanding, or rapid expansion of populations.

SEPTEMBER 5, 2004	TWENTY-THIRD SUNDAY IN ORDINARY TIME

9.46 c. The church calls all people to use their abilities, their possessions, and the fruits of technology as gifts entrusted to them by God for the maintenance of their families and the advancement of the common welfare. It encourages those forces in human society that raise hopes for better conditions and provide people with opportunity for a decent living. A church that is indifferent to poverty, or evades responsibility in economic affairs, or is open to one social class only, or expects gratitude for its beneficence makes a mockery of reconciliation and offers no acceptable worship to God.

SEPTEMBER 12, 2004	TWENTY-FOURTH SUNDAY IN ORDINARY TIME

9.47 d. The relationship between man and woman exemplifies in a basic way God's ordering of the interpersonal life for which God created humankind. Anarchy in sexual relationships is a symptom of alienation from God, neighbors, and self. Perennial confusion about the meaning of sex has been aggravated in our day by the availability of new means for birth control and the treatment of infection, by the pressures of urbanization, by the exploitation of sexual symbols in mass communication, and by world overpopulation.

SEPTEMBER 19, 2004	TWENTY-FIFTH SUNDAY IN ORDINARY TIME

9.47 d. The church, as the household of God, is called to lead people out of this alienation into the responsible freedom of the new life in Christ. Reconciled to God, people have joy in and respect for their own humanity and that of other persons; a man and woman are enabled to marry, to commit themselves to a mutually shared life, and to respond to each other in sensitive and lifelong concern; parents receive the grace to care for children in love and to nurture their individuality. The church comes under the judgment of God and invites rejection by society when it fails to lead men and women into the full meaning of life together, or withholds the compassion of Christ from those caught in the moral confusion of our time.

SECTION B: THE EQUIPMENT OF THE CHURCH

SEPTEMBER 26, 2004	TWENTY-SIXTH SUNDAY IN ORDINARY TIME

9.48 Jesus Christ has given the church preaching and teaching, praise and prayer, and Baptism and the Lord's Supper as means of fulfilling its service of God among all people. These gifts remain, but the church is obliged to change the forms of its service in ways appropriate to different generations and cultures.

1. Preaching and Teaching

OCTOBER 3, 2004	TWENTY-SEVENTH SUNDAY IN ORDINARY TIME

9.49 God instructs the church and equips it for mission through preaching and teaching. By these, when they are carried on in fidelity to the Scriptures and dependence upon the Holy Spirit, the people hear the word of God and accept and follow Christ. The message is addressed to men and women in particular situations. Therefore, effective preaching, teaching, and personal witness require disciplined study of both the Bible and the contemporary world. All acts of public worship should be conductive to people's hearing of the gospel in a particular time and place and responding with fitting obedience.

2. Praise and Prayer

OCTOBER 10, 2004	TWENTY-EIGHTH SUNDAY IN ORDINARY TIME

9.50 The church responds to the message of reconciliation in praise and prayer. In that response it commits itself afresh to its mission, experiences a deepening of faith and obedience, and bears open testimony to the gospel. Adoration of God is acknowledgment of the Creator by the creation. Confession of sin is admission of every person's guilt before God and of their need for God's forgiveness. Thanksgiving is rejoicing in God's goodness to all people and in giving for the needs of others. Petitions and intercessions are addressed to God for the continuation of divine goodness, the healing of human ills, and deliverance from every form of oppression. The arts, especially music and architecture, contribute to the praise and prayer of a Christian congregation when they help people to look beyond themselves to God and to the world which is the object of God's love.

3. Baptism

OCTOBER 17, 2004   TWENTY-NINTH SUNDAY
                                        IN ORDINARY TIME

9.51 By humble submission to John's baptism, Christ joined himself to men and women in their need and entered upon his ministry of reconciliation in the power of the Spirit. Christian baptism marks the receiving of the same Spirit by all his people. Baptism with water represents not only cleansing from sin, but a dying with Christ and a joyful rising with him to new life. It commits all Christians to die each day to sin and to live for righteousness. In baptism, the church celebrates the renewal of the covenant with which God has bound us to God's very self. By baptism, individuals are publicly received into the church to share in its life and ministry, and the church becomes responsible for their training and support in Christian discipleship. When those baptized are infants, the congregation, as well as the parents, has a special obligation to nurture them in the Christian life, leading them to make, by a public profession, a personal response to the love of God shown forth in their baptism.

4. The Lord's Supper

OCTOBER 24, 2004   THIRTIETH SUNDAY
                                        IN ORDINARY TIME

9.52 The Lord's Supper is a celebration of the reconciliation of people with God and with one another, in which they joyfully eat and drink together at the table of their Savior. Jesus Christ gave his church this remembrance of his dying for sinners so that by participation in it they have communion with him and with all who shall be gathered to him. Partaking in him as they eat the bread and drink the wine in accordance with Christ's appointment, they receive from the risen and living Lord the benefits of his death and resurrection. They rejoice in the foretaste of the kingdom which he will bring to consummation at his promised coming, and go out from the Lord's Table with courage and hope for the service to which he has called them.

III: THE FULFILLMENT OF RECONCILIATION

| OCTOBER 31, 2004 | THIRTY-FIRST SUNDAY IN ORDINARY TIME |

9.53 God's redeeming work in Jesus Christ embraces the whole of human life: social and cultural, economic and political, scientific and technological, individual and corporate. It includes the natural environment as exploited and despoiled by sin. It is the will of God that the divine purpose for human life shall be fulfilled under the rule of Christ and all evil be banished from creation.

| NOVEMBER 7, 2004 | THIRTY-SECOND SUNDAY IN ORDINARY TIME |

9.54 Biblical visions and images of the rule of Christ, such as a heavenly city, the household of God, a new heaven and earth, a marriage feast, and an unending day culminate in the image of the kingdom. The kingdom represents God's triumph over all that resists the divine will and disrupts God's creation. Already God's reign is present as a ferment in the world, stirring hope in all people and preparing the world to receive its ultimate judgment and redemption.

| NOVEMBER 14, 2004 | THIRTY-THIRD SUNDAY IN ORDINARY TIME |

9.55 With an urgency born of this hope, the church applies itself to present tasks and strives for a better world. It does not identify limited progress with the kingdom of God on earth, nor does it despair in the face of disappointment and defeat. In steadfast hope, the church looks beyond all partial achievement to the final triumph of God.

| NOVEMBER 21, 2004 | CHRIST THE KING/ THE REIGN OF CHRIST |

9.56 "Now to him who by the power within us is able to do far more abundantly than all we ask or think, to him be glory in the church and in Christ Jesus to all generations, forever and ever. Amen."

The Confession of 1967

Selections for Use in Worship

Confession of Sin

Announcement of the gospel

In Jesus Christ, God was reconciling the world to himself.
The reconciling act of God in Christ
exposes the evil in us as sin in the sight of God.
In sin, we claim mastery of our own lives,
turn against God and neighbors,
and become exploiters and despoilers of the world.
In Jesus Christ, God was reconciling the world to himself.

Prayer of Confession . . .

Declaration of pardon and new life

Hear the good news:
God was in Christ, reconciling the world to himself.
The risen Christ is the savior of all.
All who are joined to Christ by faith
are set right with God
and commissioned to serve as Christ's reconciling community.

[9.07, 12, 10]

* * * * *

Introduction to the Reading of Scripture

The one sufficient revelation of God is Jesus Christ,
the Word of God incarnate,
to whom the Holy Spirit bears unique and authoritative witness
through the Holy Scriptures,
which are received and obeyed as the word of God written.
The Scriptures are not a witness among others,
but the witness without parallel,

by which our faith and obedience
are nourished and regulated.
Listen for the Word of God . . .

[9.27]

Affirmations of Faith

In Jesus Christ, God was reconciling the world to himself.
We confess that Jesus Christ is God with us,
the eternal Son of the Father,
who became human and lived among us
to fulfill the work of reconciliation.
We believe that the risen Christ is present in the church
by the power of the Holy Spirit
to continue and complete his mission.
This work of God,
the Father, Son, and Holy Spirit,
is the foundation of all we say
about God, ourselves, and the world.

[9.07]

* * * * *

We believe that in Jesus of Nazareth,
true humanity was realized once for all.
Jesus, a Palestinian Jew, lived among his own people
and shared human needs, temptations, joys, and sorrows.
He expressed the love of God in word and deed
and became a brother to all kinds of sinful people.
In giving himself for them,
he took upon himself the judgment under which all people
stand convicted.
We believe that God raised him from the dead,
vindicating him as Messiah and Lord.
The victim of sin became victor,
and won the victory over sin and death for all.

[9.08]

* * * * *

We acknowledge that God's sovereign love
is a mystery beyond the reach of human minds.

We ascribe to God superlatives of power, wisdom, and goodness.
But in Jesus Christ God reveals love
by showing power in the form of a servant,
wisdom in the folly of the cross,
and goodness in receiving sinful people.
The power of God's love in Christ
transforms the world
and discloses that the Redeemer is the Lord and Creator
who made all things to serve the purpose of his love.

[9.15]

* * * * *

We believe that God has created the world of space and time
to be the sphere of his dealings with humankind.
In its beauty and vastness,
sublimity and awfulness,
order and disorder,
the world reflects to the eye of faith
the majesty and mystery of its Creator.
We believe that God has created us
for personal relationship in which
we may respond to the love of the Creator.
Life is a gift to be received with gratitude
and a task to be pursued with courage.

[9.16, 17]

* * * * *

We believe that the reconciling work of Jesus
was the supreme crisis in the life of humankind.
His cross and resurrection become personal crisis and present hope
when the gospel is proclaimed and believed.
In this experience, the Spirit brings God's forgiveness to us,
moves us to respond in faith, repentance, and obedience,
and initiates the new life in Christ.
We believe that the new life takes shape in a community
in which we know that God loves and accepts us
in spite of what we are.
We therefore accept ourselves and love others,
knowing that no one has any ground on which to stand,
except God's grace.

[9.21, 22]

* * * * *

We believe that God the Holy Spirit fulfills the work of reconciliation.
The Holy Spirit creates and renews the church
as the community in which we are reconciled to God
and to one another.
The Spirit enables us to receive forgiveness as we forgive
one another
and to enjoy the peace of God as we make peace among ourselves.
We believe that in spite of our sin,
the Holy Spirit gives us power
to become representatives of Jesus Christ
and to proclaim the good news of reconciliation to all.

[9.20]

Call to Prayer

The church responds to the gospel of reconciliation
in praise and prayer.
In our prayer, we commit ourselves afresh to Christ's mission,
experience a deepening of faith and obedience,
and bear open testimony to the gospel.
Let us pray . . .

[9.50]

* * * * *

The Peace

The new life takes shape in a community
where people know that God loves and accepts us
in spite of what we are.
So we accept ourselves and love others,
knowing that no one has any ground on which to stand,
except God's grace.
The peace of Christ be with you . . .

[9.22]

* * * * *

Offering

The reconciliation of humankind through Jesus Christ
makes it plain that enslaving poverty in a world of abundance
is an intolerable violation of God's good creation.

Because Jesus identified with the needy and exploited,
the cause of the world's poor is the cause of his disciples.
We are called to use our abilities, our possessions,
and the fruits of technology
as gifts entrusted to us
for the maintenance of God's family
and the advancement of the common welfare.
Let us share gifts . . .

[9.46]

* * * * *

Charge

To be reconciled to God
is to be sent into the world as God's reconciling community.
We are entrusted with God's message of reconciliation,
sharing the labor of healing enmities
that separate people from God and from each other.
Christ has called us to this mission
and given us the gift of the Holy Spirit.

[9.31]

EMERGING WORSHIP
in Congregations & Homes

A conference for pastors, musicians, and worship leaders

October 16–17, 2003
Louisville Seminary

Louisville Seminary is located at 1044 Alta Vista Road, Louisville, Kentucky

www.lpts.edu or 800.264.1839

Sponsored by the Center for Congregations and Family Ministries and
Office of Theology and Worship of the Presbyterian Church (U.S.